ALSO BY

LUDWIG DEHIO

*Germany and World Politics in the*
*Twentieth Century*
(1959)

*This is a* BORZOI BOOK,
*published in New York by* ALFRED A. KNOPF

# THE PRECARIOUS
# BALANCE

# THE PRECARIOUS BALANCE

FOUR CENTURIES
OF THE
EUROPEAN POWER STRUGGLE

BY LUDWIG DEHIO

TRANSLATED FROM THE GERMAN
BY CHARLES FULLMAN

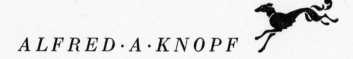

*ALFRED · A · KNOPF*

NEW YORK 1962

L. C. catalog card number: 61–9235

THIS IS A BORZOI BOOK,

PUBLISHED BY ALFRED A. KNOPF, INC.

FIRST AMERICAN EDITION

Originally published in German as *Gleichgewicht oder Hegemonie* by Scherpe-Verlag Krefeld in 1948.

TO

FRIEDRICH MEINECKE

IN VENERATION

# AUTHOR'S NOTE

THE INTRODUCTION at the beginning of this book was directed primarily at German readers. It owed its immediacy to the situation in 1945. Should I remove these pages from the English edition of this study?

In doing so, would I not, at the same time, remove the book's point of departure? Moreover, the call I then made to my fellow Germans to take stock of themselves is still of some importance and, I hope, of some interest to English-speaking readers.

It was not to just any nation that this appeal for self-analysis was addressed; it was to the last nation of the old Continent to make a bid for supremacy. This self-analysis, this search for the underlying cause of the disaster that had befallen Germany, as well as other nations before her, should lead to an understanding of the ultimate cause of the catastrophe that has overtaken the entire European system of states.

That cause is to be found in the special role of the naval powers within the system—ultimately the Anglo-Saxon nations. This study, whose Introduction deals with recent German history, proceeds to an examination of the broad vistas of modern world history, in which the Anglo-Saxon nations have balanced the powers on the old Continent with such fortunate effects.

I refer in my Introduction to Leopold von Ranke and the strictly European viewpoint that has found exemplary expression in his work; its influence has extended far beyond the country of his birth. On the other hand, the global outlook, which foresaw that a division of the world into two blocs was likely to replace the European system of states, was widely accepted in all countries around the middle of the last century. Later it was obscured only by Germany's drive for supremacy, which once more forced the course of history into the framework of the European system.

In my Introduction, in the context of the global outlook, I mention John Robert Seeley. I could have named many others in the same connection, especially Alexis de Tocqueville. Indeed, as early as the end of the eighteenth century, Gibbon spoke of the frightening possibility that a barbarian flood might engulf Europe as far as the Atlantic. But he consoled himself with the hope that 10,000 American ships would stand ready to rescue the remainder of the old peoples and carry them to "New Europe."

Does this not seem a forecast of the division of the world between Russia and America? The object of my study is to show how premonitions and prognoses such as Gibbon's have become reality in our own day.

L.D.

*Marburg, June 1960*

# CONTENTS

INTRODUCTION                                                    3

CHAPTER I  :  THE SYSTEM OF STATES UP TO THE
              COLLAPSE OF THE SPANISH BID FOR
              SUPREMACY UNDER PHILIP II

*Origin of the System of States; Charles V*        19
*Philip II*                                        43

CHAPTER II  :  THE SYSTEM OF STATES UP TO THE
               COLLAPSE OF THE FRENCH BID FOR
               SUPREMACY UNDER LOUIS XIV

*The System of States up to the Assumption
    of Personal Power by Louis XIV
        in 1661*                                   65
*Louis XIV*                                        72

ix

CHAPTER III : THE SYSTEM OF STATES UP TO THE
COLLAPSE OF NAPOLEON'S BID FOR
SUPREMACY

*The Three "World Powers" up to the*
*French Revolution* 93
*The French Revolution and Napoleon I* 132

CHAPTER IV : THE SYSTEM OF STATES UP TO THE
COLLAPSE OF THE GERMAN BID FOR
SUPREMACY UNDER HITLER

*The Conflicts Sharpen Step by Step*
*until the Powers Regroup at the*
*Beginning of the Twentieth Century* 183
*The Question of German Supremacy; World*
*War I* 224
*World War II* 247

EPILOGUE (1960) 269

CHRONOLOGICAL TABLE 289

INDEX *follows page* 296

# THE PRECARIOUS
# BALANCE

# NOTE

*For this first American edition,
the author revised some passages
of the original text of his study
and also added a new Epilogue*

# INTRODUCTION

There is a passage in Tacitus in which he speaks of the end of the reign of terror after the death of the Emperor Domitian. The most outstanding men, he says, had fallen victim to the tyrant, and those who survived had come, during half a generation of enforced silence, to prefer intellectual inactivity. It had proved easier, he concludes, to suppress intellectual life than to reanimate it. Nevertheless, the passage continues: *"Nunc demum redit animus*—Now at last life returns."

Will it be possible to say as much of us Germans? The curtain has fallen on the drama of war. To rise again? When? Or will the respite we have been granted lead to a genuine peace? Whichever comes to pass, it is our duty to seize the opportunities of the moment, great and small. The

3

task that faces us is to preserve ourselves from merely living out our days, concerned solely with the daily struggle for existence. Our task is to save our spiritual personality, which for half a generation has been in mortal peril.

We could find no better way to rally our scattered and exhausted forces for a new start than to look back into the past. Today, as never before, we must open our ears to history: not so much a *historia contemplativa*, for which we lack the necessary relaxation and leisure, as a *historia activa*, the kind of history that shows us how it all happened and teaches us which areas of the past should have continuing force and which can be allowed to slip back into oblivion. Let us look into the past in order to gird ourselves for things to come.

But which past shall we look into?

Our eyes are, of course, drawn to the lurid and gruesome scenes recently enacted before us with such violence. To understand them and absorb their lesson must be one of our objectives. But must this also be our first step? It is senseless to rush into the still burning ruins of a conflagration without first gaining a general view from outside. We shall not achieve clarity in ourselves or about ourselves, nor shall we be able to weigh destiny against guilt, if we expose ourselves unprepared to a pandemonium of charge and countercharge.

A return to more remote periods of German history promises to provide us with a broad perspective. But wherever we seek a firm foundation to stand on, we find the ground sinking beneath us, undermined throughout the centuries by the same kind of catastrophe that has convulsed us in our own time. Our history is ambiguous; it is capable, indeed, of many interpretations—more so than the history of almost any other nation—and the reading that has been handed down to us and become familiar has collapsed. We do not even possess a rounded picture of our national past comparable to what our own historians have created in writing of the past of other nations. Germany's greatest historian abandoned the "patriotic idea" of writing a history of his fatherland because he thought that German history could be understood only as the product of the general corpus of history. But he did become the master interpreter of the general history of the Western world, and of the Western system of states in particular. Ranke's conception of it has a grandeur and depth all its own.

In discussing the history of the system of states, I propose to follow in Ranke's footsteps. For it is only by stepping back inside this wide framework that we can hope to gain the detachment and perspective we need, the broad basis upon which our judgment can stand unshaken, regardless of any further spasms that may come.

Eventually, of course, a political retrospect alone will not be able to satisfy us, for our spiritual and moral existence has been called in question together with its political and material aspects. Nor am I disposed to leave the state arrayed in the divine nimbus that was placed around it in Ranke's time. To be sure, the state remains for us, as it was for him, the central factor of history: the point at which history's main lines of development intersect and its great impulses converge, the chief influence shaping our existence by virtue of order and power. This is the way we Germans have experienced the state; and by the same token, it is our experience that in times of great crisis the state's will to live operates most forcefully in the field of foreign affairs, without being necessarily or basically determined by them in the sense that would accord a dogmatic primacy to foreign policy.

5

The system of states is the largest field of energy accessible to the foreign policies of all states taken together, the sum total of their relations with one another as those relations incessantly change, conflict, and come to an adjustment again. By pointing out the main factors in the history of the system, I shall erect a framework into which the other aspects of spiritual and material existence can be fitted without difficulty.

In adopting this method, I am conscious of adhering to a fundamental tradition in the German approach to history. The destinies of other countries may demonstrate the effectiveness of other approaches. It will suffice if we find a common meeting ground with them at the end of our study.

In the years to come, we shall have to regain lost ground in our study of foreign viewpoints, and use this knowledge for a close scrutiny of our own. We shall perhaps do this with greater open-mindedness once our own approach has enabled us to appreciate the deep underlying causes of the new world situation. But while we are in our present straits and anxieties, we should not, in near panic, surrender any more of our habits of thought than a conscientious search for truth requires. For in the process, the understanding we might achieve would lose a good deal of its power to convince, a power always strongest when couched in the language of native scholarship.

To what extent is such a loss inevitable under the impact of recent experience? We can obtain the clearest answer from a study of Ranke, whose example has encouraged me to write this book. I shall refer here only to the points which are germane to my subject.

Today, contradictorily enough, Ranke seems to us both closer and further removed than he used to be, just as the morning is removed from the evening by the intervening day though closer to the evening in character than any other part of the day. Ranke confidently saluted the dawn of the day of high politics; we are entering its twilight. His devoutly affirmative outlook invested his picture of history with iridescent hues; and to his enthusiastic eye its hard contours seemed softened as if by an early-morning haze. Some of his statements glitter with metaphysical profundity, like dewdrops which the searing sun of realism will soon devour. But this matutinal air of optimism stands in cruel contrast to our evening gloom. We cannot overlook the seeds of disaster which that optimism sowed in Ranke's thought: the glorification and deification of the newly discovered state, its investment with a spiritual halo, and the indulgent treatment of its leaders—seeds, to be sure, that were to sprout only in a thoroughly changed atmosphere.

Yet however great our reservations may be, the new insight into the mechanism of politics which we owe to Ranke still remains greater. Moreover, there is nothing to prevent us from holding on to this gain, even if we link the phenomena of state life to those of other aspects of life which meant less to Ranke, and even if we see the general picture thus acquired in a different light and judge it otherwise.

The part of Ranke's insight that I shall apply to this study is his realization that the Occident has formed a political and cultural unity from the time of the migrations down to our own day. No one before him had seen this unity with such clarity and from so many angles; of course, its essence —a diversity of elements harmoniously adjusted in freedom —had never before been so thoroughly challenged as it was by Napoleon. Ranke's own experience of the collapse of Napoleon's great bid for supremacy provided the jumping-off point for historicism conceived in the grand manner; and it is precisely this experience that brings Ranke closer to us than he was to the two or three generations before us. We ourselves have, after all, gone through the same experience, though with the final auspices reversed: ours is taking us into a period of darkness; his was the prelude to a bright new era.

However, the elation that uplifted Ranke's thought also wafted him occasionally over barriers whose importance we have in the meantime learned to appreciate. Having earlier indicated one general reservation, I shall now emphasize two particular ones.

First, Ranke saw Napoleon's downfall primarily as the outcome of national uprisings among the Western peoples as a whole. He failed to stress the fact that it was Britain and Russia, the flanking powers of Europe, and through them the influence of the overseas territories and the regions of Eurasia, that had created the conditions for these uprisings. He attached significance to Russia only to the extent that she was involved in the affairs of the West; he showed no instinctive feeling for the vast potentialities of the non-Western character of the Tsarist Empire. Britain, certainly, was incomparably more familiar to him than the eastern flanking power, but Ranke, a product of the Continental interior, possessed only an indirect understanding of her involvement in maritime interests and had no vivid appreciation of the spread of the Anglo-Saxon way of life beyond the seas. He never stopped to assess the dangers that were looming up for the old lands of the Occident from the vast new territories on the periphery. His attention remained fastened on bygone perils to which the system had been exposed by the quest for supremacy on the part of individual nations among its members. Trusting in the genius of

Europe, he was convinced that the Continent would continue to overcome these threats in the future, as it had in the past.

Just as the effects of Western expansion upon the European system of states troubled him little, so he was unconcerned about the effects of civilization * upon European culture—the spiritual correlate of the political system and, in Ranke's eyes, its *raison d'être*. He was quite unwilling to see the French Revolution as a world crisis, as the beginning of a new age, as an upheaval that shook foundations laid a thousand years back. On the contrary, he was confident that the great individual states would, in the future, continue to flourish and uphold their character through layer upon layer of the general *Zeitgeist*. Living as he did in the Central European interior, he failed to sense the future importance of the new lands; and as an inhabitant of an area regarded in the West as economically and socially backward, he was equally unable to discern the dynamic rise of the coming social, economic, and technological forces. He preferred historical themes restricted in time to the sixteenth and seventeenth centuries, and in subject matter to the political and religious aspects of events; his field of vision was essentially that of the period before the Revolution of 1848; and these limitations were interconnected and influ-

---

* The terms "culture" and "civilization" are used in this book in the way in which they are being applied more and more frequently in German writing. In this sense, the benefits of civilization (political, economic, and technical) are primarily means of furthering our own well-being, whereas the values of culture (absolute ethics, the arts, religion) are rather ends in themselves. This differentiation was prepared for by Kant, influenced by Rousseau's critique of the times. Nietzsche sharply emphasized this differentiation, and Spengler finally made it one of the dominating themes of his thinking and popularized it in his work. Of course, in the reality of history "culture" and "civilization" are always somehow connected. TRANS. NOTE.

9

enced one another. Although his approach, then, might serve as a pointer to the future in regard to certain specific European problems, it emphatically needs to be supplemented for the treatment of complex global problems. Ranke built a solid structure, but some of our modern experience does not fit into it. The intention here is not to pull down his structure, but merely to extend it.

Did the generations that followed him attempt to do this? In the era in which the Second Reich was founded, his fellow countrymen pushed the venerable master aside, not because his vision was too limited, but because to their narrow-minded nationalist passions he appeared all too universal. True, this attitude underwent some change late in the Bismarck period. The Chancellor's masterly diplomatic maneuvering among the great powers reminded the Germans of the author of *Die grossen Mächte*, and they used the historian of Europe to interpret the European statesman. Bismarck's first biographer of any consequence was also, in a way, the leader of a Neo-Rankean school. But no attempt was made to supplement the Rankean conception in the direction I indicated earlier. His concepts were applied to the present without any effort to evaluate the dangers arising from the interrelated phenomena of expansion and civilization. The optimistic vitality of the unified German nation, heightened in the younger generation to a point far beyond Ranke's cool confidence, seized upon his ideas about the system of states precisely because these concepts could be used as an anchorage for nationalist hopes. The threat inherent in civilization was certainly recognized, but only within the national framework. The Germans believed it could best be mastered in a strong state, whose power would at the same time be enhanced by the exploitation of modern economic procedures.

They did, of course, devote some attention to the expansion of Europe into the world outside. But this attention was related only to national aims: the Germans demanded a share in that expansion. However, the national state of world importance they longed for could flourish only within a system of similar world powers. The Germans therefore embraced the idea that out of the European system of great powers a system of world powers could grow which would also inherit the older system's capacity to ward off any drive for supremacy arising from among its members. Moreover, they believed that Germany, by reason of her military and economic efficiency, would, under strong leadership, be just as qualified to enter the ranks of global powers as little eighteenth-century Prussia had been to enter the European circle. Thus, instead of taking advantage of their improved access to knowledge of the world and its development and reviewing Ranke's belief in the light of this knowledge, the Germans unhesitatingly applied Ranke's belief on a global basis: in launching upon imperialistic adventures they allowed themselves to be led by ideas of Continental origin. The truth is that when we Germans ventured forth into world politics, our historical publicists lost their bearings and failed to display the flair that had made Ranke the friend of kings and on occasion the counselor of cabinets. As latecomers, we were in haste to seize the opportunity of the moment and to overtake the more fortunate nations that had got ahead of us in the world, as the founding of the Second Reich had enabled us to do in Europe. We refused to ask ourselves whether the trend of world affairs might not reverse the course of events in Europe and move toward unity rather than diversity.

In World War I, Germany remained under the spell of the Rankean conception of the great powers. The urge for supremacy, or the Napoleonic impulse, was still as foreign to us in those days as were revolutionary tendencies in domestic politics. (The German Jacobins of the Third Reich were the first to bring both to fruition in our country.) We saw in Britain's command of the sea a historical parallel to Napoleon's dominance on land, and hoped that by combating that command we were paving the way for an equilibrium among free world powers. (In the eighteenth century, the French had used similar arguments to justify their struggle against Britain's superiority at sea.) Indeed, we were genuinely astonished not to find any allies. It surprised us to see naval supremacy producing effects so different from those brought about by supremacy on land. In the maritime field and in world politics in general, our experience, derived from Continental affairs, turned into a will-o'-the-wisp that lured impulsive optimists all the more into the chasm between wishful thinking and reality.

Even the catastrophe of 1918 failed to prompt a thorough review of Ranke's thought. The problem of war guilt rendered an impartial self-examination more difficult still and kept the scholars busy pleading a case. The efforts of democrats and Marxists suffered from their farfetched ideology. The swelling volume of research on Bismarck led historians right back into an era of Continental political thought; they were reluctant to criticize the grand old man whose image our self-esteem was laboring to use as a source of recuperation. Finally, the fact that Russia and the United States, the two world powers whose stars were in the ascendant, disappeared from Germany's field of vision in the immediate postwar years, distorted her view of the future. Once again, her horizon narrowed.

The fight over the Rhine with France, the nearest of the victors, revived resentments that had been fed by Continental struggles through the centuries. Even where we were not led astray by political slogans, such as the legend of the "stab in the back," pride in our wartime military achievements made us forget that they had been limited in scope to a continent. Historical thought was picked up by brilliant outsiders. They were no doubt aware of the brittleness of the system of states; but being hidebound in their Continental viewpoint, they used their knowledge to paint fantastic possibilities rather than to warn their countrymen. Unfulfilled by German history and unbroken by the vicissitudes of Germany's experiences, the vitality of the Germans still created high expectations. We still felt young. There is something frightening about a nation's habits of thought. In an age when historicism is cultivated, a view of history habitually repeated itself becomes a historical force.

To modernize our view of history is one of our great contemporary tasks. The aim of this study is to make a contribution to this process by drawing conclusions from the traditional German approach to history. I propose to go back to our beginnings in the writing of universal political history, and to Ranke's conception of the system of states. At the same time, this study aims at projecting into our own day the lines he laid down and at throwing light on Western expansion and civilization. I have tried to expand Ranke's picture of Europe to fit into a global framework—regardless of whether his early-nineteenth-century ideals are lost in the process and a diagnosis emerges that he himself never faced.

Yet even in Ranke's time a diagnosis far different from his could have been made, and the rational application of Ranke's methods might have provided Germany with plenty of warnings. This was demonstrated by John Robert Seeley, the man who laid the groundwork of modern British imperial practice. Seeley adopted one of Ranke's favorite ideas, the notion that in any state the highest principle of action is derived from its foreign policy. With this concept as his guide, he developed an approach to contemporary trends in world politics that afforded him a prophetic view of the future.

We Germans are accustomed to speaking of the two decades after 1870 as an era of world history bearing the stamp of Bismarck's thought. Seeley does not even mention Bismarck's name. He looks beyond Germany, indeed beyond the whole Continent, as if it were no more than a mountain range of medium altitude, toward Russia and the United States, the two giant powers looming into view. The United States was the product of technology, of steam and electricity. Russia would double her population from 80 to 160 million by 1920; once her regime was consolidated and her armaments and communications perfected, she would weigh upon Central Europe like a nightmare. France and Germany, the two greatest states of old Europe, would both shrink, in relative terms, to the size of pygmies and would be reduced to second-class status. As representative examples of states of a new magnitude, the two giant powers would overshadow the other great powers as completely as Macedonia overshadowed the Athenian *polis* in ancient times, or as sixteenth-century Spain and France towered above the Florentine city-state. Britain would have to decide whether to drop to the level of a European power or, by exploiting her technology, to tighten the inner unity of her scattered empire and weld it into a third world power. Proceeding from such a viewpoint, can we still speak of a system of states in the Rankean sense? According to Seeley, the two Anglo-Saxon powers were bound by a relationship closer than that between any other two states in history. He

14

maintained that the future of the planet would depend on these two powers—an utterance the more unmistakable in its implications as Seeley held that the future British Empire alone would be stronger than the Russian conglomerate of peoples. He undoubtedly envisioned Anglo-Saxon world leadership rather than a system of competing great states with national differences. He did not even consider projecting the European system on a world-wide scale. Britain, after all, had been for two centuries the eloquent protector of a Continental balance of power, but at the same time the silent champion of her own dominant role in the world at large. From her island position, it was possible to view European problems and world problems in a common perspective.

How much more difficult a task that was for us Germans! The fact that we did not command the same embracing knowledge of the globe was not the greatest obstacle in our path; rather, it was the fact that the vital drive of our nation would have been weighed down by the very insight that acted as a spur to the British. The will to live, Schopenhauer tells us, is stronger than the intellect. Before 1914, that will covered with its hand, as it were, the area it did not wish us to examine with our minds. That examination must now take place in the full light of day.

CHAPTER I

# The System of States up to the Collapse of the Spanish Bid for Supremacy under Philip II

# ORIGIN OF THE

# SYSTEM OF STATES;

# CHARLES V

**I**T IS POSSIBLE to imagine a history of the Western world that relates all events to the two principles of unity and diversity. It could, after all, be said that for more than a thousand years the pendulum has swung back and forth between a tendency toward unification, which never led to complete unity, and a divisive tendency, which never led to complete disintegration. In different epochs the two tendencies are linked with varying circumstances and forces.

Let us begin by taking a look at the Middle Ages, which will also provide us with an introduction to the actual theme of this study. In that period the unifying tendency was carried along by two currents that had their origins in late antiquity: man's yearning for the salvation of his soul and the memory of the political institutions of the Roman Empire. The exponents of these two currents were the

Papacy and the Holy Roman Empire. Their roots were linked, whether they acted jointly or in opposition to each other.

The early Middle Ages found them acting predominantly together in combating the barbarous chaos that threatened their higher interests from within, and in fighting the Magyars, the Normans, and Islam, the external enemies of the Christian West. Whereas in antiquity the Mediterranean had occupied the center of the *orbis terrarum*, with extended land frontiers as a consequence, the Italian peninsula, with its geographical unity, proved to be the natural receptacle for the spiritual and political association of Papacy and Empire; the historical events of the Middle Ages were concentrated on the Continent.

However, this co-operation between the Empire and the Papacy became looser as the reasons for collaboration weakened. The threat from outside slackened to the point where defensive action could be left to local forces, and the more firmly the religious spirit took hold among the young nations, the more the internal danger dwindled.

Manifestly, this happy consolidation of the West had fatal effects on the Holy Roman Empire, robbing it of its *raison d'être*. Its universal character evaporated until nothing was left but a hollow pretense. The Empire's close ideological and material ties with the Church prevented it from developing an independent strength of its own. Neither the sluggishly circulating economy nor the increasingly rigid social life supplied any impetus. Not even the imperialistic will among the Germans, the imperial people, maintained its original vigor.

This same development carried the Papacy to greater heights. More and more, it came to be the exclusive representative of the unifying tendency. It drew its strength from man's longing for salvation, and as the Western world recognized this as his most sublime aspiration, the Church, being the sole body in a position to promote it, took precedence over political authorities and became the most important of all organizations. In other words, the Church herself assumed a political character to the extent that the faithful were willing to obey her behests or even risk their lives in her cause. After the victory of the religious-*cum*-secular Papacy over the secular-*cum*-religious Empire, the former, in the era of the Crusades, seemed to be on the way to converting the Western world into an integrated theocratic state. The Church wielded both swords, the spiritual and the secular. In the discharge of the Church's supramundane task, the state merely acted as her handmaiden in mundane affairs: the moon that borrowed light without itself emitting any. In this introverted world, politics, as a concept, had no substance. Real war existed only as a crusade against the infidel. The cult of the eternal truths sapped and clouded men's will for the earthly life. The pulse of the economy beat as feebly as that of politics. No matter what field of activity we look at, we find dynamic movement straining to approach the static state.

However, the current of Western life would tolerate only for moments an ice coating such as had overlain the cultures of Africa and Asia for hundreds, even thousands, of years. Those with a sense of history will never cease to ponder the mystery of this abounding vitality of the Western world which was now spreading across the globe. A glimmer of understanding comes to them when they survey the course of events from early Greek times down to the present. These events began with the fertile friction between the small units of the Hellenic system of states, a friction which in a very short time brought about a development of a scope never achieved by the powerful and homogeneously organized political and cultural entities on the Nile and in Mesopotamia. Subsequently, the aging world of antiquity itself produced entities of ever-growing extent, and finally the mightiest of all, which was to spread its own: Greco-Roman civilization.

This civilization, interspersed with elements of Oriental origin, was eventually handed down to the young nations of the West by the Church, who subjected the family of the Germanic and Romance nations to a discipline that plowed up the realm of the soul with the sharp blade of asceticism. The furrow then received a variety of seed from the wealth of traditions united in the Church. Side by side and jumbled up together, the seed sprouted and grew to reach the most varied stages of development. The cities of antiquity, with their thin layer of cultured people superimposed upon a working population that was deprived of liberty, were replaced as bearers of culture by great and free peoples split up into a rich diversity of classes. Here, indeed, was a wealth of individual possibilities for friction and amalgamation, uninhibited by any leveling process such as was brought about by an invasion of barbarians in the Orient, by an onset of defensive rigidity in Byzantium, and by militant fanaticism in Islam! Truly, we sense that this European soil harbored the elements of almost incessant movement, and that enough fuel was piled up here to feed a flame of rebirth and reformation, of expansion and revolution, a flame which would not soon be quenched.

It would flicker up whenever the will to live, weary of imposed resignation, blew on the glowing embers among the ashes; whenever the questing spirit sought new and ramified paths and reviewed its relationship to the world; whenever there was a clash of opinion in all the variations of "for" and "against"; until, after confusion and turmoil, an increasingly evident movement in the general direction of power over the surrounding world set in.

The political common denominator of this dynamic diversity was the new system of states and the perpetual motion of its struggles. In this system, as in the Hellenic system, fertile friction gave rise to an immense heightening of all vital energies; the sole difference was that here the development took the form of an even bolder upward curve. At the same time, the curve continued the development of antiquity in a second, extended, coiling movement. The observer feels as if he were watching something like a spiral nebula in the vast spaces of history.

The rise of the new system of states was the result of a complicated process of erosion of the medieval structure spread over hundreds of years. Nevertheless, the new structure came into existence at a quite definite moment, the beginning of the struggle among the great powers over Italy in 1494. In much the same way, water gathers in the basin of a fountain until, at a particular moment, the basin is filled and the water overflows into a second, surrounding basin; then the process begins all over again. We ourselves have experienced a beginning of this kind which at the same time was a summing up of a long development. This happened in 1917, when the entry of the United States into the war involved the whole world for the first time in a single process and divided it into two camps.

But how did a single process in 1494 divide the great powers of that time into two camps? What made Italy, of all countries, the bone of contention and the battle prize?

Let us take up the second question first. Both in the early Middle Ages and at the height of the period, Italy had been the scene of a clash, generated by the great spiritual issue of

23

the time, between the Holy Roman Empire and the Papacy. In the later Middle Ages, however, the peninsula became the home of secular culture in its richest and most advanced form. It was here that the ice coating of ascetic renunciation first began to melt. In a climate of political disorganization in which the Christian ideals were ground to dust, the heathen ideals pushed their way out of ancient cultural soil up to the surface again. Favored by Italy's geographical position, its monopoly in relations with the Orient, and the continuing benefits of an ancient civilization, economic development moved forward and the will to live thus released found unavoidable expression in the rise of politics—an art banished earlier—to sovereign ascendancy. As no overriding body of law existed at the time of the Empire's decay and the Papacy's waning strength, there arose among the political units a lawless and pitiless struggle which saw the emergence of Caesarean tyrants. This frightful process of selection gave birth to five major states, which, unable to destroy one another, had to reconcile themselves to one another's existence in a condition of equilibrium. Thus the first system of states since the downfall of the Hellenic, or at any rate the Hellenistic, system came into being—a forerunner of the European system, whose first action would aim at the destruction of its precursor. Itself in constant danger of becoming implicated in the quarrels of the world, the new system was but a portion of a greater whole, and yet geographically and culturally self-contained enough to test out on a small scale the growth of vitality that a system of states can bring about. Indeed, when we look back with gratitude on the flowering of Renaissance culture, we must also recall the relatively short-lived Italian system of states, without which that flowering would have been unimaginable.

Among the Italian states, Venice had a salient individuality within the system. As the Italian system as a whole was the precursor of the European system, so Venice, with her insular position, was the forerunner of England.

The durability and brilliance of this dominant city were based first and foremost on its island position, which deterred attempts to conquer the city even from the landward side and made possible the establishment of a secure commonwealth of far-reaching local significance. But from the point of view of world history, it was Venice's good fortune that her insular character was coupled with an additional opportunity. The city of lagoons was not merely an island on the fringe of the Italian mainland, and on its poorer side at that; it also was an island situated between two, and for a time at the junction of three, cultural regions. Just as England later became the intermediary between the world overseas and Europe, Venice was the intermediary between Orient and Occident. So, of course, were her rivals on the Tyrrhenian coast. But these fell away one by one because, unlike Venice, they were not insular in character and suffered from continental vulnerability, as Portugal and Holland did later. And Venice's rivals in the rock-and-island world of the Adriatic, though locally well protected, lacked a rich hinterland, as did the Norwegians, for instance, at a later date.

So Venice was able to establish an empire, huge in relation to the size of the mother city, and to carry Italian expansion across the sea. Venice's maritime empire, like the future British Empire, was made up of far-flung possessions, from limited bases to the colonial territories of the three kingdoms whose flags were run up on Leopardi's bronze masts in front of the Basilica of St. Mark. Indeed, during the Fourth Crusade there seems to have been some thought of transferring the center of government overseas, to Constantinople, a movement that would have meant not merely an expansion but also a migration of power.

On overseas expeditions, the lion of Venice, unlike the British lion later, came up against a superior world power. From the fourteenth century on, the Turks prevented the island empire from spreading into the eastern expanses of the world, and in the sixteenth-century opening up of the western expanses, the Italians could play no part except in the service of foreigners.

Nevertheless, the Venetian maritime state possessed a world-wide standing in the Mediterranean and northward to the Channel which, in durability alone, far surpassed that of Athens and Carthage. Those ancient forerunners of Venice, besides lacking a secure island position, had not enjoyed anything like her large intermediary role between two disparate cultural regions.

Moreover, the strong position of Venice enabled her to play a distinguished role in the Italian state system. In the fifteenth century she spread out on the mainland to compensate for her losses in the Levant and to acquire a secure defensive perimeter. But even as a land power she retained a distinctive style. The flower of her youth served in her beloved navy: in the land forces her rulers made shift with mercenaries, who were always suspect. We cannot but admire the way this maritime city, with very little risk, went from one success to another, skillfully wielded a policy of "divide and rule," and displayed a gift for governing with a loose rein which was utterly foreign to the mainland city-states. But we must bear in mind the fact that this island state had never been enmeshed in the age-old passions of the continental struggle for existence. The cool, inherited wisdom of its regime acted like a soothing balm on the

wounds of its subject cities. These—Verona, for example—
had passed through fearful periods of agony. Whenever
feuds among the nobility were not eating at their vitals,
their tyrants used the most infamous methods in resisting
the pressure of more powerful neighbors—manifestations
of an overmature, decaying system of states in miniature.
After the Emperor had seized some of these cities early in
the sixteenth century, they were only too glad, once they
had got rid of him, to return to the accommodating regime
of the maritime city. In Treviso there had even been a
popular rising against the foreign conquerors; in those days
Venice occasionally struck a nationalist tone and focused
on herself the hopes of patriots throughout the peninsula.
In any event, it remains exceedingly instructive to observe
how high, in the face of all obstacles, the star of the insular
principle could rise, even within the framework of the
Italian system.

The external deployment of Venice's power was
matched by the individuality of her domestic character. In
her constitution, her society, her economy, in art, in intellectual life, in the whole range of human activity and in
every gesture, Venice's character contrasted sharply with
continental attitudes. Hers was arrogant, aristocratic,
bound by tradition, even in tenor, and free from obtrusive
social tensions. Spared from revolutions and autocratic
personalities, Venice was guided by sage elders, who were
conventional, ritualistic, and true to type. Eventually, this
character produced the last and sweetest fruit of Italian
culture at a time when Florence, the prototype of the mainland city-state, had long since exhausted herself in revolutionary eruptions and a dazzling cascade of unique personalities and had been reduced to a twilight existence under
foreign rule.

What lured the foreigners to Italy? It was no longer the ambition to acquire the role of protector to Rome, the spiritual center of the Occident. Rather, it was the desire to control the wealth and glamour of the worldly Renaissance life that was spread out on every side, and which, though it had been developed by the Italian system, could not command its protection. Cultural strength and political weakness, light and shadow, were united in tragic proximity. In order to overcome their weakness vis-à-vis the outside world, these free states would have had to bow to the supremacy of one among them; indeed, there was no lack of plans for such a unification, but only, as in the case of ancient Hellas, when it was too late. Had unification taken place, however, the mainspring of Italy's cultural development would have been broken.

The only country in Europe to compare with Italy in wealth and glamour was little Flanders, which was, in fact, to be the battle prize in subsequent great wars within the European system. But in the first of these wars there was no prize more alluring than the unprotected cultural garden of Italy.

What was it that made the four great powers of Europe —France, Spain, England, and the Habsburg dynasty— quarrel over this garden in the first armed struggle involving them all? Each of them had just attained a new stage in internal consolidation and external security, and therefore their hands were free for a new and bigger game.

With the end of the Hundred Years' War and the expulsion of the English from the Continent, France successfully concluded a centuries-old struggle with the island nation. Her foreign policy could move on to other areas with a surplus of

energy all the greater now that the long war had concentrated and modernized the powers of the monarchy. The
Crown had attained a high pinnacle. Feudalism had been
forced back, the Estates were without significance, and the
commonalty was interested in having the new conditions
maintained. A standing army of mercenaries had been set
up; the fiscal system was well developed and productive.
France had thus become the contemporary prototype of the
absolutist Continental national power state; she was rich
and well rounded, and had sixteen million inhabitants. Only
her navy had remained characteristically backward in both
seas. From France came the first initiative in the great
drama called the history of the European system of states.

What of England? She was vanquished, but had brought
home from defeat a new, firmly delineated state personality.
Ever since the time of William the Conqueror she had been
a state conditioned by narrow seas, like Denmark or the
Kingdom of the Two Sicilies. The transformation that
now took place in her politics was historic in the fullest
sense: she discovered the gift of the gods called insularity.
As yet, this insularity was not complete. But sovereign Scotland, in spite of her French connection, was not a serious
threat to England's rear, and Ireland, on her flank, was even
less dangerous. Certainly, many of the features that enabled
this island position to hold out such grand prospects a
hundred years later were still missing. The greatness of
Venice derived from her island situation *in conjunction*
with her role of intermediary between the Orient and the
Occident; and at that time, no such intermediary role had
come England's way. Her long-distance commerce was far
behind that of the Dutch, her export trade was undeveloped,
and her navy and merchant fleet were correspondingly un-
important. However, renunciation of her old Continental

policy permitted England to cultivate her economic life, particularly the woolen industry and shipping, without heavy expenditure on arms; to settle accounts, as had been done in France, with her brawling feudal nobility; and, again as in France, to establish, without too much regard for Parliament, a popular monarchy as the pacemaker for a new society in town and country. Even at that time, the downgrading of the military factor in England signaled a law of development different from the one operating on her old Continental adversary.

But how great could the offensive power of this new policy be, as practiced by a nation of four million people, and how much influence could that policy have on the main currents of history beyond the Channel? Was a surplus of power building up here too?

Spain showed another variant of this development. Here, too, a popular absolute monarchy arose and the great nobility was subdued. But these modern features were combined with archaic elements. The chivalrously contested, centuries-old religious struggle had stamped the national spirit, but whereas the introverted Middle Ages had developed a driving force expressed in crusades and knightly orders, its offshoots were now combined with the energies of a national power state, which, closely allied with the Church, formed an explosive mixture. In the age of religious wars then opening—but only in this age—Spain, a late arrival among the nations, was fated to be a continental power. To be sure, commerce and industry, in fact the whole modern ethic of labor, could not flourish here; hence the role of Jews and Moriscos. The very characteristics that had carried the nation upward limited its possibilities of development. Its rocketlike rise was touched off, above all, by the union of the two kingdoms of Castile and Aragon into a combined realm which, though only half as densely populated as France, nevertheless boasted seven million people. Here, indeed, a new state personality took shape, which was intent on filling the geographical vessel formed by the Iberian Peninsula. The expulsion of the Moors—which, like the expulsion of the English from France, was the conclusion of centuries of struggle—was the most important stage on the road to this goal. Henceforth only Portugal stood aloof.

But side by side with the trend toward concentration, a tendency toward expansion beyond the peninsula was already in evidence. The most important of these expansionist enterprises, from the viewpoint of world history, led to distant, unknown territories on the periphery of the western ocean; it opened new avenues to this adventurous, warlike nation, without at the same time interfering with its continental character and causing Spain to develop into a naval and commercial power. This chance success was out of all proportion to the energy expended. Its importance did not become manifest until centuries had passed, and need not be discussed at this stage of my study.

By contrast, Aragon had for centuries been systematically reaching out into the Tyrrhenian Sea in pursuit of its attractive, nearby prizes and had conquered the rich grainlands of Sicily and Sardinia; even the Kingdom of Naples owed allegiance to a bastard line of the House of Aragon. Here, then, in the south of the peninsula, the threat to the freedom of Italy became discernible and not for the first time. Spain's forces, like those of France, having warded off dangers on the outer rim of the Continent, stood ready for action in the center.

If we now again review the progess of the three Western powers taken together, we realize that the development of power had shifted in their direction, continuing a tendency that had set in at the zenith of the Middle Ages with the decline of the two central powers, the Holy Roman Empire and the Papacy. The overseas discoveries were to give fresh impetus to this development.

So far, my observations have not touched on German territory. Could counterbalancing forces be expected to arise there? The first of the great nations to appear, Germany had long since lapsed into a paralyzing chaos. But here, too, new energies were astir which, had a happy synthesis evolved, might also have produced a rejuvenated and firmly outlined state personality. No external enemy had forced a common effort upon the Germans since the Magyars were repelled. Still, the Turks might now have acted as a salutary rallying incentive, just as did the Moors in Spain and the English in France. Continental states draw strength from a continental adversary. Moreover, out of the depths of its debasement, new prospects for the Emperor's office arose under Maximilian through the union of his hereditary lands with Burgundy. Was this the harbinger of a national Habsburg Empire which would guard the frontiers to the east and west? Did it mean that the policy of the dynasty was to coalesce with the interests of the nation; that a geographically fluid area was to acquire political shape; that territorial disintegration was to be brought to a halt; and that the nebulous tradition of a universal emperor was to become anchored in a German monarchy? And this in good time to prevent the hurricane of the coming Reformation from harming a newly consolidated Reich? The path the Habsburgs might have taken to a national Reich at that time appears to us far less paradoxical than the road traveled by Prussia to the Second Reich.

Be that as it may, possibilities of a quite different and

much more paradoxical character were soon to be realized when the Spanish succession opened up new vistas for the House of Habsburg. For the time being, however, under the vacillating Maximilian, everything was still in a state of flux. The erratic foreign policy of this indefatigable prince did not spring from genuine strength. The Reich was a figure on the chessboard of Europe, and its role was difficult to fit in. The disjointed Habsburg possessions, with their radically dissimilar political and social structures, were not of the material from which an imposing power, poised for action, could be formed—in spite of their combined population figure of nine million, the unique wealth of the Netherlands, the prosperity of Austria, and the existence of a partly well-trained bureaucracy. Both the vulnerability of the Habsburg territories in the field of foreign policy and their divergent interests stood in the way of such a development of power.

Yet they were held together by a force quite different from that which was taking shape in the three national states, a force which, with the system of states in its infancy and still in a malleable condition, was powerful enough to produce tremendous effects. The policy of dynastic inheritance, flourishing on the border line between private and state interests, had always found its classical setting in the vast and pivotless regions of Central and Southeastern Europe. Here the princes of the House of Luxembourg had swiftly amassed their great family heritage, and here, overnight, the Dukes of Burgundy had established their splendid realm, which now passed to the Habsburgs as the principal heirs. Here, too, in the ensuing centuries a constant succession of new territorial combinations, held together by the dynastic bond alone, were to be tied and dissolved. Here the state remained for a long time in a condition of youth long since outgrown in the West; and the more poorly the most populous nation in Europe (there were twenty million Germans around 1500) was placed for homogeneous expansion, the more ravenously expansionist the family policy of its dynasties became. More than any other, however, the House of Habsburg, growing with great opportunities, developed an uncanny energy in pursuing its dynastic aims and in playing a historic role in world affairs as a roving counterpoise to national states with local ties. Like some giant creeper, the House of Habsburg sent out tendrils that gathered tree after tree into its domain. In this it was fortified and consecrated by a natural alliance with the old universal ideas of Empire and Papacy, ideas which hovered with fewer and fewer roots over the Western world.

These, then, were the four great powers that became linked, as enemies or allies, in the struggle for Italy. At first the main contenders were France and Spain. After violent swings of the pendulum, their forces achieved an equilibrium, and a division of the peninsula between them seemed likely.

However, the election of Charles I, King of Spain, as the Emperor Charles V of the Holy Roman Empire drastically changed the situation. The balance that had only just begun to function was challenged, not merely in Italy but in the Western world as a whole. Barely in existence, the system was put to a most severe test: it was threatened by the specter of supremacy which was to reappear so often in the following centuries.

Now the unifying tendency was reactivated by the House of Habsburg. It was advanced by surpassing diplomacy and the co-ordinated application of all the instruments of power at the disposal of that heterogeneous mass of lands which had accumulated through an avalanche of legacies, and was soon to be further increased by the addition of Hungary and Bohemia. The method, proven in the Reich, of counteracting disintegration by building up strong dynastic possessions was applied to the entire Western world. In the face of resistance from the Pope and from France, that method achieved in the first sweep a degree of success that would have been inconceivable after the consolidation of the balance of power system in later centuries. Was this to be the dawn of a modernized Carolingian Empire which would succeed in assimilating the fast-rising forces of the new age?

To be sure, in the West these forces were already in the service of the national state. But Spain, with her religious tinge, was well equipped to serve as the main supporting pillar of an empire sanctified by religion; and in Central Europe, in Germany and Italy, no nations had as yet crystallized. If the Habsburgs now gained mastery of the area south of the Alps and added it to their lands to the north of them, they would have assembled a gigantic family domain which, coupled with Spain, could indeed function as the solid base of an imperial hegemony. In 1494 the attacking French King had probably planned to use the conquest of Italy to win the imperial crown and with it lasting supremacy over the Western world. Now Habsburg supremacy seemed to hang on the possession of Italy. The manner in which the dominant position in Italy fell to the Habsburgs while the transalpine starting base crumbled away need not be recapitulated here in full. Perhaps, however, I should single out some of the factors that will be of importance later in this study.

The battle for Italy was a battle between the House of Habsburg and France, but it was at the same time the death struggle of the Italian system of free states. Today, the record of this death struggle cannot fail to move us more deeply than ever. We watch these small, politically impotent states with their glittering cultures and their corrupt morals come into collision with states of a different magnitude, and go down to destruction in such unforgettable catastrophes as the Sack of Rome and the conquest of Florence by the Medici in alliance with Spain. So it was that the freedom of the glittering, corrupt, and impotent *poleis* of antiquity crumbled before the onslaught of the Macedonian state. And as the downfall of the Hellenic system of states in the ancient world led the noblest minds to introverted philosophy, so there arose on the ruins of the Renaissance system the great movement of contemplation and change of heart that is so misleadingly called the Counter Reformation. The revulsion came all the faster as the masses had not broken faith with the Christian way of life, and the culture of the upper classes also rested on a foundation of Christian tradition, albeit often obscured. Holy ascetics appeared, a metaphysical moral outlook was established, and the arts, while retaining the forms of the ancient world, learned to give expression to the revived Christian values. The spirit of Italy, far from being destroyed, was transformed, and remained the preceptor of Europe. In reverting to the universal ideals of the Church, it now prepared the way for the militant Catholicism that in the second half of the century was to impart powerful and violent impetus to the unifying tendency within the European system of states, although too late to support the imperial designs of Charles V. A factor in his failure was the shortsighted suspicion of the Popes, and one of its sources, the natural antagonism between Papacy and Empire, never quite disappeared even later. But the main factor was, of course, the decadence of these secular-minded Popes whose concern for the petty interests of their Italian state, if not of their families, so often made them forget their responsibility toward the interests of Christendom.

Only one Italian state preserved its freedom, and the events of our own time have taught us to appreciate the successful defense of the insular liberty of Venice no less than the collapse of the mainland states. In the very first phase of the struggle for Italy, even before Charles was elected Emperor, the island empire, accustomed to wielding the "divide and rule" principle, suddenly found itself confronted with a fearsome, closed phalanx of Continental states: in the League of Cambrai, France, Spain, the Emperor, the Pope, and some smaller Italian states had entered into an alliance against Venice. What a mustering of force against a city-state of not quite two million inhabitants! Its most populous mainland provinces fell forthwith into enemy hands; its army, bad as ever and led, as always, by a foreign *condottiere*, was cut to pieces. Panic broke out on the mainland, but on the island itself *sang-froid* prevailed. Within a few months, Venice had mastered the crisis by exploiting the dessensions in the enemy camp and had regained her mainland territory. She was to last for another three hundred years, enjoying the colorful evening of her thousand years of history. For a long time after her victory over the League of Cambrai, Venice remained the foremost Christian naval power in the Mediterranean; she was the principal victor at the Battle of Lepanto (1571), which broke the naval might of the Grand Turk; and in many subsequent battles she proved to be the bulwark of the Western world against the infidel.

However, while Venice alone was able to evade Spanish domination, and France for her own sake tried vainly to defend Italian liberty, the opposite development prevailed north of the Alps. There, thanks to the alliance of the princes with France, German liberty was not merely preserved; it was able to strengthen its hold. In Italy a system of states went down; in Germany the outlines of a new one became visible. And if the destruction of the Italian system was initiated by the rise of the European system, the latter was no less responsible for the dissolution of the Reich into a fluid collection of semi-sovereign states. Habsburg imperialism was, after all, the enemy of both German *Libertät* and European freedom.

Charles V was dependent upon his alliance with the concept of a universal Church. Whereas in Italy that idea was temporarily weakened by the secularization of the Papacy, it was shattered forever in Germany by the reaction to that secularization. The Reformation invested the opposition of the princes with a religious aura and started the final disintegration of the Holy Roman Empire. It destroyed the old basis of imperial supremacy at the very moment that the exhausted Emperor thought it consolidated. In any event, the fate of Germany as a political nation was moving into the shadows. The Emperor's victory would have subordinated Germany to universal aims as one instrument among others for achieving them, and so would have overridden German interests; the victory of his opponents fell short of serving German interests and subordinated the idea of the Empire to the aims of the princes.

The belated victory of the princes and its enduring effects can be understood only if we take into consideration the various counterweights that kept the fate of the Emperor in suspense and were connected with French policy as the natural rallying point of all resistance. A general accounting of this kind would have to adhere closely to Ranke's line of thought. In elucidating this first struggle for supremacy, Ranke was able to show his full mastery precisely because the battle was fought essentially within the confines of the old Continent. I shall here dwell on only two items in that account: the role of England and that of Turkey, the two states on the wings of the old Continent.

England's classic policy in recent centuries has consisted in creating a counterweight to the strongest Continental power of the day. Was this policy taking shape even at that time? Was England attempting to tip the scales, or side with the weaker party, in order to redress the balance? There are many indications that at the outset Cardinal Wolsey understood English policy in this sense; Henry VIII was heard to say: *"Cui adhaereo praeest."* But this was wishful thinking rather than reality. After the election of Charles V, the influence of the island kingdom—not yet playing an intermediary role between two worlds—was not strong enough to support a successful balance of power policy; and for that very reason English leaders could not be expected to pursue it consistently. Characteristically enough, Wolsey had as yet no conception of the importance of a navy to England. And Henry VIII, who had a keen instinct in regard to the future of his country, was not fitted by temperament to steer foreign policy with a steady hand. He relapsed into schemes for Continental conquest and, instead of consistently backing France against the superior strength of the Emperor, dreamed from time to time of acquiring the French crown. England's insular position had to be fortified by new circumstances before the island kingdom could become a decisive factor in Continental affairs. Until that time, the system would lack the mainspring that was to ensure its flexibility in future struggles for supremacy.

It was therefore all the more important that a nation— Turkey, in this instance—existed on the Continent which could function as a spring. Turkey formed a counterweight to the unifying tendency represented by Charles V, just as, after the closing stages of the Peloponnesian War, the Persians shifted their weight from one side to the other and back again whenever Athens or Sparta made a bid for supremacy. Like the Persians of old, the Turks combined the instruments of power of oriental despotism with the military techniques they had adopted from the West. Although both were actually mortal enemies of the opposing culture, they became guarantors of its political form. Both times, fortunately, the short-lived strength of the barbarian alien power, committed as it was in other parts of the world as well, did not suffice to convert the guarantee into dominion. Nevertheless, the loss of huge cultural areas to the barbarians was the price that the systems of states had to pay for their continued existence. In the sixteenth and seventeenth centuries, in particular, this price was an enormous one.

At the time of the Crusades, the offensive of the Occident against Islam had provided an opportunity for a demonstration of Christian unity. Now not even Islam's assault upon the Christians could forge a unified defense among them. The alliance of His Most Christian Majesty of France with the Grand Turk showed up the weakened nature of the universal religious outlook in a particularly frightening manner. Nevertheless, this introduction of the power of Turkey into the diplomatic and military game played a most significant part in preserving the freedom of the system of states. Charles V, whose lands threatened those of his French adversary on two fronts, was now himself caught up in a two-front war that lasted for decades. Certainly, his struggle against the infidel lent his imperial position a moral justification which also worked to his advantage in practical terms—for example, in bringing some German Protestants to his aid. But the damage he suffered in that struggle was much more serious. Had there been no damage, he might conceivably have settled accounts with Italy and France far sooner and much more decisively and, having established his authority in Germany, might have attempted to round off his work by setting up a new order in the Western world through the medium of a Council. As it was, he began the German campaign with the last dregs of his strength and was unable to make good the setback caused by the defection of Maurice of Saxony. Last of all, Turkey, as well as France, dispatched armies to contest the supremacy that the Emperor believed he had won at Mühlberg. This is not to say that it was primarily the Turks who brought about a decision against the Emperor—his enterprise was built on altogether too many brittle premises —but Turkey undoubtedly contributed to the decision.

The geographically enclosed character of the Occident, a peninsula, had provided natural support for all unifying tendencies. Now, however, that enclosed area had been opened wide toward the southeast, and the introduction of Turkey into the political maneuvers had strengthened the tendency of the Occident to split up. For centuries afterward, the Franco-Turkish alliance remained a weapon in France's struggle against the Habsburgs. But the aging Ottoman Empire was never to regain the importance it enjoyed in the sixteenth century.

A fresh and youthful power from the vast eastern territories, the Orthodox empire of the Tsars, took Turkey's place, was drawn into the system in turn, and had the same detrimental effect on the French bid for supremacy as the Crescent had had on that of the Habsburgs.

To assess the significance of this development, one need

only imagine an absolutely, instead of a relatively, closed Western world at the beginning of the modern era. If we assume a continued spread of civilization, we cannot doubt that the unifying tendency, the tendency toward supremacy, would have mastered the divisive tendency at some time and under auspices of some kind. How tremendous were the forces at Napoleon's disposal which favored unification! If the consolidation of the European states into one unit nevertheless failed again and again to materialize, the main reason was that regularly, just before the moment of achievement, new powers were brought into the maneuvers to serve as counterweights: the Islamic regions on the eastern margins of the Continent under Charles V, and under Philip II the Western overseas territories and their European exponents, the maritime powers.

# PHILIP II

BEFORE I proceed to justify this latter contention, I want to show how Philip, in spite of the reverse suffered by his father, Charles V, could renew the struggle for supremacy, and with better prospects than his predecessor.

Did not the weakening of the Habsburg position in the Empire and the division of the House into a German and Spanish branch compress Philip's power base to a degree that rendered impossible the erection of a solid structure of supremacy? Here it must be said that even if the Spanish King could expect no accretion of strength from Germany, he also had no cause to fear the obstacles from there that had so often thwarted his father's plans; aggressive ambition was alien to the Protestant princes, and, if left in peace, they retired with equanimity from the glare of high politics into the twilit lethargy of their humdrum German lives. Their dangerous link with France was loosened, particularly as the French religious wars were confusing the issue. At first, the German branch of the House of Habsburg was gripped by the same lethargy; instead of increasing its power through a policy of inheritance, it took to dividing inherited property, and even indulged in questionable dealings with the heretics. But in Rudolf II a product of the Spanish court ascended the throne, and the Counter Reformation, in a systematic plan of attack, seized one important position after another. By building new dams, it confined, stage by stage, the effect of the great breach of the 1550's; and in the western parts of the Empire each of its successes could also be regarded as a direct success for Spain. For the Counter Reformation served to consolidate the chain of Spanish possessions on the Rhine, which, from the Netherlands down as far as Italy, had exerted, and continued to exert, an almost unbroken strangle hold on French power.

The progress French expansion had made through the acquisition of the three bishoprics had not been a lasting one. In Italy, France could go no farther; in the field she was no more of a match for the Spaniards than she had been in the days of Charles V, and she was compelled to conclude a peace without advantages. Far worse, she became involved in a thirty years' religious civil war. Thus, the religious dissensions which had undermined the position of Charles V in Germany now indirectly benefited his successor, sapping the power of France, his main Continental adversary. They achieved what no victory in battle had brought about, the penetration of Spanish diplomacy and Spanish armies into the heart of the country. Indeed, the creeping vine of the Habsburg policy of dynastic marriages was to be able to send its tentacles reaching for the throne of the very country that had been the *de facto* champion of the Continent's freedom against Habsburg supremacy.

In England, this policy, in the Emperor's own lifetime and to his joyous gratification, had actually reached its goal, if only for a few short years. The marriage of Philip to Mary the Catholic was, in truth, contrary to everything the classic policy of the England of the future would prescribe. How far the island still was from assuming its role in world history! To be sure, England soon threw off the fetters fastened upon her by Spanish diplomacy, but not before she had eased the way for Spain's triumph over France at Cateau-Cambrésis. Elizabeth had to continue maneuvering with great skill for many years, for the Counter Reformation had links stretching to Ireland, Scotland, and England herself, and threatened those countries with the horrors of the Continental religious wars.

If, in Philip's time, England was still unable to act as the main counterweight to his drive for supremacy, the Turks, who had discharged that function in his father's time, were no longer in a position to do so. Eastern despotisms swiftly pass the zenith of their greatness. The naval victory at Lepanto invested the King of Spain with the halo of the Occident's champion against the infidel, and its glory shone ahead to light up the goal, almost within grasp, of welding the European peninsula into a political and spiritual unity.

Yes, a spiritual unity as much as anything! The dream of Charles V seemed on the verge of coming true, albeit in a form he had not envisioned. His ambitions were wrecked primarily by the Turks, the French, the Protestants—and the Pope. We have seen how the first three of these adversaries were beset by weakness. The fourth, now strengthened, had become the ally of Spain. Although the Pope had not acquiesced in the role the Emperor's Council policy had allotted to him, the old antagonism between these two repositories of power was losing its edge. The new Cluny Reform, the Counter Reformation, was finally reaching the papal throne. It had grown out of the union of Italian piety, which had emerged from the catastrophe of the Renaissance to return to the old path, and Spanish devoutness, which had never left it. Uninhibited by the provincial ambitions of the Papal States, the Pope's vision now encompassed the entire West, indeed the whole world. The great spiritual task of combating the heretic, formerly sacrificed to paltry, short-term secular objectives, brought the holder of spiritual power as close to the holder of secular power as was possible without compromising the otherworldliness of the rejuvenated religious principle. In Rome, even more than in Paris, the Protestant threat served the purposes of Spanish power. The sails of Spain's universal policy were swelled by the favorable wind of a powerful universal spiritual movement, something the Emperor's policy had all too obviously lacked.

It was a movement that was in perfect harmony with the Spanish soul—being largely an outgrowth of it and nurtured by it—and was thus able to fire the deepest energies of the nation. It fused the national and universal, the political and religious impulses into an indivisible unity which served a world-embracing missionary task at a moment when Central Europe was lapsing into bondage or lethargy and the Western powers were wrestling with the problem of refashioning themselves. Under Charles V this unity had not yet been fully felt. In his reign the Spaniards, like all his subjects, had in varying degrees felt themselves harnessed to an alien idea. Philip—with his dignity, consistency, and devoutness—became their national hero. He was not always traveling, as the Emperor had been; he was not regarded as a foreigner. Under him and through him, the rambling power of the Habsburgs found a firm national basis. A monarch does not need a wealth of talent to achieve a wealth of effect, particularly if he combines with the religious aura surrounding the crown a rocklike conviction of his own mission and an absolute mastery over the conduct of affairs.

Philip II was served with the same devotion as was Tsar Nicholas I in the nineteenth century, and for similar reasons. Spain's economic backwardness remained her Achilles' heel. The expulsion of the Jews and the Moriscos, a popular action, had certainly been no help: it had eliminated the competitors of the Christian craftsmen, but not their archaic economic outlook. The flow of precious metals from overseas and their vitalizing effect upon the efficiency of the state seemed a fantastic windfall. The fact that they undermined the efficiency of the economy even more did not immediately become apparent. From the short-term standpoint, that influx represented an enormous asset to the Empire at a time when the decision concerning its future standing was close at hand. In Charles V's time the Spanish colonies had not been sufficiently developed to place their treasures at the Crown's disposal. Now those colonies were adequately opened up; moreover, after absorbing Portugal, Philip added to them all the Portuguese colonies, thus uniting the entire overseas possessions of the white race under his scepter.

Even this cursory review shows that Philip was indeed well placed to resume his father's game with new trump cards. What circumstances wrecked his grand design with such abiding effects that a third attempt on the part of Spain was out of the question?

At this point, I should discuss the double-edged role of these overseas territories and the manner in which they came to spell the doom of their Spanish rulers in the course of the rise of the naval powers.

To what extent was the rise of the Netherlands associated with overseas possessions? I referred earlier to that region as the second-richest country in Europe, a close second to Italy; it was favored by industry in the south, and in the poorer north by the development of fishing, shipping, and seaborne trade. While in the course of the sixteenth century industry declined, partly as a result of English competition, the maritime element in the life of the country underwent a mighty upsurge, precisely because of the overseas discoveries. To be sure, the Dutch had no part in them, nor did their ships and capital operate in the new oceanic areas. But they had previously employed their matchless merchant fleet in a huge long-distance trade exchanging products from east and west and from north and south, a process extending from the remotest corners of the Baltic to the Iberian coasts; and this middleman's role gained new importance as soon as it became necessary to ship to the northern corners of Europe the colonial riches piled up in the harbors of Portugal and Spain. But at first the commerce of the Netherlands benefited only indirectly from this new ocean-going trade. If we look only at the growing superiority of their tonnage over that of any of their competitors, or at their increasingly consolidated position in the western and northern waters of Europe, a comparison with Venice comes to mind. However, when we examine the role of the Netherlands in world trade side by side with Venice's role in the Far Eastern trade, we realize that the Netherlands were still restricted to the medium hauls, the European hauls, and had as yet no share in the long voyages to distant shores beyond Europe.

How adequately was that special position in European waters protected against disturbance from the Continent? And did it provide the basis for a politically independent state? This was put to the test in the Revolt of the Netherlands. In that struggle, the southern provinces, including Antwerp, which were largely bound up with the mainland, were subdued by the armies of Spain, the dominant Continental power; the northern provinces, being surrounded and crisscrossed by water and both threatened and protected by it, held their own. Once again we are reminded of Venice. Just as the one factor in Venice's greatness—the role of maritime intermediary between widely separated regions—reappeared in the rise of the Netherlands, though at first in a form less marked, so the other factor in that greatness—the advantage of being situated in a delta, the amphibious setting—now also proved its worth. But here again the advantage was less marked, as there was no genuine insular citadel of the kind formed by the islands of the Venetian lagoon.

The religious movement was an added factor in the Netherlands. But without the two circumstances I have indicated, it would not have been enough to keep Holland for long out of the clutches of Spain. It inflamed the masses and rendered them fluid, so that they could be recast in the mold of a new state. But it did not itself ignite the Revolt, which owed its origin to secular impulses that transcended denominational boundaries. The religious movement was rather a reflection of the Spanish system, in which political and religious impulses had become fused. Opponents adjust to each other in battle. As soon as the Spaniards ceased to be dangerous, the tolerance of the Dutch unfolded, while in Spain obdurate intolerance ran riot.

However, did all the circumstances collectively suffice to ensure victory for the insurgents? Doubtless they were able to delay the advance of the Spaniards, who struggled against the waters without a fleet, their best infantry pitted against a nation of seamen which was happy to leave land fighting to foreign mercenaries, as were the Venetians. Nevertheless, the rebels could not prevent their powerful enemy from slowly pressing forward. Holland's strength, though reminiscent of that of Venice, was inferior to it. No matter how great the indirect profit the seafaring Dutch were reaping from ocean-going traders, what was lacking was an absolutely insular position and long voyages to overseas coasts.

The fate of the system of states was decided by England. Her key role was due to her island position, but also to her maritime power, which she had only recently acquired in the battle for the ocean approaches to the overseas territories.

We left England already withdrawn from the Continent but still uncertain and unsteady both in her external posture and in her internal character; already inclined toward industry and shipping, but without long-distance trade to match that of the Dutch, her sea power effective only in home waters. Then, under Elizabeth, nation and state braced themselves with marvelous resolve, and finally put forth a degree of strength that enabled this small country for the first time to play a role in world history and to inaugurate a development that was to continue unbroken until 1945.

The connection between England's rise and the existence of overseas territories was much more evident than in the case of the Dutch. All European colonial settlements were still in the hands of the two Iberian nations—indeed, since 1580 they had been in the hands of the Spaniards alone. Yet the ocean areas brought to the island kingdom an accretion of strength that was fraught with decision.

Overseas expansion and the system of states were born at the same time; the vitality that burst the bounds of the Western world also destroyed its unity. The Turks were involved in each of the two processes. We have seen how, through their alliance with France, they frustrated the unification of Europe under the Habsburgs in the first half of the sixteenth century. But even in the fifteenth century, by blocking trade with the Far East, the Turks had stimulated exploration of new routes to India and thus promoted the discoveries which in the end were again to tilt the scales against the Habsburgs.

The first to make headway in the field of discovery were the Portuguese. Like the Spaniards, they combined the old crusading zeal with modern ambitions for power; but being the smaller nation and without hope of expansion on the Continent, Portugal could turn only to the sea. Her teachers were the Italian naval powers whose ships so often put in at Lisbon, the best ocean harbor on the peninsula, and who were themselves already pushing as far as the Azores. The commercial spirit of the Italians, their Renaissance zest for discovery, and their scientific methods became strangely intermingled with the chivalrous fighting tradition of the Portuguese.

The bold and consistent endeavors of three generations were rewarded by the growth of a network of Portuguese bases studded about the distant Indian Ocean. Mamelukes and Turks tried in vain to rip asunder this web in which the fabulous riches of the East were enmeshed and captured. The link with Europe was made secure by a chain of settlements along the far-flung routes. An unprecedented feat had been performed: thanks to its shipping, to a technique that is, a European nation had spread to remote parts of the globe, just as a plant reproduces itself at great distances by means of its winged seeds.

Portugal's legendary glory was as fleeting as a meteor. Not that this fantastic lunge into distant territories incurred any retribution. The colonial empire remained firmly in the hands of the mother country, like a gaily colored balloon on a long string in the hands of a child. But the parent herself proved vulnerable. Portugal's long-distance trade discharged the intermediary function between two worlds as well as Venice's had ever done, but the country lacked any kind of insular, or even amphibious, security. In 1494, Portugal had to concede to her Spanish rival a demarcation line cutting the globe into two halves; and in 1580 she lost her independence, together with all her overseas possessions, to Spain, not to regain it for two generations.

Spain had in the meantime forcefully built up her own colonial empire. Overnight and almost fortuitously, a continental state became, paradoxically, an overseas power. For compared with the systematic voyages of the Portuguese, the discovery of America occurred almost by chance. Characteristically, the initiative of a foreigner played a decisive role. Columbus, the Genoese of Lusitanian stock, had served his apprenticeship among Italian and Portuguese explorers. He forsook that milieu because his visionary projects could not be fitted into the framework of systematic enterprises, and made his way to Spain. There he found a continental society almost devoid of maritime and commercial tradition. He was enjoined to wait until the great continental task of the state, the expulsion of the Moors, had been carried out. In his impatience, he was already turning his gaze toward England and France when at last Granada fell. He set sail under the flag of Castile, and with this first undertaking Spain won the prize of prizes, harvesting what Portugal had sown.

Was Spain capable of exploiting the treasure that had fallen into her lap? Certainly not in the manner of the heroic Portuguese mariners and merchants. But she succeeded in her own fashion, through soldiers and monks. They did not create a broad-meshed network of bases; nor was there a process of colonization from settlement to settlement.

What came into existence was a mainland empire beyond the seas which embraced whole continents and millions of people, an empire imbued with crusading spirit and governed in the politico-ecclesiastical style of the mother country. Here, after a period of appalling atrocities, a start was made on spreading the kingdom of Christ; the colored subjects were shown some respect, and intermarriage with whites was encouraged. Economic activity, however, was confined in the main to the mining of precious metals.

From 1580, then, Philip held both the Spanish and the Portuguese colonial empires in his mighty hand. Did not this colonial monopoly appear to be the harbinger of Spanish supremacy in Europe? Was not the end of the European system of states in sight?

To understand how it was saved, we must take stock of England's transformation under the impact of events overseas before she herself owned so much as a square foot of land there. England was immediately and profoundly stirred by the news of the discovery. No Englishmen captained the first English voyages, but, as elsewhere, Italians—Venetians, in fact. The emerging naval power was piped aboard by the retiring naval power.

But neither in the northwest nor later in the northeast were the results achieved comparable to those attained in southern latitudes. In the long run, it was these latitudes that attracted all enterprise, as a magnet attracts iron. There was no necessity for the state to take the lead. The island setting provided private initiative with facilities unknown on the Continent. It was from the ranks of the old Company of Merchant Adventurers that England's heroes, the buccaneers, emerged in those days—pirates, traders, and organizers of capitalist enterprises, who developed into discoverers of every kind and became the pioneers of the great maritime history of their country. Excluded from legitimate overseas trade by the mercantile monopolies of the Iberian countries, these men raided the far-flung sea routes to foreign colonial empires, garnered fantastic booty, and attained a superiority in shipbuilding and seamanship that made them the true heirs of the Vikings. Elizabeth, maneuvering cautiously, disavowed them as need arose, while silently furthering their ends. With growing determination, she continued the policies of her father, and encouraged industry, commerce, and shipping, as well as the navy.

As the Queen had no thought of abandoning any advantage, a collision with Spain became increasingly imminent, although neither she nor Philip was bent on open war. Gradually, the two countries took up opposing positions on all fronts. In England, almost as much as in the Netherlands, the religious difference had an inflammatory effect, however little Elizabeth, like William the Silent, might of her own volition give it priority. The Queen helped the French Calvinists and above all, after the murder of William, the Dutch Calvinists. She thus piloted England for the first time to the leadership of a kind of Continental coalition against a dominant Continental power. Simultaneously, this constellation of forces for the first time made manifest England's vital interest in controlling the great river deltas —the first line of defense of the British Isles against attack by a power supreme on the Continent. The decline of France cast England in the historic role of Spain's adversary. The balance of power policy, an unformed wish under Wolsey, became a reality. Yet even at that time, it consisted not merely in the defense of a European equilibrium but necessarily, too, in an aggressive drive for England's own predominance on the seas. This drive was so successful, and

Spain's losses at the hands of the freebooters so fearful, that, if the sum total of all Spanish efforts on the Continent was not to be nullified, Philip was left with no choice but to challenge the English as the backers of Holland even before he subjugated the Dutch, and smash both at one tremendous blow. The execution of Mary Stuart, itself precipitated by the machinations of the Counter Reformation, forced the final decision by flouting the honor of Spain while destroying Philip's hopes of a rift in the ranks of his island opponents similar to the division among his Continental foes.

Thus, the supreme Continental power, seemingly at the peak of its strength, entered the lists against the small and untested island power: Goliath against David. Venice's insular mode of existence had, after all, crystallized only in the more restricted framework of the Italian system. Now, for the first time in the European setting, two ways of life confronted each other. Their derivatives have remained face to face right down to our own times.

It is the peculiar characteristic of naval warfare that it compresses into days and hours crises which on land may be spun out over decades. Here a decision momentous for the history of the world was brought about by a *single* battle, and it has symbolic significance down to the very details.

The Spaniards were proud of the fact that the greatest naval victory of the previous century had been gained under their command. But the action at Lepanto was a Mediterranean battle, fought out at close quarters with drawn cutlasses and small-bore guns. Spain's ocean-going ships had a long record of backwardness, and now the call came for a fleet of 132 men-of-war to be equipped on a gigantic scale for the Atlantic. How could the design of the ships fail to show a lack of maritime tradition—to say nothing of the seamen, some 10,000 of them drummed up from every harbor in the Mediterranean? The fighting men on board, 22,000 strong, were perfect specimens of their kind, under officers of fine bearing. But they were perfect only for hand-to-hand combat in the execution of tactics which, to all intents and purposes, translated the conditions of land fighting into naval terms. These fighting units were like a tract of continent on the high seas, foreign bodies on the ships' decks.

The English had at their disposal no more than 34 actual men-of-war with 6,000 men on board, but their ships were small and handy, well adapted to Atlantic conditions, and equipped with long-range artillery firing broadsides from gun ports. Gun crews, soldiers, and seamen were knit into a living unity with the ship; the relationship between officers and men was flexible, not rigidly authoritarian in the feudal Continental style. Alongside the men-of-war proper, and almost five times as many in number, were ships the Spaniards could not match—privateers, with a total strength of 10,000 men, their crews welded together in a hundred actions. They were the vanguard of the new maritime England, at their head Francis Drake, the embodiment of England's transition from the age of the freebooters to that of a great naval power.

Nothing was needed but a gale to complete the havoc wrought by broadsides fired at safe range among the huge, unwieldy Spanish galleons with their packed complements of men. The Armada shared the fate of the Persian fleet at Salamis and foreshadowed that of the Russian fleet at Tsushima: in each case, the squadrons of a giant continental power with long voyages behind them were sent to the bottom in the home waters of the small opposing naval power. The Armada also brings to mind Austria's host of knights in armor that succumbed at Sempach to the plebeian spears of the Swiss. At any rate, the tactics of the Swiss could be learned, whereas Spain could not hope to procure ships' crews like those of the English, even if she could have raised the funds to fit out a new Armada. She entirely lacked that intrepid breed of merchants steeped in the ways of the sea. She had no Francis Drake.

Drake is an object lesson in the sources from which England, at one of the most fateful hours in European history, drew the strength to save the liberty of the system of states by staking her own freedom. The very rivalry in the sea approaches to the colonies had developed the maritime energies of the island people so swiftly that they soon surpassed those of their enemies, who, for all their colonial monopoly, had remained hidebound in continental attitudes. *Afflavit et dissipati sunt*: it was a whiff of air from across the sea that scattered the Armada. It was the new territorial elements in the game, the ocean areas, which, at the height of this struggle for supremacy, acted, if only indirectly, as the decisive counterweight by raising the naval powers, England and Holland, and the insular way of life to world stature.

Paradoxically enough, Holland achieved this stature earlier than England, although the latter could claim the decisive battle. England might be compared to a ship with an ungainly hull that cannot too readily be set on a fresh course. The patterns of life and interests of the landed gentry prevailed there alongside those of industry and urban commerce, the free spirit of Shakespearean late Renaissance at court alongside the religious spirit among the ordinary folk. Compared with the Continent, the island had its own rhythm of development. Even after the battle, the Queen remained prudent and denied her support to the war party, whose adherents were eager to make the jump from naval to colonial power and attack forthwith the whole massive block of Spanish overseas possessions. Close to home, Elizabeth did prepare an extension of her power: the personal union with Scotland promised a valuable addition to England's insular strength. More than a generation was to elapse before England, having scored her great defensive victory over her external enemy, overcame the retarding factors in her internal affairs and, under Cromwell, sallied forth with aggressive intent and all her pent-up strength into the maritime world.

How different was the case of little Holland. There national life had long since centered on trade and shipping. As soon as the effects of the Armada's defeat had made themselves felt, and the full weight of Spain, now sorely impaired, shifted and fell on France, the Dutch in their turn followed England's example and threw all their energies into long voyages across the oceans. Their merchant fleet far exceeded its English counterpart in size, and having been saved by the English, they used their superior maritime potential to leave their saviors behind. They, too, avoided the firmly knit bloc of the large old colonies; but they boldly attacked and seized an impressive number of small Portuguese bases and founded a trading empire similar in character to that of the commerce-minded Lusitanians, whose heirs they now became.

Like the Portuguese, the Dutch were vulnerable, but for different reasons. The amphibious landscape of Holland afforded a more effective defense against attack from the Continent, but in other respects Holland labored under disadvantages.

The nearby English with their sea power and their much larger and purely insular base proved to be redoubtable competitors on the seas once Cromwell had eliminated those factors that impeded the development of the nation's strength.

Nor was Holland free from domestic frictions. The House of Orange, representing the land front and striving for a monarchical position on the Continental model, was backed by the army and the lower levels of the fanatically Calvinist population of the towns; the affluent upper-class burghers, representing the maritime front, were interested in shipping, commerce, and sea power. In religious matters they were inclined toward tolerance. They saw the foundation of the public weal in private wealth, while the House of Orange saw it in the military and political aggrandizement of the state. But however violently these conflicting trends might agitate the nation, the sea remained the focus of its energies, and in the long run the wealthy burghers gained the upper hand. The importance of the army diminished with the decline of Spain, while the war now breaking out was fought essentially in naval engagements, and proved to be excellent business for the rich: "Land war brings hunger, sea war brings plunder." Certainly, this naval war was fought against an opponent with fat colonies and a feeble fleet. A later naval war, fought against the maritime strength of England, was to have quite different consequences.

For the time being, however, the land basked in sunshine. Sturdy and self-confident, the Dutch built up their own special island—or, rather, amphibious—civilization, which, like its Venetian forerunner, left its own imperishable memorial in art. The amorphous character of their political life (the States-General was once called a Congress of Ambassadors made up of 2,000 sovereigns) contrasted sharply with the clarity of organization in the leading Continental absolutist states. Yet this amorphousness differed fundamentally from that of Germany or Poland because it throbbed with vigorous modern life. In an island setting, the people and the social system, with their invisible reserves of strength, are always of more account than the visible attributes of the state. The free citizens of the Dutch welfare state, the wealthy masters of the seas, looked down with pitying contempt on the power states of the Continent, their tyrants, their constraint upon conscience, their militarism. They saw themselves as the repository of a higher political morality, as the advocates of a rational, enlightened world order based on peace and justice against the brute force of senseless continental wars. Naval wars, waged for the freedom of the seas—waged, in other words, to break the Spanish overseas monopoly—were, of course, a different kettle of fish!

In short, the secret of Holland's world position as a naval power—and the same is true of England—was a whiff of overseas air. It was from the new territories beyond the oceans that these small but supple organisms drew the strength that enabled them, during the decline of the Ottomans, to take over the latter's role as the counterweight to any Continental power seeking supremacy. In fact, these countries performed that function with far greater consistency and effect than the Turks had ever done; and England was to maintain her grip on the role for centuries to come.

What of Spain? As a logical consequence of the rout of the Armada, her star dimmed more and more. Nor was her failure against the naval powers the end of the matter. Philip tried in vain to recoup his loss by extending his Continental position. He pursued this aim with redoubled energy and haste, just as his successors in the struggle for dominance would do in analogous situations. He shifted his pressure from Holland to France. There were still to be some hopeful moments for him when he had troops quartered in Paris, Provence, and Brittany, and when his envoys, acting on behalf of his future son-in-law, were negotiating with the French States-General about the succession to the throne. But the very conspicuousness of Philip's victories engineered his failure. It aroused the slumbering national feeling of his opponents, as his father's triumph had done after the battle of Mühlberg, and as would happen again and again in the fluctuating struggle between the Continental powers. Even the French Catholic extremists in league with Philip came to be ashamed of their ally. Moreover, counteraction from England was making itself felt.

Above all, Henry of Navarre, by his conversion, removed the barrier separating him from the majority of his countrymen. The French, who had had their fill of anarchy and of the arrogance of the foreigners, saw in the re-establishment of a strong monarchy a return to their national way of life. The thirty years of French religious wars ended with results diametrically opposite to those produced by the Thirty Years' War in Germany. The Pope himself, in defiance of all Spanish admonitions, made his peace with the renegade and, in doing so, recovered freedom of action and the possibility of playing off two Catholic powers against each other. The hour of Spain was past. Forsaken by fortune and friends alike, she became the first power to suffer, albeit at a crawling pace, the fate of an exhausted aspirant to supremacy.

Spain's heroic, desperate effort to master a great and sacred task in the face of all obstacles, and despite these to capture the glory within her grasp, had led her into reckless squandering of her substance. The effects of this prodigality could be seen most clearly in the nation's economy. More and more frequently, too, the silver-bearing ships were seized as prizes and failed to arrive. In its depleted condition, the organism could no longer be shocked into activity by stimulants. Interest on debt devoured income in advance, and three times under this regime the state was formally declared bankrupt. *Sint ut sunt aut non sint.* Religious fervor and warlike pride had carried Spain to the pinnacle of her power; their effects on the economic outlook of her people now hastened her downfall.

The Empire, by virtue of the mere size of its lands as well as the bravery of its troops, maintained its position at the head of the Continental powers, just as some great ship of war, though its mobility has been impaired in action, remains an opponent to be reckoned with on account of its firepower. Or, as Sully put it, the Empire was like a wrestler with the muscles of a giant whose heart has grown weak.

# CHAPTER II

## The System of States up to the Collapse of the French Bid for Supremacy under Louis XIV

# THE SYSTEM OF STATES

# UP TO THE ASSUMPTION OF

# PERSONAL POWER

# BY LOUIS XIV IN 1661

I_N AN irrigation system, the closing or opening of a high-level sluice is sufficient to dry up wide areas or fertilize others with moisture. So the defeat of the Armada dried out the veins of the Spanish lands while it swelled those of the opposing countries. However, the political and economic decline was so gentle that more than two generations passed—generations still filled with Spanish feats of glory on the battlefields and even more so in the fields of the mind—before the aging dominant power retired to the second rank, yielding place to her principal Continental adversary. Not until the Peace of the Pyrenees in 1659 and Louis XIV's assumption of power in 1661 did the wave of France gather majestically, to attain its proud crest a century after the defeat of the Armada.

The broad trough between these two waves is packed with incident in many forms and ramifications. But they lack paramount significance. They merely paved the way for a decisive turn in world history. A brief characterization of this period will suffice here.

The absence of any great central issue caused the island world and the Continental world to break apart. On land, Spain was no longer a serious threat to Holland, and at sea she was for the most part thrown on the defensive. Thus the battles in the Netherlands lost the overriding importance as a focusing element which they had possessed in Philip II's time. Britain * was able to devote herself to her domestic problems without being forced into conflicts abroad. Under Cromwell, she was at last in a position to come to grips with her outmaneuvered Dutch rival without fear of endangering their common insular interests vis-à-vis the Continent. Not until the French drive for supremacy did they renew their alliance, which had first been forged to resist Spanish supremacy. Until then the naval powers turned their backs, as it were, on the Continent.

On the mainland, Germany now became the principal theater of war. The two Habsburg lines were once more making common cause. The Spanish branch needed German backing, while the German line, which had stood so long in the wings, awoke from its stupor, and the old objective of Charles V, the subjugation of the Empire, came into

* England and Scotland were not completely united in one political entity until 1707, when the Act of Union merged England, Scotland, and Wales in the United Kingdom of Great Britain. However, the term "Britain" had been used informally ever since the union of the crowns of England and Scotland in 1603; this earlier usage has been adopted in this book. Trans. Note.

66

prominence once more alongside Philip's objective, the subjugation of the Netherlands. No sooner had the Emperor's
hand reached out for the decisive blow than Sweden intervened, and France, her strength mounting under Richelieu,
threw her power into the scales. As a result, Germany was
converted unequivocally into a fluid system of states, a
process whose groundwork had been laid by the Religious
Peace of Augsburg. The Empire paid with its own impotence for having warded off Habsburg supremacy; in fact,
Europe's freedom and German *Libertät* had been interde-
pendent for a hundred years.

The price paid was the more terrible since, in the seventeenth century, the threat of Habsburg paramountcy had
long ceased to be as great as it was in the sixteenth. With
Spain's decline on the one hand and the rise of the naval
powers and France on the other, a victory for the Emperor
in Germany could scarcely have had much effect in a westward direction, no decisive effect, that is, in terms of world
history. It would have meant little in the Atlantic area if
Austria had achieved a foothold in the Baltic, a landlocked
sea. Indeed, how could a power seeking supremacy have
emerged from remote Vienna?

The same was true of Sweden. Her power did not reach
as far as the Atlantic Ocean or into the depths of Eurasia. It
stopped short of both the great maritime and continental
areas of the future.

Whereas the exhausted German Habsburgs acquiesced
in the Peace of Westphalia, the Spanish branch went on
fighting doggedly in isolation, even though the secession of
Portugal and the loss of the Portuguese colonies had manifestly weakened Spain. With the Peace of the Pyrenees, to
which she was finally forced to accede in 1659, the gates
were closed on a magnificent century and a half of history.

Unremitting exertion had consumed Spain's moral as well as her material substance. But even her accelerated decline was to be a downward glide, not a plunge.

Moving at the pace of Spain's withdrawal, her adversaries fanned out, France on the continent, the maritime powers on the seas.

Under the two Cardinals, the French crown broke the resistance that the nobility was able to offer even after the conclusion of the religious wars by Henry IV. Amid all the jostling, conflicting interests of the Continent, a powerful state apparatus could develop only on the basis of absolutism. Although this revolution from above did not destroy the ornate edifice of feudal society, it razed its fortifications, the boltholes of active resistance to the state. The well-proportioned, dominating structure of a modern army and bureaucracy began to rise from amid the antiquated masonry. A strictly royalist attitude toward the state increasingly permeated the middle classes and drove back what was left of the older outlook among the upper classes.

As for the naval powers, Holland had already reached the stage of full maturity, but Britain, like France, was still climbing out of a welter of internal struggles to a new height of prestige abroad. While France pressed forward on her centuries-old course as a continental state, Britain hastened toward her destiny as a great maritime island power. What Holland had achieved decades earlier, Britain now accomplished: she turned full face toward the sea.

Only a gallant advance guard of maritime England had sailed into action in 1588. Under Elizabeth's circumspect leadership, the country merely went through its apprenticeship at sea. There was even a sharp setback to follow under the first two Stuarts, whose minds were never stirred by the maritime spirit. What fascinated them were the absolutism of the Continent and the glitter of its great courts, and this fascination extended to all the upper ranks of society—the landed gentry of the old school and their close allies, the Anglican Church and the ancient episcopal cities—all of which were still unaffected by industry and sea-borne trade. Rallied against these forces about the hostile Parliament were all the forces of movement: certain sections of the aristocracy (thanks to its principles of heredity, no clear line of division existed between the nobility and the middle-class capitalists); the countryside as a whole, with its sheep shearing, its consequent interest in exports, and its increasing manufactures; and lastly the young towns, where cloth-making, commerce, and shipping predominated. These groups were dependent for their well-being on maritime prestige. They were deeply conscious of its ignominious decline, of the advantages their Dutch competitors derived from it, and of the low esteem in which their own country was held abroad because it was unable to render effective aid to the German and French Protestants. Militant forms of the Baptist faith and Calvinism spread among these circles; and in her Civil Wars, Britain finally experienced—belatedly, because of her island position—the heat of both religious and political passions.

Under the Tudors, absolutism had earned its national *raison d'être* through the suppression of feudalism and the inauguration of an insular policy. But the more thoroughly absolutism discharged its task, the more superfluous it became. Self-assured people had come to the fore, men able to pursue on their own initiative the course already laid down. At this very moment the Stuart monarchy put a curb on this development. It is true that the colonization of North America began at this time, but the Crown allowed it to happen rather than fostered it. On the Continent, the greatness of a state rested upon an absolute monarchy, upon its army and bureaucracy, upon the grand strategy of its foreign policy. The opposite was the case in the island world. In Britain and Holland alike, the rise to maritime greatness involved holding the monarchic element in check; the navy was developed in place of the army; and government by the people instead of government by bureaucracy became the rule.

However, Britain's population, large and complex as it was in comparison to Holland's, needed more than two generations of domestic struggle to express and consolidate its new character. After the execution of Charles I, the legitimate monarchy was excluded and a revolutionary regime established. The surging breakthrough in the direction that the current of English history was to follow so majestically and serenely in the future, brought, as in Venetian history, a personality of Caesarean cast to the pinnacle of power on the island. Cromwell's tyranny, backed by the army of the Revolution, jeopardized the British way of life in a manner different from that of the Stuart monarchy, but no less forcefully. Yet, in the long run, the sound, forward-looking factors in his regime prevailed. The amorphous nature of his power spurred him to look abroad in order to justify himself in the eyes of the domestic opposition. He successfully launched Britain on the path of maritime imperialism; and to her great good fortune, his contradictory plans for an expansive policy on the Continent never matured. He built up the navy. Elizabeth's, compared with his, was a mere infant.

The navy had remained basically loyal to Parliament, which advocated a maritime policy. Cromwell now sent it into action against Holland, which, however closely akin in religion, was Britain's rival on the seas. Dutch commerce had benefited greatly from the long wars with Continental Spain. But in the brief war against the island nation, in which her trade was broken, Holland found her master. She bowed to the Navigation Act and fell back into second place as a naval power.

Cromwell also struck a mighty blow at Spain and sealed at sea the defeat administered to her by France on land. He finished off by offensive action what the defeat of the Armada had begun in a defensive battle. Now the maritime energies of Britain, which had been pent up over forty-five years of Stuart rule with only a modest outlet afforded by emigration to North America, poured forth into the world. Both in overseas trade and naval strength, Britain gained supremacy, favored, like Venice, by two interacting factors: her island position and the new role which fell into her hands, the role of intermediary between two worlds. Unlike the great Continental powers, Britain could direct her undivided strength toward the sea; unlike her Dutch competitor, she did not have to man a land front; and towering over her rival in size and vigor, she no longer had to fight grave domestic dangers. Thus it was that Britain acquired a title to world power, and the insular principle, Holland's slow decline notwithstanding, achieved a new level of strength alongside the continental principle.

To be sure, the Restoration again brought uncertainty into British foreign policy, for, in the main, the last two Stuart kings understood the insular spirit of their country as little as had the first two. But their continental tendencies, although destined to jeopardize their own throne, could not divert the maritime aspirations of the nation from the chosen course.

# LOUIS XIV

A YEAR after the restoration of the Stuarts, Louis XIV took the reins of government into his own hands. A century after Spain had been lifted to the heights, French power began to rise.

I shall here single out those factors in the new battle for supremacy which emphasize its structural similarity with the one that went before and the one that came after: *eadem sed aliter.*

A comparison of Louis XIV's prospects with those of Philip II will be particularly enlightening because the two rulers not only pursued similar ends but did so by similar means. Both their realms belonged to the category of the military-*cum*-bureaucratic Continental power.

To take the external situation first, it is obvious that the initial Continental position of France was far more modest than Spain's had been, to say nothing of their respective situations overseas, which admitted of no comparison. In the preceding century, the divisive tendency had made great strides; its progress was marked by the rise of the naval powers, of France herself, of Sweden, by the progressive dissolution of the Holy Roman Empire, and by Spain's downfall. To advance the tendency toward unification now, in the face of this richly diversified array of states, was a far more difficult undertaking than it had been in the early days of the system.

But even when we examine the internal resources of France, we find her at a disadvantage: she had at her disposal no universal spiritual force such as the Counter Reformation, which had acted as a spur to Spain's energies in the sixteenth century and which had brought her friends into line and confounded her enemies. In fact, the universal ideas of the Middle Ages had lost their influence on the formation of political entities.

Yet the new France was abundantly endowed with potentialities of her own special kind. Whereas the Spanish domains had been scattered and disparate, the French dominions were firmly knit and homogeneous, possessing internal lines of communication and a population twice as large as that of Spain proper. Pulsing through France was a worldly, dynamic vigor that was concentrated on enhancing the power and glory of the national monarchy, had made the Gallican church an instrument of political power, and, following a tradition cultivated since Francis I, did not shrink from alliances with Turks or heretics. This élan breathed into the French economy a kind of life that the Spanish system had never been able to generate. Of what avail had the wealth of her mines been to Spain? Colbert learned modern methods of amassing wealth from Holland, Spain's opponent. Holland's new forms of economic activity, rapidly grown from maritime origins, were to be transplanted to France by careful planning and with the aid of the bureaucratic apparatus grafted onto her economy from above.

For the first time, a Continental country began, with rationalized energy, to compete with a naval power. Against the islanders' free spirit of enterprise, France pitted the full weight of her manpower under state discipline. She used her resources of power to achieve prosperity, not as an end in itself but as a means of increasing those resources of power. Europe's first standing army, a creation of Louis's, was based on a taxation system developed by Colbert on mercantilist lines. However, a cardinal point in the program of this system of acquiring wealth was expansion overseas. A French colonial drive interposed itself with tremendous verve between the older colonial empires. There had been no lack of initiative in this direction since the time of Francis I; indeed, France, with her extensive Atlantic coast, had a far larger maritime region than Spain. But this region, for one thing, lay in the shadow of France's conflicts with Spain, and had to take second place to Continental concerns nearer at hand; at the same time, it was overshadowed by internal conflicts, and was more cruelly afflicted by the wars of religion than almost any other area in the center of Europe. Both causes seemed to have been eliminated at the start of the new regime. Would they remain so? Or were they inherent in the nature of the French body politic?

At the outset, the rejuvenated state under its young monarch swelled with unbounded self-assurance and with a quite unanimous national sensation of strength which might well serve as a substitute for the missionary zeal of the Spaniards. And if France, as she stepped onto the stage of world politics, was not allied with any spiritual force of truly universal appeal, the glory of her national spirit generated a power of attraction that recognized no frontiers. France was moving toward her *grand siècle*. With the god of opportunity smiling upon her, who could predict what limits would be set to her powers?

Louis's first warlike action was directed against Spain. Of Spanish blood on his mother's side, he never, in his stiff-necked pride, denied this descent. From the very beginning he proudly claimed it as his due to occupy the place of Catholic Majesty in the world. It could already be foreseen that the last Habsburg on the throne of Spain would die childless. When that moment came, France must be strong enough to broaden her own base decisively by adding to it the most important segments of the Spanish inheritance and so bring about a turning point of history such as the union of so many scepters in the hand of Charles V had represented. That was the long-term goal. In the meantime, Louis must keep hard on the heels of his failing adversary and, in pursuance of long-nurtured tendencies, push forward his eastern frontiers in sudden thrusts at the expense of the Spanish Habsburgs, the German branch, and the Empire.

Yet Louis's incursion into the Spanish Netherlands achieved only limited success. It was diplomatic, not military, resistance that checked him.

The shift of power heralded by Louis's action constituted the first threat to the balance of power as a whole since 1588; and events within the European system of states thus reacquired key importance for the duration of this regime. The maritime powers, which had so long kept their backs turned to the Continent and were for the second time pitting their strength against each other, shelved their differences, turned jointly to face the rising dominant power, and compelled it to treat its predecessor with forbearance. For Holland had long since ceased to regard the Spanish Netherlands as a sally port against her territory; rather, she considered them an advanced buffer. Again, in the eyes of every farsighted person, any threat to Holland was also a threat to Britain's obvious interests. From Philip's time until the downfall of the system, the Netherlands remained its storm center. The delta of the Scheldt and the Rhine was the key to the world domination for which Louis was striving. His very first move in pursuit of his grand Continental plans brought him into conflict with the interests of the maritime power; and having failed to foresee the collision, he swore vengeance.

In the maritime theater, too, a collision was at hand. Mercantilist France had her own special reason for demanding the "destruction of Carthage." She wanted to become the heir of her instructor in trade and colonial affairs. Colbert made haste to build a powerful navy.

Thus Holland, because she had acted as peacemaker, became the objective of the next war; and, as in Philip's time, the freedom of the European system of states was to stand or fall with the freedom of the Netherlands.

However, Holland could be softened up for attack only by diplomatic preparation. *Divide et impera.* Not until Louis had separated the two naval powers, which had just united to thwart him, could he hope to isolate and wipe out Holland, a country over which France had a sixfold superiority in population figures, to say nothing of the way the Dutch had neglected their land armaments. The destruction of Holland would constitute a victory in both the Continental and maritime spheres, for in the long run probably not even Britain would be able to contest French expansion overseas once France had the maritime potential of the Dutch at her disposal.

The improbable happened. French diplomacy divided the naval powers and, moreover, managed to form an alliance with the British against the Dutch. Two circumstances helped it in this. First, public opinion on the other side of the Channel had not yet fully recognized the danger so suddenly looming from France and had failed to see that the roles of friend and foe were being switched; the prospect of a commercial rival's easy destruction in a third war had its attractions. Second—and this was Louis's covert trump card —the Stuart King himself had been drawn into the net; not only was he corrupted by the hope of support for his plans to rule as an absolute monarch and Catholicize his country, but he was also bribed by immediate French subsidies. A grotesque juxtaposition: on the Continent, a monarch who was the creator and pivot of the state; on the island, a king who had become the most dangerous enemy of the country's true and inherent future, of its liberties and independence.

Louis, then, hoped to eliminate both naval powers at one blow—Holland in open war and Britain by a secret alliance. Yet the breakthrough to signal success was denied him. Even in isolation, Holland proved strong enough to repel the sudden attack. Finding itself deserted and faced with the threat of extinction, the amphibious state defended its land positions by breaching the dikes and summoning the waters to its aid. At sea its heroic navy held the combined fleets of the attackers in check. But the actual deliverer of the commonwealth was a Prince of Orange, just as a member of that family had been its co-founder. The House came into its own whenever the land front was in peril. The plutocrats were not equal to the task, and the reins were torn from their grasp, though the republic was not converted into a monarchy. The States-General remained an ellipse with two poles, and the House of Orange patriotically accepted this equivocal state of affairs. Louis tried in vain to tempt the twenty-two-year-old William. The prince, no Stuart, was not prepared to bargain away his country's freedom for the sovereignty of a small principality.

Holland, then, heroically survived the kind of panic that occurs in the history of island states whenever their insular integrity is suddenly placed in jeopardy. Probably Holland

on her own would have been as little able to resist indefi-
nitely as the Netherlands had been a century earlier. However, *fortes fortuna adjuvat*: public opinion in Britain
grasped the situation, Parliament insisted on peace negotiations, and for the time being Holland was saved.

But, we may ask, whence came the stoutness of the
Dutch who had barely managed to prevent the French from
flooding across Europe? Unquestionably, their strength
came from the link that bound the country to overseas territories. As an exponent of the spirit of the new transoceanic
territories, Holland was able once more to summon the
strength for a last feat of historic proportions.

Now, however, a new and typical state of affairs arose.
After her failure against the naval power, France, like
Philip II before her and Napoleon and Hitler later, transferred her unbroken energies to the interior of the Continent, and even the hastily formed coalition of the two Habsburgs, the Holy Roman Empire, and some of its princes
could not offer effective resistance to Louis's standing armies
with their superiority in armaments. Moreover, Turkey, the
old ally of Francis I, reappeared on the scene, and the Emperor found himself exposed to tremendous pressure from
east and west at the same time. Europe was overcome by a
feeling of impotence in the face of Louis's provocative
breaches of ancient property rights and watched helplessly
as the French frontier was systematically pushed eastward.
Meanwhile, France continued her expansion overseas as
well. Spreading his plumage like a peacock, the Sun King
savored triumph after triumph, and with each his *hubris*
and his sense of power grew, even faster than his power
itself.

Might he not one day try to repeat his spring at Holland's throat? *Reculer pour mieux sauter?* Who can tell
whether Holland in her plutocratic obesity could have put

forth another heroic effort? In Philip's time, after all, she had been saved only by the actual intervention of England.

From the long-term point of view, the future of the system unquestionably depended on Britain. It would be lost, and the future of the island with it, if the Stuarts were to remain at the helm and whittle away both the country's independence and its liberties at home. Despite growing resistance in Parliament and throughout the country, it was by no means certain that public opinion would recognize the exigencies of the Continental situation in time, or that the nation would produce farsighted new leaders, men with the ability to act.

Fortunately for the system, the genius of Europe now became embodied in a man who, rising above the selfishness of a single state, planned and worked for all the states threatened by France. Again and again in the course of the great struggles for supremacy, the sense of solidarity among the threatened parties has torn down the barriers raised by their special interests, but perhaps never so completely as in the person of William of Orange. Unable to rule as a monarch in Holland, he became a European statesman. His deft and patient hand wove, thread by thread, the flexible net in which the Sun King, dazzled by the glare of his own power, was to be worn down. William's delicate diplomacy had already achieved considerable success on the Continent. The splitting up of territory which had become more and more frequent since 1588 offered wider scope for coalitions than would have been possible a hundred years earlier. But their structure remained fragile as long as it was not cemented by the gold of the combined naval powers. Only in the larger setting of London could William play out his role as history's first organizer of a large-scale encirclement, a role he had created on the smaller stage of The Hague.

How ironical it was that a Prince of Orange, of all people, should be called upon by both parties in Parliament to ascend the British throne. Had not Cromwell engineered the exclusion of the Princes of Orange from all office in their own country in order to weaken Holland? But the same Cromwell had also conceived the idea of a constitutional union between the two naval powers. To that extent, his wish was now fulfilled by the Glorious Revolution. Not that considerations of foreign policy had been of primary importance in producing that Revolution. However, interwoven with the domestic struggle for power, they were contributory factors; and both sources of tension were brought to a head by the religious issue, which, arriving belatedly, retained its importance north of the Channel longer than it did farther south. The revocation of the Edict of Nantes created among Protestants a belligerency reminiscent of the mood prevailing in Philip's time; and the effrontery of James II in moving—in alliance with France—to introduce Catholicism and absolute rule heightened the unanimous public wrath. William himself proceeded with cool tolerance. As a European diplomat, he had succeeded in enlisting the help not merely of the Habsburgs but even of the Pope. In Britain, he exploited the wave of religious feeling and acted with masterly speed to assume control of the whole country. This foreign prince, schooled by his experience in Holland, understood something the Stuarts had never grasped: the real position of the monarchy in Britain. The more clearly he assessed the role of public opinion, the greater his actual influence on affairs became.

In broad outline, Britain's character as a maritime nation had settled into its final shape. After negotiating a last set of rapids, her history flowed on serenely down the centuries. The nobility may have remained the ruling class,

but the nobility of the island nation was so variously interwoven with the life of the entire country, particularly with
the exponents of its capitalist economy, that the dominant
influence of the aristocracy ensured a beneficently even
tenor in the conduct of affairs.

Louis was not the first, and would not be the last, Continental ruler to miscalculate in his estimate of the British
people. His knowledge of Britain was confined to the Court
of St. James, and he missed his opportunity to check William's enterprise when he might still have been able to do
so. While the net was drawn tighter around him, the fighting strength of his Continental opponents was invigorated
by subsidies from the overseas cornucopia of both naval
powers. Blood and gold made common cause. Together,
Britain and Holland were far more difficult to overcome
than isolated Holland had been. It was no longer sufficient
to breach the advanced Dutch dike; henceforth, the more
powerful British dike behind it stood in the path of French
inundation. Leadership within the coalition of the naval
powers passed to Britain, and, behind the scenery of the
personal union, Holland lost her status as a great power.

Louis then, like Philip before him, was forced to raise
his stakes. Nothing could help him but a landing in Britain
—an island denuded of troops—and a restoration of the
Stuarts. But Louis's defeat at La Hogue repeated, as it
were, the rout of Philip's Armada in the Channel. Once
again, the navy of the dominant Continental power proved
inferior to that of the purely naval power. The efficiency
of the French seamen may have been as greatly superior
to that of the Spaniards as Colbert's mercantilism was to
Spain's metals policy; but a disastrous disharmony beset
French planning down to the very details. The soul of Continental France and the soul of maritime France would not

merge. Fundamentally, Louis did not understand the sea; and instructions issued from his cabinet to his admirals speeded the downfall of his battle fleet.

Like Philip, Louis was not in a position to build a new navy. The impoverishment of his great realm, now entangled in William's net, continued inexorably, despite its rational mercantile policies. It was accelerated by the King's irrational love of ostentation—an expression of the progressive *hubris* of the aging monarch. This *hubris* would reappear, as an occupational disease, to threaten great kings in coming struggles for supremacy. The Habsburgs had been saved from it by their ascetic piety; but owing to the universal demands of this piety, their policies, too, had been pushed to extremes.

If France had manifestly passed her zenith at the battle of La Hogue, her decline, like that of Spain before, ensued by degrees. As Britain, content with her defensive victory at sea, still held aloof from the Continent during Louis's Third War, he managed to retain the bulk of his Continental possessions.

An external event then brought the failing strength of France surging back once again. The great opportunity that for forty years had been the goal of Louis's yearnings presented itself almost unexpectedly to the elderly King in the most alluring form. In the will of his Spanish brother-in-law, Louis's grandson was named heir to Spain's dominions on both sides of the oceans, an intoxicating prospect in the maritime as well as the Continental sphere. Forgotten or misunderstood were all the warnings of past years. Louis rushed blindly into temptation and soon found himself entangled once again, this time more deeply, in the net of a great European coalition, which was again directed by Britain's money diplomacy. Gone, with the rise of the naval powers, were those early-sixteenth-century days when the European system was not as yet capable of preventing the accumulation of many crowns on the head of Charles V. Gone, too, since La Hogue, was Louis's hope of defying the naval powers in their own element. He was forced to fight the War of the Spanish Succession on land, while far out to sea cruised British ships of which no one spoke but whose actions outweighed many a glorious victory on land.

This time Britain's contribution was not confined to the operations of her fleet. For the first time since the fifteenth century, she threw a sizable army into the scales—no longer for purposes of conquest on the other side of the Channel, as Cromwell had still dreamed of doing, but in pursuit of a shrewdly reasoned naval policy. The aims of that policy would be jeopardized if France remained strong enough to absorb Spain. For if that should happen, she might try at the peace table to get a hold on Spain's overseas territories and then bolt and bar them to her rivals. To conquer the massive bloc of this colonial empire was beyond Britain's strength, despite her command of the sea. This time, therefore, she found herself obliged not merely to support her Continental allies with subsidies but also to strengthen them with an expeditionary force, which would also put her in a position to control their actions. At the head of this force she placed a man who continued William's diplomatic work with the instruments of war. Just as William had created the prototype of the coalition statesman, so Marlborough originated that of the coalition commander. He proved himself a master at co-ordinating all resources on sea and land, in the diplomatic as well as in the military field. When he fell from power as the result of the change of government in 1710, France's resistance had been thoroughly broken.

To eliminate it entirely would not have profited Britain; she was not making war on the dominant Bourbon power in order to revive Habsburg supremacy on behalf of Austria. When the coalition that Britain had founded and controlled had served its purpose, she coldly tore it apart. More than once, perfidious Albion, ensconced on her island and possessing longer leverage, treated allies with a ruthlessness that might have jeopardized the prestige of a Continental country. On that occasion she bargained out a separate peace with Louis, who doggedly and successfully defended his own and the nation's honor with his last ounce of strength. The downfall of a state that has striven after supremacy always shows marks of a gloomy grandeur to match the splendor and *hubris* of its preceding triumphs.

The Emperor and the Holy Roman Empire had to make the best of the situation created by Britain. In the last analysis, they had both been nothing more than auxiliaries.

Although the peace treaty recognized the Bourbon prince as King of Spain, it relieved the naval powers of most of their fear that the spirit of France's mercantilism would permeate the Spanish colonies; the farsighted new equilibrium in the European balance of power system guaranteed that the treaty's cunning provisions in this regard would be observed. The process of splitting up the Continent was advanced still more by the distribution of the Spanish domains. The rise of the new kingdoms of Sardinia and Prussia was characteristic of this development. The Bourbons on both sides of the Pyrenees had lost so much strength that they could not have renewed Louis XIV's enterprise even if they had been completely united. Remote Austria, on the other hand, had not gained nearly enough strength to make a bid for supremacy. Although her reluctant acquisition of the Spanish Netherlands as an exclave carried her into the maritime zone, she would never be permitted to pursue an effective maritime policy. In occupying the Netherlands, Austria was merely acting as a sentinel watching France on behalf of the naval powers. Even her acquisition of Spain's subsidiary lands in Italy facilitated Britain's penetration of the Mediterranean. On these coasts, too, the British navy now posted its strong sentries. Here, as elsewhere, its aim was to prevent any power in quest of supremacy in the future from breaking out of the ring that it was gradually drawing around the Continent.

To Britain, the balance of power in Europe, whose guarantors the naval powers remained, was not an end in itself but merely the prerequisite of her supremacy beyond the seas. There the roots of the island's strength had lain since the time of Elizabeth, when England herself did not own a square foot of land overseas. There, too, her territorial expansion now made increasingly powerful strides.

Following the pattern set by the imperialist practice of the Dutch, Britain established posts and naval bases, particularly in the East and West Indies. In the West Indies, these stations also served as bases for the smugglers' traffic with the Spanish colonies on the American mainland. Britain was too weak to seize these colonies by military conquest, but the Peace of Utrecht provided her with ways of penetrating them commercially by legitimate—and, even more, by illicit—means. She secured for herself precisely what she had prevented France from obtaining.

British penetration of the Portuguese colonial empire was more pronounced still. Portugal was Spain's natural enemy, and when Spain became Bourbon, Portugal exchanged French for British protection, never to leave it again. Britain tacitly inherited Portugal's sea power at the same time that she took Holland's in tow. Supremacy at sea can be extended less conspicuously than dominance on land.

However, Britain was not content with a policy of commercial colonization. She began to develop large colonial territories in the manner of Spain. Superior in sea power to any of her Continental rivals, she had an additional advantage over all of them: the basis of her sea power was much broader than that of the Venetians or even that of the Dutch. Moreover, Britain was one of the great old national states of the Western world, and boasted a richly diversified society. Unlike Holland, she did not specialize in shipping and commerce. Her economy, resting on a broad agricultural foundation, supported a population three times that of the Netherlands. In contrast to the Continental peoples, the British were not involved in fierce struggles for existence, and so this surplus strength could be channeled into emigration.

It took Britain a long time to recognize her own trump card. In the insular world, society often takes the initiative before the government. We have seen this in connection with the development of British sea power, which was fostered by the Merchant Adventurers and buccaneers. Similarly, in the seventeenth century private initiative, acting independently of, and almost against, the state, started the first great wave of emigration to North America. The first Stuarts, with their Continental outlook, simply tolerated it. They would have restrained it had they been as strong as the absolute monarchs on the other side of the Channel who were their models. For the people who embarked in the emigrant ships were members of the home opposition, and this remained so, *mutatis mutandis*, under the succeeding revolutionary regime.

From the very outset, therefore, a spirit of opposition

86

took root on the far side of the ocean, an unbridled urge in the part of the settlers to build a life of their own fashioning in ecclesiastical and political affairs. Economic considerations took second place. What attracted the settlers there were not the sources of wealth generally exploited in colonial economies of the day. North America called for hard work in a hard climate. Merchants and adventurers were not the only ones who voyaged to the new lands. The magnet of freedom attracted members of all classes. What was created was not just a loose chain of colonies laid out along the coast, but a new nation with a new pattern of life. (One may be reminded of the Germans pushing across the Elbe on a broad front in the Middle Ages: there, too, a new nation with new patterns of life came into being in the wake of the Emperor's official policy.) With no need for much state planning, the whiff of ocean air brought to life natural forces which in the seventeenth century fostered colonization as they had favored shipping in the sixteenth.

In the War of the Spanish Succession, the British colonies became involved in local friction with the French settlements. The conflict between the Continental and the island way of life, which was being fought out in Europe, was projected into the territories of the New World.

These French settlements in North America were different from the British colonies. They were the fruit of a state-planned and state-controlled colonial policy closely integrated with the broad lines of the power policy pursued by the mother country. They were as different from their Anglo-Saxon neighbors as a formal baroque garden is from a rambling English park.

Not that the great maritime zone of France had lacked spontaneous native forces urging colonization, or that the internal disorders during the wars of religion had not supplied incentives for emigration. But these forces and incentives did not flourish in the Continental climate as they did in the island air. The authoritarian regime of Louis XIV afforded them no scope.

But it did possess a capacity of a special kind for developing colonial territories. The Spaniards had demonstrated that a Continental power state could conquer and organize mainland territories overseas. The mercantile, seafaring Portuguese, in handling the plantation economy of their Brazilian colony, displayed a less impressive aptitude. And the Dutch showed none at all: they gained a grip on Brazil for a while but were unable to maintain it; to do so, they would have needed a land army and the suspect assistance of the Princes of Orange.

In fact, France applied the methods of Spain in masterly fashion, having perfected them with the mercantilist practices that Colbert had learned from the Dutch. He knew how to wield his military and bureaucratic instruments of power to penetrate into the depths of the continent in movements embracing large areas. The scattered British settlements only gradually gained ground in a westerly direction. France, like Spain, was adept at handling the natives: her hunters and traders were their good friends, the English farmers their natural enemies. In the manner of Spain, too, France cemented her relationship with the Indians by enlisting the aid of the Catholic Church. Furthermore, the authoritarian methods and firm hand of France ensured the lasting loyalty of the immigrants, and were able to turn their disciplined manpower to good account for military purposes.

If all the plans of the maritime powers for conquering the Iberian colonies foundered, why did not Britain's schemes in regard to the French colonies suffer the same fate? For one thing, the Iberian nations, the sixteenth-century masters of the sea, had been able to consolidate their overseas possessions at leisure and at a steady pace, for a small body of immigrants had been sufficient to re-mold the numerically large, but docile, native population. In the vast and sparsely populated regions of North America, however, only brisk immigration could have ena-bled French colonies to defend themselves, especially as, since La Hogue, the mother country had been losing con-trol of sea communications.

This point shows us the drawback of the French sys-tem. Whereas the British emigrants came from the ranks of the opposition, Louis, who declared that he had not made his realm Catholic in order to deliver up his colonies to heretics, did not permit the Huguenots to emigrate. Thus, as Frenchmen are as a rule reluctant to leave their native soil, and could only expect to find the same authoritarian forms of social, political, and ecclesiastical life on the other side, no large-scale migration took place. Whereas around 1700 the British settlements already sheltered a white popu-lation of a quarter of a million, the French colonies could not boast one tenth of that figure, although both had come into existence at about the same time.

With that kind of proportion between the forces on the spot, it was only natural that the provisions of the Peace of Utrecht relating to the American colonies reflected the de-cline of France. The British were able to spread through the coastal region of Canada and make future communica-tion between the hinterland and France still more difficult. Nevertheless, the position of the French remained suffi-ciently strong and deeply rooted to enable them to resume the fight at an appropriate moment. In the New World, as in Europe, the wave of French power was slow to ebb.

On the whole, the European system of states had stood its third test with a far greater margin of safety than it had the two previous challenges. Louis XIV, in his unifying drive for supremacy, was never able for one moment to pose as great a threat to the liberty of Europe as had the two great Habsburgs. Against this drive, the divisive tendency prevailed all the more conspicuously, the more arrogantly it was contested by the Sun King. At the end of the seventeenth century, as at the close of the sixteenth, the maritime powers had proved to be the backbone of this divisive tendency, the counterweight to, and antagonists of, the tendency toward supremacy. Yet they were preserved by their very nature from the temptation to strive for hegemony in Europe themselves. In the insular sphere, a concentration of forces nevertheless took place which contrasted sharply with the disintegration on the Continent. But it was a concentration of sea power alone. Britain inherited more and more of the naval prestige of her predecessors in the Atlantic. She assumed by degrees the prestige of Spain and France, the two great land powers, as well as that of Portugal and Holland, the maritime powers. This was in part a result of Britain's insular position, which allowed her to concentrate all her strength at sea. At the same time, and above all, this development was due to the discovery of the new overseas territories, which conferred on the island its great role of intermediary between two worlds.

This intermediary role is the very foundation of the singular importance of sea power in the framework of the entire system. Since the defeat of the Armada, the lines along which that system has developed have been mysteriously influenced by overseas factors. The freedom of the system and overseas expansion bear a causal relationship to each other.

90

## CHAPTER III

# The System of States up to the Collapse of Napoleon's Bid for Supremacy

# THE THREE "WORLD POWERS"

# UP TO

# THE FRENCH REVOLUTION

Not only the overseas territories but also the continental territories in the East contributed constantly to maintaining the balance of the system. There was no question, of course, of any expansion by the West, of conquest and migration. Rather, it was a case of individual Eastern powers pushing westward. But to achieve success, they tried to gain admittance to the diplomatic maneuvers of the Western world and to have themselves included in its system as marginal figures. For the sake of attaining equality of status in the military field alone, they were at pains to go some way toward adapting themselves to Western civilization.

I have already discussed the Turks. Drawn into the system through their alliance with France, they at first played an outstanding role in trimming the balance under

Charles V. They lost that role mainly because the maritime powers became the counterweight to any power seeking supremacy, but also because the Turks' own barbarian strength crumbled swiftly. In the process of adapting themselves to the West, they never got beyond superficial borrowings of military techniques.

Their enemies and successors, the Russians, towered above them in every way.

Whereas, in the West, power moved from the center of the Continent to the Atlantic coast, magnetically attracted by the vastness of the overseas regions, power in the East was magnetically drawn by the oceanlike vastness of the continent itself. We observe this phenomenon even in the framework of German history. The territories of the East, being unsaturated with political power, offered better possibilities for expansion than the much-divided Holy Roman Empire. This German shift of power culminated in the Habsburg state, which saw the fight against the Turks as a Westernizing mission. The Germans, cut off as they were from the oceans, might have found scope in that mission for continental expansion on a grand scale, but power gravitated past Germany to a point farther east. Although the loosely knit Polish state, with its weak ethnic core, was not destined to become a rival, Russia certainly was. This vigorous nation found itself with the chance to grow unchecked in all directions. The Russians, unlike the Turks, were distant cousins of the Western peoples both ethnically and in mentality, and this kinship became the source of great possibilities for assimilation. These can be strikingly illuminated by the parallel, first suggested by Jakob Burckhardt, between Russia and Macedonia, between Peter the Great and Philip.

Macedonia was a country without access to the sea, built

94

into the solid mass of the Balkans and peopled by remote cousins of the Greeks. A monarchy of about 32,000 square miles in area, it differed both in character and order of size from the *poleis* of the Hellenic system of states, which, geographically as well as culturally, was minutely individualized. Toward that system of states—seaward, that is— Philip forcibly turned his people. A semi-barbarian, he became the enthusiastic disciple of the Greeks, only to outwit and overpower his teachers. The secret of his meteoric rise to power lay in his forcible grafting of the aging Greek culture onto a young, educable people. In this process Hellenic culture was stylized into Hellenistic civilization; the scale became larger but the roots of creative power deteriorated in the alien soil.

Analogous features can be seen in the physiognomy of Russia. Her physical dimensions and uniformity contrasted with the highly articulated, complex European peninsula. Mastery of the vast distances was made easier by mighty river systems that were not separated by towering mountain ranges. Here, there was space for a potamic empire comparable to the ancient empires of Mesopotamia and the Nile Valley. The rivers and the horse provided sufficient cohesion. Here the soil had no such binding, individualizing, distributive force as it had in the West; the muzhik of the *mir* did not cling to a patch of ground. Colonizing migrations had endowed him with an extensive outlook; the Western mind always thinks intensively. Politically, this was the natural home of unbridled absolutism built on Byzantine and Oriental foundations, an absolutism stiffened by Ivan the Terrible to monumental rigor. Links with the West were insignificant. The young Leibniz still spoke of Russia, Persia, and Abyssinia in the same breath, and would even call the unknown empire "old Turca."

Then came Russia's "Philip," who once and for all turned the country's face seaward, toward the European states. Peter was an admirer of Western culture in the same practical sense as Philip of Macedon had been of the Greek. Through a reign of terror, he imposed on his people European techniques of every kind: the techniques of warfare at sea and on land, economic techniques, the techniques of administration. He mated methods borrowed from the West with the spirit of the patient, malleable human material of the East and with the tradition of a despotic Eastern regime. The explosive mixture thus created, the very secret of his reign, sent the power of Russia soaring upward.

This power bore the marks of civilization to an extent that would not yet have been possible in the Western world. There, too, with the slackening of religious ties, the tendency to acquire power for its own sake by rational methods emerged more and more blatantly—and this, properly understood, is the common denominator of civilization. Since Spengler, we have become aware that the late period of a culture offers increasing scope to civilization, which is always present, until the latter seizes control of the absolute spirit in religion, art, and science. But a study of Russia, as of Macedonia, shows that this development progresses faster in the vast peripheral territories than at the center. Culturally backward marginal areas are the soil in which such a development flourishes best; whenever masses and dynamic vigor become more important than perfection, a drawback may turn into an advantage.

Even before Peter, Russia was spacious and populous enough to provide the quantitative prerequisites for a power characterized by civilization. For this condition to become a reality, however, Russia needed a creative ruler who would break away from many native traditions without allowing foreign ones to overwhelm him; a ruler who would assess both the old and the new according to their useful-ness in gaining him power, and ruthlessly harness both to that end, regardless of their original absolute spirit. At an early stage, Peter surrounded himself with foreigners, eman-cipated himself from native belief and tradition, inwardly forsook the cultural matrix of Russia, and, in doing so, stripped off fetters that might have hampered his will to power. He thus became the founder of an entirely new Russia, and to that extent a personality of a historical emi-nence such as the consolidated West had long since ceased to produce. He, and he alone, was the hinge on which the destiny of the Russian Empire swung from the Orient to the Occident, from a culture sunk in apathy, isolation, foreign domination, and despotism to a civilization with world-wide contacts and power.

Step by step, the new was installed as the old was dis-mantled, each move conditioning another.

The new had of necessity to originate at the center of power, that is, in the army and navy. As naval armament was an innovation, the question of dismantling did not arise in this field. The shift of emphasis toward the sea, though planned by Peter's predecessors, was first put into effect by him. It was the passionately conceived nucleus of his think-ing. Only by making that thought a reality, either in the south or in the north, could he hope to approximate to the West, to achieve equal status, to penetrate the maneuver pattern of the system and gain ground in it—in other words, to link his state to the current of Western civilization and arouse the latent strength of the Russian giant to action on a grand scale. His new capital was to become the Amster-dam of the North. He familiarized himself with all the techniques of the naval powers, from shipbuilding to com-

97

merce. But he could not, and would not, admit the liberal spirit of their regimes, their human freedoms: such things would have acted like poison in the intracontinental empire which he ruled as a despot.

However, in the war with the Swedes, arming on land proved to be far more important than naval armament. The enemy was Peter's stern preceptor: the new instrument of war was forged in the fires of war itself, and the foundation of the modern Russian military state, unshaken to this day, was laid between battles. The patient, readily drilled, easily replaceable, death-defying manpower of the East proved to be superb material for the mechanical tactics of those days. The sons of the nobles were brought up as officers. Thus a pliant weapon was placed in the hands of the supreme commander, a machine in which human instruments were welded together, men who, severed from traditional ties, saw obedience to their sovereign's will as their highest duty.

But this constructive process could not take place without some destruction. The unreliable old Strelitzi, who were accustomed to living in civilian comfort with their wives and children, mutinied against the furious new pace of existence, and were overtaken by the same fate that later destroyed the Janissaries. Thus the forces of Old Russia were robbed of their military weapon, and reactionary elements that dared to oppose the new course, even through the Tsarevitch himself, could be burned out. The spiritual weapon of the reactionary forces was blunted by bureaucratization of the Church. Orthodox caesaropapism, which was not evolved in ignorance of the conditions of German Protestantism, invested the Tsar with a concentration of power over his subjects' lives and souls such as the great Catholic monarchs could not attain. Peter built the native church organization into his system as a useful bridge between the old era and the new. Inevitably, this took place at the expense of a genuine religious spirit; at the expense, that is, of the root of Christian culture and therefore of the true counterpole of civilization. Replacement of the Patriarchate by the bureaucratic College of the Holy Synod facilitated and masked the manufacture of the new human instruments. And state education, wherever its beginnings were to be found, operated even more effectively in the same direction. The new man was needed not only in the armed forces but also throughout the bulging bureaucracy which served them. The bureaucracy created the necessary financial basis by means of a system of intensive tax collection.

In setting up his bureaucracy and his army, Peter, of course, learned a good deal from the absolutist states of the West. But here, contrary to his experience in his borrowings from the island world, he established intimate contact with the spirit of the models as well. Both the absolutism of the West and the despotism of the East were manifestations of the continental power state and, in the technique of acquiring power, more akin to each other than either was to the maritime states. Although the Western monarchies were two hundred years ahead in the development of militarism and bureaucracy, Peter's state caught up with its teachers. It put their experience to use on a vast *tabula rasa* and was able to maintain the dynamic thrust of the native despotism while driving back the native forces of reaction. This system was related to that of the Western power states in somewhat the same way that the massive brick churches of the Baltic are to their French models—the Baltic version simplified and strengthened, yet showing exotic Asian traits of its own.

But the very suddenness of the success of this violent

artificial synthesis was purchased at the price of internal tensions that diminished its fruitfulness and solidity. The fabricated structure did not completely replace the native growth. The imposing façade of this civilization—and the art of the empire was really a Hellenistic façade—concealed the smothered discontent of the outraged soul of a people. Henceforth, people and government lacked the natural harmony which in Western states at the height of their power brought a rich flowering of the national spirit. The greatest glories of the Russian mind would be achieved in detachment from the state, and even at times in opposition to it; and the smothered discontent would seek release not merely in outbursts of reaction but also in sudden revolts, once Western techniques were followed by Western ideas. To substitute for an organic evolution of society from below, this empire would again and again require the highest degree of initiative from above, a process which alone had created it. Again and again, the urge for expansion would burst forth. Though inherent in the Russian nature, this urge was unleashed as never before by Peter's sudden switch to Western civilization.

Was not this drive, from the very outset, the motive force of his system? It needlessly touched off war with Sweden; it supplied the energy for the breathtaking improvisations that, after all the reverses, paved the way for victory. Because of that urge, the country's internal evolution and its external acts could be interwoven to a degree not to be seen again until the wars of the French Revolution. And so invigorating was that urge that Peter's state was scarcely born before it developed, in the cradle, the powers of Hercules.

To understand the effects this state had on the European system, we must consider its situation before Peter.

Russia was the continental flanking power in relation to Europe—indeed, she was a continent on her own. She could as little be outflanked as, for quite different reasons, could Britain, the western flanking power with command of the sea. Just as Britain was able to retire into splendid isolation on her island, so Russia could withdraw into the oceanlike immensity of the Eurasian lowlands, there to remain secure from assault until she was herself ready to break out and attack. This qualified continental status afforded Russia advantages which, though diametrically opposite to those of the island situation, were nevertheless comparable to them.

Peter found some of the main features of this continental position already developed. This was particularly true, in the east, of Siberia. Russian fur trappers had already crossed it as far as the Sea of Okhotsk in the first half of the seventeenth century, and had fanned out in the empty expanses on the obscure side of Asia with the same rapidity as the French trappers in North America.

In both these new regions a development was under way which, though it did not penetrate to the consciousness of the old cultural world, was to cast a shadow over its destiny. In Europe, bloody battles could not change the deeply worn course of the stream of history. The sources of the future lay in the immense outer regions, and events there, unheeded elsewhere, were deciding the direction it would take. Nevertheless, whereas huge tracts of land in North America were to change hands more than once, Siberia, in spite of the primitive communications—or perhaps because of them—remained firmly attached to the motherland. For in these regions which were cut off from the outside world, the immigrant, unlike the emigrant to overseas territories, depended entirely on his link with the homeland for the satisfaction of his needs. How could he ever secede? Moreover, the extensive outlook that was part of his make-up found fulfillment in the featureless expanses beyond the low threshold of the Urals which seemed to be an extension of Russia's own spaces. Thus this immense territory developed a power of cohesion that never faced a test. Yet it was to remain an empty vessel until the latest phase of civilization brought uprooted peoples to fill it.

In the north, the Russian Empire before Peter had stretched as far as the Arctic Ocean, but had not reached a single point on the Baltic; in the south, it had extended as far as the Caucasus, but had nowhere touched the Black Sea.

In such a situation, with rear and flanks protected, Peter, the great Westerner, decreed his empire's expansion toward the Occident and the warm seas at the very moment when the Western world was entering the War of the Spanish Succession in order to beat off Louis's last thrusting bid for supremacy. In circumstances of this kind, a state weaker than that of the young Russian Hercules would have been compelled to enter the struggle as a partisan shifting his allegiance from one great power to another. It is indicative of Russia's attitude from the start that, to the displeasure of both parties, she steered an independent course.

Not that the question of supremacy could be a matter of indifference to her. The very nature of the conflict compelled Russia to oppose any unification of the old Continent, which could only work to her detriment. It is a fundamental law that the outer regions in the west and east function, directly or indirectly, as counterweights to a concentration at the center. But Louis's star was already fading, and independent action in the rear of the Western struggle promised larger gains for Russia than joining the phalanx of an alliance. Moreover, an alliance would, in any case, lead indirectly to a weakening of France. For all three of Russia's possible opponents could be regarded as pillars of the structure of French diplomacy: Poland on occasion, Turkey and Sweden almost regularly. To envelop these three with alliances, to mount military attacks against them, to sap them from within, was henceforth the main normal aim of Russian foreign policy. Working methodically, sector by sector, along her western frontier, Russia executed a large-scale operation similar to that carried out by France on a small scale on her eastern frontier.

This continuous expansion resulted in nothing less than a regrouping of the European system of states about two poles, a situation comparable to that which had arisen in the middle of the seventeenth century. At that time, the two maritime powers were grouped about one pole, and the two great land powers with their adherents about the other. Now, one circle enclosed the final Anglo-French battle for the Atlantic, while the other marked Russian expansion at the expense of the states confronting her. These two circles intersected in Germany.

On the whole, however, the trough between Louis XIV and Napoleon was filled by events as complex and fluctuating as those which took place in the trough between the defeat of the Armada and the battle of La Hogue.

This intricate pattern of events becomes manifest when we consider it from the commanding position of the two flanking powers.

I shall therefore return to Russia and her mode of procedure on the three sectors of her Western front. Peter applied himself to all of them.

Action in the southern sector commended itself not merely because of the enticing proximity of the coast, but also because such an initiative offered the possibility of combining a modern expansionist policy with the old idea of Russia's religious mission and its drive toward Constantinople, while at the same time gaining acceptance for Russia in the eyes of the West as the champion of common Christian interests. However, the Tsar soon abandoned this first line of advance because the Emperor declined to enter into an alliance with him in view of the impending War of the Spanish Succession.

Accordingly, the decision was taken to thrust northward. Poland was available as an ally for a move against Sweden, and the Baltic coast offered greater prospects than the isolated Black Sea. This predatory war began with the Russian defeat at Narva. But it soon became evident that Russia's qualified continental position made it possible for her, as for Britain, to open a war with a defeat and end it with victory. Peter practiced the principle of *reculer pour mieux sauter*; he withdrew into the depths of his empire, and there displayed a power of reorganization of which his enemy had not thought him capable. When Charles XII finally followed him deep into the Russian interior, the decision the Swedish king had been seeking turned against him with a vengeance. His rash venture into the Ukraine miscarried. The winter wrought havoc among his heroic troops, who, thanks to the obstinacy of their commander in chief and in the teeth of their generals' advice, were called upon to continue operations without going into winter quarters. By laying waste his own country, Peter put every conceivable obstacle in the way of the Swedes' advance through desolate and marshy terrain, an advance that carried them farther and farther away from their base. While the Russians were easily able to replace their numerically larger losses, the heroic army of Sweden melted away until it was destroyed by a superior Russian field force during the stubborn siege of the fortress of Poltava. By reason of their military and technical capabilities, the prisoners of war were not the least important booty taken by Peter that day. Thus, even Russia's first war with a great Western power brought all those factors of strength into play which this giant empire would command in the two struggles for supremacy in the nineteenth and twentieth centuries. For Peter's empire, the battle of Poltava had the same kind of significance that the defeat of the Armada had for maritime England: the threshold of a new era of history had been successfully crossed.

For Sweden, this battle was the beginning of the end of her great-power status. The heroic folly of this end bears the accidental stamp of the monarch's personality. But the fact that this personality was idolized was no accident and the end as such was inevitable. The sands had run out for the Swedish military monarchy the moment it was confronted by a military monarchy of a quite different order of magnitude. Yet Charles's proud, inherited will to power knew no resignation; his patriotic sense of honor turned to extreme stubbornness, which became inextricably bound up with his spirit of adventure. At the price of most of her external possessions, Sweden was barely able to salvage her independence from defeat; and though threatened again and again by internal disintegration and by the eruptions of the Russian volcano, she finally achieved equanimity and a thriving, if placid, existence, at times apart from world politics and at times sheltered by its conflicts.

Pursuing her program of Baltic expansion, Russia seemed unwilling to content herself with the surrender of Swedish territory. While Russian influence gained ground in Stockholm, it simultaneously consolidated its position in

Copenhagen; and after Russian armies had marched across Germany's coastal belt in wartime, they were followed in peacetime by the Romanov policy of dynastic marriage. Last of all, Prussia owed her acquisition of Swedish Pomerania and a new rise in her fortunes to Russia's spring tide. Here, then, the eastern flanking power had begun to do its work of splitting up Continental territories in the same way as its western counterpart.

Prussia remained separated by Poland from her admired Russian patron; but if he continued his forward pressure, this powerful patron might well turn into an adversary.

The dark shadow from the east that had fallen upon Sweden all but enveloped Poland. Her great neighbor could thwart any revival of her power.

Thus Peter had either opened up or undermined the northern and central sectors of his offensive front. Only in the south, in the Turkish sector, was he forced to sacrifice his initial gain.

Even in Peter's time, Russia, however European her deportment, frequently surprised Western diplomats by her actions in the Asian expanses which were unknown to them. For Peter, though occupied with Europe, did not forget Asia; at the end of his reign he even established relations with China, and from his intervention in the Persian disorders brought home as booty not merely two provinces but also Baku.

The pinnacle of power he reached, particularly in his last years, can perhaps be most tellingly measured by the fact that in that period the eastern flanking power aroused the suspicions of its western counterpart for the first time. Britain, only recently rid of her concern over French hegemony, saw looming out of the depths of the Continent a new opponent who threatened the position of the maritime powers in the Baltic and at the same time exerted pressure in the direction of the Persian Gulf. In the Baltic, Britain at once reacted vigorously by holding a shield over the stricken body of Sweden. A future world conflict was signaled in these years, though only by a flicker of distant lightning. With Peter's death, the tension eased.

For more than a generation, his throne was occupied by insignificant or unworthy personalities, and Russian foreign policy was clouded by intrigue and passion. Yet the hope, still expressed more than once by Frederick the Great, that the young power would vanish as suddenly as it had appeared was not to be fulfilled. The huge, enigmatic empire remained erect, a menace to the world of Western culture, as if uncertain what use to make of its ungainly powers.

In the western sphere, the Atlantic area, the shift of emphasis in events was all the more definite. We shall gain the best general view of this from Britain's commanding position. For up to the end of the Seven Years' War, if we look at the situation from the global standpoint, Britain, operating in the area where the orbits of East and West intersected, had maneuvered herself into a position of advantage not merely over Russia but also over the German powers. Human and national sympathy for the German heroes of the Seven Years' War must not distort our view of the importance of their deeds.

It becomes strikingly apparent how great a success the island kingdom had attained at the Peace of Utrecht. In 1588 it had barely succeeded in defending its independence; by 1713 it had victoriously advanced the policy of a general balance of power in Europe and of its own dominance beyond the seas. Without conquest in the Continental style and without striving for supremacy in the Continental sense, Britain acted for two decades as an unobtrusive arbiter. In doing so, she was even able at first to make use of the support of France, who, though exhausted, was not mortally wounded. But for the society of the *ancien régime*, now aging in pleasurable indulgence, desperate re-enactments of heroic efforts that had failed held no appeal.

Nevertheless, just as Spain in her decadence under Philip III and Philip IV had been capable of considerable feats in defense of her status, so was France in her decline under Louis XV. As soon as her strength revived somewhat, her ambition was again aroused, and so was her sense of rivalry with Britain. France was able to register her first great success—a surprise success gained while the surrounding world basked in freedom—in the War of the Polish Succession. Although she lost her influence in that distant kingdom to Russia, she gained neighboring Lorraine, the hinterland of the projecting Rhine bastion, in a fortunate passage of arms with Charles VI and the Empire. At the same time, the Spanish Bourbons drove Austria out of southern Italy. Collaboration between the Bourbons, which Britain had tried to stave off at Utrecht, nevertheless did come to pass, and not for the last time. Britain became all the more disturbed as the weakness of her old Austrian ally also became manifest in a new war with the Turks.

Moreover, she found cause for uneasiness on yet another battleground. In this epoch, for the first time, the struggle for colonies came to the fore as a leading issue. The importance of the colonies grew continuously and organically, whereas that of the Eurasian region increased spasmodically. In the seventeenth century the spark of war had flashed across the oceans from the Continent. Now the process was reversed, and the spark flew back from the overseas territories to ignite the intricate web of European relationships. However, the wars that broke out in this fashion in the Old World produced their most important results in the New. The issues were shifting. Even in the War of the Spanish Succession, concern for trade with the Spanish colonies had been the primary stimulus acting on the maritime powers. Now the French exponents of mercantilism and commercialism were goaded by the sight of Britain's new trade boom, even more than they once had been by the sight of Dutch prosperity. In these years of financial opportunism following the great armed clash, a fever of speculation spread across to the Continent from Britain. Even the Emperor tried to use his newly acquired Netherlands as a platform for gaining access to overseas trade. In France the colonies inflamed the imagination of the public as never before; and greed for personal profit easily merged with the patriotic consideration that colonial wealth was the prime factor in increasing the power of the state. Industry and the credit system had not yet cleared the roads to wealth that France would use in the nineteenth century.

The French colonies everywhere were now locked in combat with those of Britain: in North America, in the East Indies, and in the West Indies. There were many points of friction. The most conspicuous of them were not to be found in the great American colonial territories, but rather in the small settlements, particularly in the West Indies. Profits far greater than those to be had in North America beckoned in the Caribbean, where a flourishing plantation economy crossed paths with the well-established smugglers' trade between the islands and the Spanish colonies on the mainland. In the eyes of British statesmen, too, what generally counted most in the assessment of the value of a colony was not size or opportunities for settlement, but the balance of trade. Britain's colonial settlements were, after all, the result of a migration of people rather than of any deliberate initiative on the part of the state. They were regarded above all as markets and, possibly, as an incentive for the expansion of shipping and of the navy—thereby occupying, as it were, a lower plane.

Thus the struggle did not break out in those colonies, but in the West Indies in 1739. At the outset, it took the form of a war between Britain and Spain, the first instance in which the spark of war leaped from the New World to the Old.

Because of the close link between the two Bourbon lines, France was drawn into this war, the more so as she also found herself confronting Britain on the Continent in the great struggle which had flared up over the survival of the Habsburg monarchy. Anglo-French antagonism remained the key issue in the West for a generation; the period from 1748 to 1756—that is, the eight-year interval in open warfare between the end of the War of the Austrian Succession and the beginning of the Seven Years' War—was in truth only an armistice.

It is remarkable how successfully the ambitiously refurbished French fleet at first engaged the British navy, which had once again neglected its armament. A familiar picture reappeared: thanks to their organizational ability, the Continental power states gained the advantage until the indolent islanders mobilized their material and moral reserves. After a while, in spite of all the efforts of the French, their natural inferiority in the maritime sphere became evident. But this was counterbalanced by France's successes in Europe. Two souls dwelt in her breast, and even now the real ambitions of the nation lay in the sphere of Continental warfare. After all, her British rival could be dealt perilous injuries in the Netherlands, Britain's Achilles' heel; and this was precisely what France did in the War of the Austrian Succession. The issue in this war was the survival of the German Habsburg empire, just as the survival of the Spanish Habsburg empire had been the issue in the preceding wars of succession. To a certain extent, the second war revived the diplomatic picture of the first, for once more Britain went to the aid of Austria against the two Bourbon powers. However, the failing strength of France did not suffice to lend this new war the character of a fight for supremacy. She was now merely one power among others. Her successes in the War of the Polish Succession had not restored her old dominance; they had only shown that France had risen from her nadir while Austria had passed her zenith. A progressive leveling of the Continental states was taking place as the natural result of the balance of power created by Britain. Russia, the flanking power, was contributing her share to this process. By her very nature, she, like Britain, acted as a check to any bid for supremacy, in this case that of France.

The most striking expression of this leveling process was the rise of Prussia. The great had perforce grown small so that a small state might grow great. Operating in the area where the eastern and western spheres of interest overlapped, Frederick the Great could enter into partnership with all the main powers, occasionally even with the older German great power, at whose expense he had acquired his own title to great-power status. Like Bismarck later, Frederick had come up in the world as a master at exploiting the leveling process and thus complicating the European system in a trough between two waves. Both he and Bismarck were adept in the art of using the special circumstances of such an interlude and their own hazardous mid-

**111**

dle position to make capital out of shifting their allegiance. Audacious, unscrupulous in snatching at booty, and both unshakable and circumspect in defending it, they risked their existence at a time when the "haves" were in no mind to put forth a supreme effort.

In Frederick's time there was not the slightest reason to suppose that this Prussian mentality, which had developed between struggles for supremacy, would one day itself give rise to such a struggle. Frederick's ascent had not yet carried him into those strata where the weather of world history is brewed. But his influence in the German arena, on the destinies of the nation abroad as well as at home, was already all the greater. He smashed the receptacle of the Holy Roman Empire before the coming nationalist movement had a chance to fill it with a new content. He pushed back the Habsburg state which had so often served as a shield against Frenchman and Turk. In its stead, a country on the culturally backward fringes of the Protestant world now shot into prominence, from small beginnings, as a power based on a military civilization. That country acknowledged no master but its own success. It was open to alliance with one and all. Its continuing poverty and the artificial character of its starting base only served to increase its expansionist zest. Frederick, the one and only, Frederick the solitary, the guiding genius and co-creator of this power-seeking enterprise, a man purged of human warmth and detached from the ways of his native soil, completed the work, begun by his father, of training human instruments at once pliant and plucky. He instilled into them a spirit that regarded the performance of any task as the fulfillment of duty carried out stoically and heroically. Here, as in the not so very dissimilar case of Russia, the forcible union of Western techniques with malleable Eastern human material produced an explosive mixture—the whole a late development that was to make its way, by devious, unforeseeable paths, down to our own time, and finally become a factor in shaping world events.

After the war of the Austrian Succession and the first two Silesian Wars, a British observer might have drawn up a preliminary balance sheet somewhat along these lines. The key issue of Anglo-French rivalry had undergone no substantial modification. Britain's superiority in the overseas territories and French superiority in the Netherlands had simply been brought into the balance by the restoration of the status quo. But France's efforts had been far more taxing than those of Britain, who, in her usual fashion, had made her contribution to the war mainly through subsidies, that is, by using the troops of her allies rather than her own. Austria, her ally, in jeopardy at the start, had once more consolidated her position, and was again available as Britain's "Continental sword." However, Austria's operational effectiveness against France was impaired by her rivalry with the Prussian upstart. Prussia's success, while not welcome to Britain, did not really alarm her. Although it had been achieved mainly in association with France, in accordance with the tradition of the German princes—primarily the Protestant ones—Frederick, who had proved that he believed in flexibility, not loyalty, could be lured away again from his French connection. Russia, too, offered a means of reinsurance against a new growth of French power. During the last stage of the war a Russian army, acting in support of Austria, had made an appearance on the Rhine in order to expel French influence from Germany, just as that influence had been driven from Poland in the War of the Polish Succession. A tendency on the part of any nation to dominate the old Continent would always cause the flanking powers to shelve their antagonisms and join forces. At that time, however, conditions in Central Europe were in the main of interest to London only insofar as they provided counterweights to France. Britain's primary interest lay in the Atlantic area.

It was generally felt that the calm created at Aix-la-Chapelle would not last; the Atlantic rivalry, the main issue of the struggle just ended, had not been settled. The same was true of the rivalry between the two German powers, however much lower it might rank from the vantage point of world history. These sources of conflagration were still smoldering, both ready to blaze up again in another war.

But in what diplomatic form would these interests merge? At this point, the leveling off and instability of power relationships were dramatically demonstrated in the celebrated reversal of the alliances. Except for the two rival pairs, each country involved might link up with any other. Almost everywhere the watershed between opposite decisions was so low that ample scope was left for intrigue and chance. But once the diplomatic pattern had been rearranged, Britain, who in the real struggles for hegemony had shown such mastery in weaving a network of grand coalitions, saw herself reduced to an alliance with the small Prussian upstart. And France, who at the peak of her strength never joined forces with another power of top rank, was found marching shoulder to shoulder with Austria and Russia. She hoped that by helping the Habsburgs to reconquer Silesia she herself would, directly or indirectly, come into the possession of their territory in the Netherlands and, in doing so, strengthen her Atlantic position vis-à-vis Britain. It became evident that France was abandoning her old aspirations in Central and Eastern Europe. With France in retreat, Russia could stop opposing her and, following up Peter the Great's Baltic policy, contemplate the conquest of East Prussia—in other words, a drive into German territory past a weakened Poland. In contrast to her situation at the beginning of the Northern War, Russia had long since become deeply involved in the power combinations of Central and Western Europe and, while herself unassailable, was in the happy position of being able to choose the country at which she might direct her aggressive designs.

What of Prussia? How could Frederick, that master of the diplomatic game, commit the error of signing the Treaty of Westminster, which offended France, his old ally, drove her into the camp of his Austrian enemy, and thus engineered his own suffocating isolation on the Continent? He believed himself the victim of chance. However, one may point out that, as a Continental, he viewed the old Continental Franco-Austrian rivalry in absolute terms, and failed to appreciate fully the higher importance of another factor in contemporary French policy, her sharpened maritime rivalry with Britain. One thing is obvious: "naval matters were beyond him." He failed to comprehend the immense significance of the overseas struggle between the two Atlantic powers. The North Americans celebrated Frederick's victories, and Pitt declared that he had won Canada in Germany. But Frederick, who had contributed so much to this conquest, saw its true import hardly more clearly than Voltaire, who scoffed at Canada as "a few miserable acres of snow."

Yet, viewed from the standpoint of world history, those few acres of snow were the prize in the Atlantic struggle. Even more unequivocally than in the preceding War of the Austrian Succession, the Seven Years' War broke out in, and over, the colonies. But this time the stake was the

North American colonies, and the two rivals were fighting for the future of a continent. Today the historic significance of their fight is plain for all to see. At the time it was probably sensed by only a handful of people on both sides of the Atlantic. The spark of war was generated by local tensions. But so fateful was the sense of rivalry on both sides that the local fire could not be quenched.

The difference between the insular and continental outlook, now projected into the colonial framework, was again shown impressively in the final struggle. The insular group had at its disposal almost half a million settlers, who by then had begun to develop a political will of their own and who envisaged the entire North American continent as an area of expansion. The French-speaking whites numbered only a fifth of that strength. France sought to compensate for this by centralized military planning; she strengthened the link between Canada and her colony of Louisiana in the Mississippi delta, an area as yet completely undeveloped, by setting up bases in the vast region in between. For reasons rooted perhaps in basic national instincts, lines of fortresses had played an important role in French strategy ever since the sixteenth century. At any rate, the grandiose sweep of that planning made the British colonists feel that they were excluded from the interior of a continent which had been granted to them as far as the Pacific by royal charters. The guns went off of their own accord.

The outcome could have been in doubt only if France had been able to bring the superior strength of her armies to bear on that distant field of battle—in other words, if she had had command of the sea communications. In the long run there could be no question of this. Quebec fell, and at the Peace of Paris in 1762 the French had no Eu-

ropean asset, as they had had at Aix-la-Chapelle in 1748,
to use as a bargaining counter. America was lost to them
forever.

There was scarcely any difference in the case of the
East Indies. There, transparently disguised as allies of native princes, the two European rivals had been fighting for
half a generation; and again it was the French who switched
from traditional commercial policy to territorial policy on
a large scale. There, too, the final victory went to their opponents, who held command of the sea.

Only in the West Indies did France salvage some precious fragments from the wreckage of her first colonial empire.

There were no two ways about it: after all the ups and
downs of twelve years of war, the decline of monarchical
France, heralded as early as the end of the War of the Austrian Succession, had continued overseas as well as in Europe. Overseas, it had led to losses that could never be
recouped. In Europe, a long period of sickness, comparable
to Spain's, was in store for France. In 1762 the Peace of
Paris sealed the defeat of Louis XIV, as the Peace of the
Pyrenees in 1659 had sealed the defeat of Philip II.

If in the Atlantic contest France had been weighed once
again and finally found wanting, Britain's success sent the
curve of her two hundred years of maritime history soaring.
Who would henceforth contest the islanders' right gradually
to appropriate the maritime and colonial prestige of the four
Atlantic states on the Continent as their sole heir? And
how could the Continent, split more deeply and diversely
than ever since Russia's appearance on the scene, once
again give birth to a power with serious pretensions to
supremacy? Britain, the exponent of the growing importance of overseas territories, herself seemed bound to grow

—a Janus, with one face turned toward the Continent to trim the scales of the balance of power and the other directed at the sea to strengthen her maritime dominance.

The leading Continental powers had often suffered heavy reverses at the very peak of success because the slumbering energies of their opponents had been awakened. Now Britain experienced a setback; but it was her own people in America who, awakening to full consciousness of their strength, rose against her. Britain's rise, which had been due to her dominance in the maritime sphere, now encountered a most serious threat from that very quarter. This maritime sphere had drawn the energies of Europe from the interior to its western shores, had developed naval and colonial power, had enhanced both in the maritime states, and had finally concentrated them on the island lying off Europe's west coast. Now a migration of power from that island itself began. Just as the water filling the basin of a fountain overflows into a second basin, power now moved from the island farther west across the ocean. The ring closed. The whiff of ocean air had produced a flowering in Western Europe, last of all and most of all in Britain. Now a movement in the opposite direction set in. The colonial areas, which as the servants of European states had indirectly helped to secure the freedom of the system of the Old World, now wished to gain their own freedom and be their own masters. The principle that new territories drawn into the game act as counterweights to balance the system against any bid for supremacy revealed its cloven hoof. As the price of its freedom, the Old World of the West had to watch the beginning of a migration of power.

The colonial failures of the four Atlantic states on the Continent are clearly explained by the dead weight of the

Continental conflicts which again and again acted as a drag on progress in the maritime sphere. Now the favored island itself had to accept failure, because in this particular case the advantages afforded by its insular character were transformed into as many drawbacks.

The blooming of the spacious American colony was brought about, not by the state, but by a society and its people, by free and ebullient forces which, acting in political, social, and religious opposition to the mother country, created a new home for themselves. In the vast expanses of this territory, these forces had developed more and more pronounced traits of independence of an intensity unknown in Europe. Hippolyte Taine observed that the nature of Western man is marked by faith and tradition. Faith the emigrants had carried with them as their most precious possession, but a great deal of tradition had been left behind. In the midst of a mobile struggle for existence— in place of the security that came from living on native soil—art, poetry, and custom lost much of their creative power. Their place was taken by an unparalleled vigor in economic development which drew spiritual resilience from the old belief that success comes to the elect, and from the new faith in the paramount importance of utility. This expansive entity, rid of French trammels since 1762 and conscious of its immense youthful strength, would tolerate no British fetters either. The colonies of the Continental powers, with their small white or racially mixed populations and their authoritarian regimes, remained loyal to the mother countries. The two million white settlers in New England, on the other hand, represented the freedom-loving forces of an insular society in an intensified form; and these people, to whom rising maritime Britain had owed her best years since the defeat of the Armada, now turned—from motives springing from their innermost selves —against the country of their origin.

European statesmen foresaw this turn of events immediately after the signing of the Treaty of Versailles, indeed even earlier. In Britain itself, in 1762, the question had been debated whether, in view of the mood of New England, it would not be wiser to leave Canada to the French and take from them instead their valuable possessions in the Antilles. This shortsighted commercialism had been defeated by the powerful new imperialist trend that soared high above the mere mercantile and fiscal exploitation of colonies. There emerged the concept of a world-wide maritime empire, whose core should be formed by the lands around the shores of the Atlantic, all with equal rights under the Crown, and it seemed altogether possible that within this bloc the center of gravity might one day shift to America. Would Pitt, the protagonist of the imperial idea, have been able to maintain the empire in the form of an ellipse with two foci? The fact that this question can be posed at all throws light on the relationship between the two Anglo-Saxon states in the generations that followed. The gulf separating them was not unbridgeable. But with Pitt's fall, more narrow-minded considerations again came to the front; and Britain, who has so often made shift with second-raters, this time had to pay a bitter price for the disappearance of a man of the first rank. The monarch, too, once again proved to be a handicap. George III, with his German and Continental cast of mind, lacked the island spirit. Intent on maintaining the authority of the throne, he merely succeeded in sharpening the conflict.

Nevertheless, without European support, the American rising would have been doomed. A study of the diplomatic and military situation shows clearly the extent to which the old insular advantages failed to take effect this time. Britain was accustomed to operating at the head of coalitions, crushing dominant powers on the Continent, establishing a balance of power in Europe, and consolidating her own ascendancy beyond the seas. This time, however, the balance of power was so perfect, and the dominance of France so completely broken, that the normal motive for a Continental war could not be found, particularly as the rivalry between Prussia and Austria also had lost its intensity. The Continent remained quiet, and this calm seemed to rob British power of its old magic. For the first time, France, in alliance with Spain, was able to wage a purely naval and colonial war against her old rival. Moreover, the seafaring neutrals, bent on protecting their trade, formed an alliance, under Russian leadership, which destroyed privateering, one of Britain's most potent weapons. Even Portugal, indeed even Holland, joined this alliance, and Britain, completely isolated, found herself obliged to declare war on Holland. What an upheaval of the old and well-tried foundations of British power!

Was this the manner in which the Continent could overcome the exploiter of its disunity, after all attacks by individual powers had foundered on Britain's almost mystical invulnerability? A Continent lastingly unified might have succeeded. This alliance occurred but once, and was short-lived. The common antagonism of the land powers toward the naval power could not overcome the more lively antagonisms among the land powers themselves. Supremacy at sea does not hold the same terrors as dominance on land —and how soon France was to make another bid on land!

However, the brief period in which the Continentals made common cause sufficed to render the subjugation of the American colonies a prospect more hopeless than ever for the mother country. Now that Britain could no longer count upon allies, the weakness of her armies was glaringly exposed on the impassable terrain of that vast theater of war. She could vanquish the largest European land powers, but not the insurgent bands on that distant island—for America *was* an island as much as Britain. Britain was not even able to secure her sea communications—the sinews of her power—against the pack of her opponents. She was, in fact, compelled to look to her own security while fighting at widely separated points overseas.

The American colonies gained their freedom. The hub of Britain's world-girdling empire was cut out at the very moment when the idea of an empire had barely taken shape. As guardian of the European balance of power, Britain had humbled her European rivals. Now she was humbled by them, likewise in the name of the balance of power. She now paid her own toll to the European fate she had in-flicted on others. Thus the old Continent lost its birthright.

Yet the jubilation on the mainland over Albion's fall was premature. Britain preserved her direct relationship with the world outside Europe. To begin with, she main-tained her hold on Canada—for the very reason that there were no English settlers there. The local French Catholics feared the rule of their fanatically Puritan neighbors more than the negligently tolerant regime of London. Who, indeed, could have foreseen then that the expansionist Yan-kees would never round off their huge territories by an-nexing Canada? More important at the moment than the retention of Canada was the fact that, commercially, the secession of the colonies worked out almost to the advan-tage of the motherland: the ambitious free country be-came a better trading partner than the colonies had been. After a while, its energies were absorbed by the newly acquired hinterland, and, contrary to France's expectations, it failed to confront Britain's shipping and her navy with permanent competition. Britain's strength vis-à-vis the Continent remained unimpaired, the more so as she acquired in the East Indies a substitute for the territories she had lost.

It proved impossible to establish a maritime balance of power as a counterpart to, and extension of, the balance of power in Europe. Those who counted on the creation of such a balance rashly applied European experience to a sphere in which other premises operated; and the developments of the nineteenth century were to underscore this error again and again.

Was France, at least, able to record a return to her old colonial status as a reward for her efforts? Actually, only America benefited from French intervention. France's aim had been to bring into being an overseas power that would support her; that power became the young cuckoo in the nest of the Atlantic states. It was the disunited states of Europe that were the godparents of the United States of America; the United States gained from their dissensions. Measured by the standards of European battles, those fought in the American War of Independence were insignificant enough. Measured by their future importance, they far surpassed those that were so much closer to the focal point of politics. The weight on the long arm of a balance has a greater effect than a far larger weight on the short arm operating near the fulcrum of the scale.

While in the West the overseas world was growing increasingly in importance—indirectly through the medium of Britain and directly through the breakaway of the United States—Russia, the other flanking power, suddenly advanced to a new level of prestige in the East. The Anglo-

Saxons, content to have Europe held in check by the balance of power, poured out their energies into the uncivilized expanses of the overseas territories. In the meantime, the energies of Russia were applied in the opposite direction —from the uncivilized expanses of Eurasia toward the Occident, the ancient cradle of culture. Britain, one of the bearers of Western culture, was at liberty to spread it across the seas, of which she held command. Russia had to gain access to the maritime lanes of Western life, and gorge herself on Western civilization, before she was capable of using it to fertilize the vast spaces of the East. What her systematic advance threatened was not Russian dominance in the sense of Spanish, French, or, later, German supremacy, but the much more serious danger that in the long run this colossus would clasp one member after another of the old family of nations in its tentacles and wrench it out of the existing framework. It is true, of course, that Russia was striving not merely to approach the West physically but also to penetrate the Western mind intellectually. However, as we know, this process never really went beyond the point of a civilizing assimilation; incalculable forces deep down in the Russian nature remained hidden from view by the Western veneer, just as the glaze of Hellenism had covered similar forces in the empires of the Ptolemies and the Seleucids.

The new Russian expansion started in 1762, the year of Britain's triumph over France; it was also the year in which Catherine II seized the throne. If it is true that empires are maintained by the forces that have created them, then Peter's empire, to remain vigorous, repeatedly stood in need of a ruler of his own stature. In 1762 Russia had just survived, without losing ground, the confused regime of the three women who had followed him. Now, at long last, she made powerful strides under the control of a fourth woman, who had the capacity to make purposeful use again of Russia's innate strength. No Russian man could have discharged this task better than this German woman. At once the seductive incarnation of the Western mind in its latest manifestations and the ruthless mistress of her Eastern subjects, she was perfectly equipped to parade, on the two levels of this Hellenistic setting, both her own person and the empire in all their glory, evoking wonder as the Semiramis of the North.

Her first tour de force was the removal of her inferior husband, Peter III. In his naïve folly, he had let victory over Prussia slip through his fingers. What would the course of Germany's history have been if East Prussia and the entire Baltic area had fallen into Russian hands at that early date? All the genius of Frederick the Great would not have sufficed to preserve him from the fate of Charles XII; chance, in the shape of a fool, was needed to protect him. Prussia, the youngest of the great powers, was at the same time the most vulnerable to mortal injury. Her founder himself was reluctant to have her ranked as a genuine great power.

As Catherine could not hope to retrieve the opportunity her husband had lost, she turned her back on the Baltic region and confined her attention, all the more successfully, to nearby targets. What Peter the Great had begun on Russia's western front by defeating Sweden, Catherine continued with enterprises against Poland and Turkey, systematically rounding off the empire in the process.

Her operations, pursued in accord with the changing international situation, break down into three periods.

The first, lasting until the end of the American War of Independence, was marked by the struggle of the Atlantic powers and the opportunities it offered for Russian action. France still regarded Russia's three western neighbors as the bastions of her old supremacy—even though they were crumbling—but her arm no longer reached far enough to protect them against the Tsarina. And Britain rejoiced over Russia's progress only to the extent that it kept France pre-occupied. The German powers, exhausted by the Seven Years' War, were too weak to grapple with Russia individually and too jealous of each other to join forces against her. Catherine played with consummate virtuosity on the in-strument provided by this situation. After the War of the Bavarian Succession, she formally assumed the position, now beyond the capacity of France, of the courted arbiter in the *querelles allemandes*. This was the heart of the mat-ter: the energies of the much-divided Continental nations could easily be rallied against one of their number aspiring to dominate its sister nations, but not against Russia, the outside power with her more limited objectives. Thus, when Russian diplomacy sought allies in the rear of its enemy neighbors, the sovereign egoism of Prussia and that of Austria were in turn at Catherine's disposal, even though qualms and premonitions were felt in both Vienna and Berlin as they received a share of the Russian booty. Austria had every reason to fear that her Occidental mission against the Turks and her drive for southeastward expansion would have the wind taken out of their sails; and Prussia could not but fear the loss of Poland, the buffer separating her from the Russian colossus. Yet their mutual suspicion left the two German powers no choice but to vie with each other in offering their services to the fortunate giant who used them.

The First Partition of Poland was the Prussian King's masterpiece of diplomatic technique. It established the long-desired territorial link between the bulk of the country and East Prussia, and at the same time resolved Austro-Russian tension in the Balkans, which had threatened to unleash another great war. In reality, Prussia's co-operation with Russia was a *societas leonina* favoring the bigger power, and Frederick's success more a proof of his dexterity than of his strength. Russia remained the mightiest figure in the game. Through undermining her Polish victim by peaceful means and successfully concluding a war against the Turks, she had brought matters to a point where partition appeared to the alarmed German powers as the best way out of a precarious situation.

It was not long before Catherine, by extending Russia's power to the Black Sea, gave her empire a second window on the world. Soon she was threatening Constantinople, not only by land from the north but also by sea from the west. A large Russian fleet sailed all the way around Europe and destroyed the Turkish fleet in the Aegean. For the first time, the arm of Russia reached out as far as Greece, there to set off uprisings against the Turks. Indeed, she was already making contact with the rebellious Egyptians, who would henceforth so often draw the eyes of European diplomats to their country. As if by the wave of a wand, the northern power had become a southern power. The cabinets of Europe shuddered. Measured against the eastern empire with its unlimited possibilities, the dimensions of Western Europe seemed to shrink, as the states in the Hellenic system had once shrunk beside the empires of the Diadochi.

However, the international situation was now starting to change, and to the detriment of Russia. The second period in the development of Catherine's foreign policy began with the reappearance in world affairs of Anglo-Russian antagonism, which had first flashed up on the horizon at the end of Peter's reign. Britain had had to accept Russia's leading role in the League of Armed Neutrality at sea because all her own forces had been absorbed in the Atlantic struggle. Now that this fight was over and France, in her exhaustion, was tottering toward revolution, the question arose whether a Russian victory in a new war with Turkey would really serve Britain's interests. Until then, any Russian victory over the Ottomans had been interpreted as a blow at the French; but a Russian penetration of the Mediterranean was an altogether different matter. London accordingly engineered diversions on the Continent: it encouraged Sweden to go to war, and allied itself not only with the Turks but also with Prussia. Austria, after all, was at that time associated with Russia, and, given the rivalry between the two great German powers, an alliance between London and Berlin was natural. This course also commended itself by reason of Prussia's coastal location; for it was by way of coasts, those of the Baltic and the Black Sea, that Britain had to tackle the Continental giant. Fortune favored the British. A new occupant of the throne in Vienna robbed Catherine of her German ally against the Turks; and the Ottomans' surprising resistance foiled the Tsarina's widely laid plans. How often the fatalistic heroism of the Ottoman army was yet to make amends for the rottenness of the Ottoman state!

Now more than ever the younger Pitt felt encouraged to drive Russia into a corner. A large Prussian army was to march on Riga, and a British fleet was to be dispatched to Kronstadt. An ultimatum to Catherine was imminent. But, curiously, Pitt at the last moment withdrew from the diplomatic action, humiliating the Prussian King, who had just informed the Sultan of the impending declaration of war on Russia. The Prime Minister had realized that public opinion in his country, still accustomed to viewing the world from the maritime standpoint, could not so swiftly be convinced of the new danger looming up from the depths of the Continent. His retreat was yet another proof of the fact, documented in the peace negotiations of 1714 and 1762, that Britain felt strong enough to ride roughshod over the interests of her "Continental swords," and confident nevertheless of being able to win allies again if need should arise. Pitt himself brilliantly displayed this capacity for recruiting allies as he forged the coalitions of the Revolutionary Wars.

The last phase of Catherine's rule is interlocked with the beginning of these wars. At the end of her life and of the *ancien régime,* she was able to bring home unprecedented spoils from the Second and Third Partitions of Poland. Once again Britain's attention was diverted in the West. But this time the two German powers were also engaged there; weakened, disunited, and covetous, they were incapable of resisting baits and threats. But the role of Prussia, who betrayed her recently adopted Polophile policy, was the more ignominious.

Thus the old policy of the Eastern powers obliterated a national state of the West, originally almost as large as the German Reich, at a time when modern nationalism, coming from the West, was starting to regenerate state life. Poland was hacked to pieces in the diplomatic slaughterhouse according to the yardstick of lifeless statistics, and then parceled out with equanimity to foreign masters; these, separated from her by history, by language, and most of all by religion, possessed few of the prerequisites for assimilating, at that late date, such vast booty. Poland might be no more than a shadowy marginal region of the

Occident; but in her there slumbered the mysterious vital forces of a Western nation with nineteen hundred years of history, with its own language and customs, and with religious and spiritual traditions. The nineteenth century was to awaken these forces, and the Poles, conscious of their rights, would rise against the mechanical civilization of an absolutist regime that had been imposed upon them, even though this civilization might, in its own way, offer some progress. Just as the *poleis*, in which Hellenism achieved its crystallization, summoned up the last of their ardor to resist being incorporated in a greater Hellenistic empire, so did this Western nation revolt against being absorbed into the empire of Peter the Great.

For it was Russia, who had taken the lead in the Partitions, that carried off the lion's share as a matter of course. The Western world had never witnessed expansion on this scale. The earlier Habsburg expansion had taken place within the framework of personal unions. Indeed, no major territorial changes of the past, even in Italy, had led to such encroachments as were here carried out by alien centralized bureaucracies.

An observer looking out from the old Continent at either the Anglo-Saxon or the Russian periphery might have noted a darkening of the horizon. But the West had not as yet exhausted its possibilities to the same extent as had ancient Hellas when it fell under the shadow of the great Hellenistic states. Within a few short years, undreamed-of energies, generated by the masses and by technical advances, were to burst forth with the violence of a geyser. Once more, the mainspring of the old system of states would be wound up. Again, the rhythm of waves and intervening troughs would renew itself, and for another century and a half the

Continent would hold its place at the center of the world's destinies.

Nevertheless, its rejuvenation was bought at the price of a revolutionary spread of civilization—at the expense, that is, of culture. When that civilization was able to extend its influence into the vast outer regions, the star of the old Continent finally waned.

# THE

# FRENCH REVOLUTION

# AND NAPOLEON I

THE MARCH of civilization within the comprehensive scheme of life is in itself a phenomenon that runs all through the recent centuries. It is the most conspicuous expression of a slow and many-sided process that nevertheless follows a single consistent line of development: the evolution from the world-denying asceticism of the Middle Ages to the vigorous mastery of the world in our own day, from renunciation of earthly life to positive acceptance of it, from a pessimistic to an optimistic view of life, from a relatively static to an extremely dynamic attitude. It is as though frozen matter were thawing out and melting under a rising sun. The sun first overcomes the frost on the southern hillsides and sends melted snow trickling down into the valley. But greater and greater avalanches of dormant life are set moving until they come thundering down and whole worlds of historic life patterns are swept away by swirling floods.

In such an epoch the roar of melting waters rises in crescendo, and the sight of plunging avalanches fills the souls of men with wonder or dread. The end of the eighteenth century was such an era. Dynamic evolution in economic and political life rose in a bold curve. And behind it all was the intensified, naked lust for power.

This intensification was not a uniform process. The nations took part in it one by one, not together. In one place it affected one aspect of life, elsewhere some other; it first mobilized one group of people within a nation, then another. It also touched off enormous reactions: mixtures of the old and the new took shape and assumed a life of their own; for example, the concept of nationalism. The development was less than ever a placid stream; rather it was a maelstrom, indeed a seething upsurge. But for all that, the course of nineteenth-century history entitles us to say that the actual agent that provoked this movement was a heightened and optimistic will to live, a spread of the thirst for worldly power, bringing in its train a new and furious phase of the struggle for existence. Tradition, faith, and beauty, the calming agents in this struggle, were driven back along the entire front in battles that swayed back and forth. However magnificent the manifestations of the threatened spirit that were left behind in art, poetry, and religion, the retreat could not be reversed.

This new intensification of the optimistic will to power over the external world, which was soon to feed such unparalleled volumes of energy into the mill of high politics, took different forms on both sides of the Channel, and these in turn reacted on each other. Toward the end of the century, the part amicable, part hostile controversy between the Anglo-Saxon island world and the French Continental world came to be the "balance" in the clock of developments—and not only in politics.

In Britain, the state did not play a significant role, either as a retarding or as a promoting agent, in the new advance of civilization. Besides being free from the motive forces of the Continental struggle for existence, the state lacked an extensive organization within the country, as well as both the will and the chance to intervene on a broad front. Private initiative had long occupied a front-rank position in this setting of insular security and broad maritime scope. Moreover, it was ennobled and nourished by its fruitful alliances with utilitarian philosophy, applied science, and those movements in the Protestant faiths that fostered worldly activity. In Britain, where the acquisitive drive of the middle classes colored the entire national life, the Industrial Revolution began, in the eighteenth century, as the spontaneous product of untapped energies in an adaptable society. It was to bring about a momentous change in the physical pattern of human existence.

Here the importance of coal, which brought the island prosperity, was discovered. Coal, shipped on a new network of canals, achieved in forty years a tenfold increase in the production of iron—which, for lack of wood for fuel, had been about to move to America. Machine production penetrated the old home craft of woolen weaving, and created the new factory-organized cotton industry which obtained its raw material from overseas and marketed some of the finished products there. Britain, the land of sea power, shipping, and world trade, the country that had risen to world status as a colonial power, now became the world's industrial power. The economic revolution brought her a huge accretion of strength at the very moment when, hav-

ing lost her American colonies, she faced a showdown with
the political revolution in France. As the reserve in the fight
against Philip II, the young maritime England of private
freebooters had been the deciding factor; so, now, the young
industrial Britain of private enterprise was to prove her
worth as a reserve against Napoleon I.

The progress of civilization, unlike that of culture, can
be measured by the findings of statistics, a science which,
characteristically, began to develop in the late eighteenth
century. Statistics record as a key figure the fact that in
the reign of George III, between 1760 and 1820, the population almost doubled, from 7½ to 14 million; the rise was
due to new medical methods that kept so many people alive
and new economic techniques that provided them with a
livelihood.

This rapid development was a purely practical affair;
its motive power was not supplied by theories. It affected
only certain quite definite areas of life, and left others close
by completely untouched. The old structure of state and
society was not pulled down, but merely altered and added
to. Faith and tradition retained their standing precisely because they had not been cast in a rigid form by an absolute
power state, but had remained elastic and fluid. This free
island—this country alone—provided room for the very
new side by side with the very old, without risk of chaos.
Wealth and opportunities for emigration mitigated unavoidable tensions. The harmony between unconscious instinct
and conscious interest pervaded life with a healthy rhythm.

In France, the relationship between state and society
was the antithesis of the one in Britain. Under great sovereigns and statesmen, it resulted in a kind of efficiency that
Britain could not match, and did not need. But the dangers
that threatened France when her destinies were in the

hands of insignificant rulers were all the greater. The Continental system with its military and bureaucratic apparatus, its artificial pattern imposed from above, tended to become rigid; it could not be reconstructed without injury to class interests previously promoted or tolerated, nor indeed without a temporary weakening of the whole structure. Now in France, too, fostered by the mercantilist policies of the state, a self-assured middle class had developed; its impetuous instincts—in the economic, social, and intellectual spheres —were pounding against the steep and rigid dike of a political order created or guaranteed by the state. Furthermore, that country, set up to be a military power state, had been worsted both on the Continent and overseas and had seen its prestige abroad drop to a low ebb. How, under an insignificant ruler, was it to develop the authority to put through the internal reforms that were needed to restore its effectiveness in the face of the selfishness of the privileged classes and the discontent of the Third Estate? Joining forces with polemical writers, the Third Estate attacked faith and tradition in all their forms, for the most part taking its standards from the insular countries—first England, then America. So great was the power and influence of the Anglo-Saxon world even then that the grandest of Continental nations began to stray from its innermost traditions, without regard for the different nature of the laws governing the struggle for existence beyond the Channel and the Atlantic. There, society had been involved in an imperceptible, practical evolution since the seventeenth century; on the Continent, everything propelled the body politic toward spasmodic development, revolution from above or below. There, the new civilization set in motion the wheels of industry; on the Continent, the wheels of politics.

In the given circumstances, the Revolution could have been averted only by a revolutionary on the throne, a ruler who could have reorganized the nation and swept it along with him in a great new effort in power politics such as was soon to burst out as a wild growth.

In its early stages, the Revolution seemed bent on the very opposite of such an arduous plunge into power politics. A yearning for happiness sent the dreamy gaze of the revolutionaries wandering to places where the blood-drenched glory of the power state was unknown—toward distant America or, at least, toward nearby idyllic Switzerland. Yet, in a breathtaking rush, the fight against the rusting old power state gave birth to a new power state whose giant shining machine was as much superior in performance to its predecessor as Britain's new industry was to the old crafts. Soon the enchanting spring blossoms of great popular ideas lay strewn on the ground, and their fruits horrified those who had admired the blooms. The tiny step from opposition to power seemed to transform the people who took it.

The world witnessed, for the first time, a succession of events whose typical character was to become apparent only through the events of the twentieth century. For the first time the decadence of a great Continental power coincided with a rapid melting of social and intellectual concepts under the impact of the swift advance of civilization.

The first phase was marked by a welter of sentimental rhetoric in which noble emotions were corroded by instinctive and covetous impulses. Chaos reigned in the second phase; the unexpected collapse of the state apparatus on which national life had depended created a vacuum that attracted human passions, among them the lowest. To the astonishment of the protagonists as well as the spectators, the third phase brought about a paradoxical, and yet logical, climax. A new power state was improvised by the passions that had been unleashed. The Revolution could save its achievements only by reinforcing one-hundredfold the centralized instruments of power; and the revolutionaries wielded them without scruple, though they had attacked the privileged for using them. The genius of the state absorbed the most bizarre elements. A new despotism sprang from the new liberty. The twin scourges, terror and propaganda, were born. The old faith, the old traditions, were mocked. All calming influences on the will were eliminated, and life based on personal impulse was deified in the national myth, which all intellectual life and education were made to serve. It was used to justify all crimes which served to intimidate or destroy the opponents of the Revolution and to bind its adherents in solidarity as accessories. For the first time—for a few moments, as it were—the totalitarian state, the Continental power state in its ultimate revolutionary form, raised its head. The absolute monarchies paled beside it. The new state was an end in itself, and felt entitled to use men and things on a scale never before envisaged. The metaphysical personality of the old Occident was challenged in new terms by politics, and in the course of this drastic process the seething torrent of the masses was canalized and controlled.

Of course, the bureaucracy helped; but control was made possible primarily through the party, the new sovereign of France. The Jacobins, a small, minority organization of fanatics, operating ubiquitously as terrorists and propagandists, kept the fellow-traveling masses in ferment.

They succeeded simply because their rule had something to offer to a very large part of the population: participation in public affairs; equality before the law, in administrative practice and in economic opportunity; and removal of the humiliating sense of social inferiority. The property of the nobility and the Church was seized and pumped into the stream of the nation's economic life. In sum, the domestic achievements of the Revolution constituted a mass of booty which the new society would never again allow to be torn from its grasp. At the same time, the nation's fortunes abroad experienced the beginning of a rise which seemed without limit. Any man who successfully guides a nation in world affairs can smother all domestic dissensions.

The Revolutionary Wars touched off a new wave of domination whose ebb and flow showed steeper outlines than had any of its predecessors. Those earlier waves had reached their crest in a process lasting several decades, and had just as slowly ebbed away. The new wave reared up abruptly out of the uttermost depths of the trough, only to crash down with equal abruptness. Louis XIV's initial position had been inferior to that of Philip II. How much more inferior to both was that of the Revolution! We have observed how in the eighteenth century the outer regions of the West and East began to rob the ancient central region of light and air. At the outset, therefore, the Revolution entered the great struggle not with a sense of its own strength but rather with the courage of despair. Not that it had been attacked from abroad. In fact, it was not primarily considerations of foreign policy that made the Girondists eager for war; they sensed in it, rather, the cure-all for their internal difficulties, the final justification for every use of violence. Then, to be sure, violence grew beyond their control; and it was left to their executioners and successors to develop those subtle possibilities of terror that crushed all political opposition. War, once it came, lent the terror a national aura, and terror and war boosted each other. The fate of the country was chained to the fate of the party.

Victory for France was bound to mean victory for the Jacobins, her defeat their physical downfall. With the September massacres, they had burned their boats behind them: they could not capitulate.

It was a game for high stakes, but those who played it saw beyond the abyss of inflation and famine, of disorder and discontent, which threatened to engulf them if peace were maintained; they sensed the explosive forces that war in an atmosphere of revolution might unleash if love of the native soil merged with thirst for the unforgotten, intoxicating draught of supremacy, and if fanatical awareness of a revolutionary mission combined with lust for plunder. Success was with them.

The expulsion of foreigners followed hard on the heels of the September massacres; the old social order and moral code of the West were not permitted to sit in judgment on France's reign of terror. But France purged herself of it by her own efforts.

How was this accomplished? The Terror lacked, of course, the technical means that are at the disposal of to-day's "civilization" and make every single citizen dependent at any moment upon the whim of central authorities. Moreover, Frenchmen of the *ancien régime*, although, as Continentals, far more obedient to the government than the island peoples, were not as yet so domesticated as they later became under the impact of modern administrative methods. But a factor of greater importance was the inferior quality of the rapidly changing government personnel, who, amid their daily struggles for power and sheer survival, could not rise above amateurish, makeshift measures. The Terror became both more frightful and less effectual for being conducted on dilettante lines. Instead of holding the threatened victims down individually, it united them in opposition. The toxic medicine was administered to the nation in the wrong doses. Thus the very success of the system abroad undermined its domestic position; once the foreigners had been expelled, terror could no longer be justified on patriotic grounds.

Power slipped from the grasp of the party, from political parties as such, and fell into the hands of a victorious general, a danger against which revolutionaries ever since have remained on their guard. In an era of revolutionary wars, military dictatorship proved to be the ready-made middle road between the extremes. To some, it offered security for their revolutionary achievements; to others, protection against the Revolution's arbitrary ravages; to all, it offered justice, order, and prosperity at home and glory and booty abroad.

Napoleon raised the power state of Louis XIV to the level of the new age. He stabilized revolutionary society, adjusted the army and the administration to it, and infused government and nation with the old Continental spirit of authority. He created an instrument of power that was sharper, more pliant, and more potent than any the Continent had ever seen before. But having been forged in haste and under duress, it was even more rigid and inflexible than the power structure of the legitimate and Most Christian Kings. Napoleon concluded a peace of expediency with the Catholic Church, and so secured for his regime a special kind of luster against a background of Jacobin persecution of the Church; but he was not disposed to share power over men's souls with a spiritual authority. Unlike the Orthodox and Protestant churches, the Western church, historically the antithesis of any secular civilization based on power, offered resistance to the Emperor's caesaropapist ambitions. Thus his reign, which had begun with a Concordat, ended, as it must, in a conflict with Rome.

In the fight against the free mind, which he had inherited from the Jacobins, Napoleon never allowed a moment's respite. Whereas material interests of every kind were encouraged, intellectual activities that were not consistent with government policies were considered subversive and forced into silence. Only the sciences, the handmaidens of civilization, were cultivated intensively. The arts, too, particularly architecture, profited after a fashion; they were given the task of depicting the spirit of the Empire in monumental works. The last of the uniform Western styles was taken in all its rigidity from Roman imperial forms. It gave appropriate expression to life as conceived under Napoleon: an *imperator* had arisen again to guide to belated unity the manifold elements of a waning culture.

In fact, the twenty-two-year era of the Revolution and the Napoleonic Empire labored more forcefully than the era of Louis XIV for the unity of the white world. It had at its disposal the new magic formula of social upheaval. With its aid, France in decline produced a rejuvenated military power that towered above those of her Continental adversaries. By the same means, she also generated an ideological power which multiplied her material strength many times over. Just as the magnetic mountain in the legend draws the iron parts from a ship, causing it to collapse, so French propaganda disrupted the ideological forces on the other side. Napoleon understood how to wield this propaganda; and the bouquet of revolutionary achievements looked all the more alluring in his hand for being well arranged and firmly bound. There was not a country in which the new empire did not find a powerful body of supporters. As had happened in the age of the Wars of

Religion, Europe split into two armed camps, and the rift cut through the nations themselves. It spared only Britain and Russia, though for very different reasons. Yet how greatly transformed were the causes of this new division! Since the time of Philip II, much of the religious spirit had melted away, to swell the stream of civilization with its waters. The personality of Napoleon promised to confine this stream in an orderly course, and his followers instinctively interpreted his expansionist Caesarism as a reasonable concomitant of the great crisis. Those with a classical training were struck by the parallel with Caesar and Augustus, which was harped upon by the propagandists, and in Jena, Hegel declared he had seen the *Weltgeist* mounting his steed.

Certainly, a comparison with the Spain of Philip II shows at once where the new world power, for all its roaring dynamism, lagged behind the old. Of France overseas, nothing was left but some insecure fragments, and the state of the navy was not much better. In the English Revolution, the navy had felt itself the representative of maritime opposition to the Stuarts, whereas in the French Revolution, the officers of the navy, which owed its development to the Crown, remained royalists. Some of the warships went over to the British; and the decay of the navy was not so easy to put right as was the decline of the army by a *levée en masse*.

Thus the new struggle for supremacy presented an ambiguous picture. Countering France's vastly enhanced power of expansion on the Continent was the barrier cutting her off from overseas territories—the evil heritage of earlier generations. Could this barrier be breached by new methods operating from an enlarged Continental base? If not, could not this base itself be extended, beyond the confines of Europe, to Africa and Asia? In other words, could not the British scale of the balance, having already lost weight through the secession of the American colonies, this time be made to rise with a rush? On the seas, shipping had mastered global distances for three centuries. Was not the new civilization perhaps equipped to do likewise on the mainland? Would it bring about the victory of the new Rome over the new Carthage? The struggle between the continental and the maritime principles now broke out with greater violence than ever before—an epilogue to the earlier struggles for supremacy and a prologue to future, German, struggles.

However, no new technique of war was as yet available. The progress of invention and engineering in this field was slow. Nevertheless, the political revolution resulted in a revolution in land warfare such as had not been experienced in the past three centuries. The spirit of a country is always reflected in its military establishment. The uprising of the French masses swelled the army; the abundance of manpower enabled the nation to accept losses with equanimity; and the patriotism of the enlisted men made it possible to shape tactics and strategy in an elastic and more mobile form. The concentration of new moral energies led to swift thrusts deep into enemy territory and campaigns that aimed at annihilating the enemy. Looked at as a whole, these campaigns are a manifest expression of the sharply intensified struggle for existence.

At the beginning, the Revolutionary Wars were confined to the framework of the old Continent; for the time being, neither Russia nor Britain allowed her policies to be deflected from their traditional course.

Catherine II, of course, hated the Revolution as the Continental antithesis of Peter's absolutism. She wished for nothing better than the restoration of the Bourbon monarchy to its original standing. But she wanted the German powers to pull the chestnuts out of the fire while she herself absorbed Poland. "I am racking my brains," she remarked at the end of 1791, "to find ways of maneuvering the courts at Vienna and Berlin more deeply into French affairs."

Now more than ever the British, on their island, felt safe from the French upheaval. For the time being, the younger Pitt was quite happy to see Britain's adversary sink into chaos. He had no interest in reviving the monarchy and restoring order. He prophesied a long peace and reduced the strength of the army. Britain took some time to realize that a new kind of opponent was evolving on the far side of the Channel.

Austria and Prussia, however, were closer to the volcano. They felt the tremors in the social foundations they shared with France. The rivals clasped hands, while in their cabinets nervous foreboding over the new and unknown quantity alternated with carelessness—the characteristic opening phase in conflicts with a revolutionary opponent.

The disastrous campaign of 1792 demonstrated that the forces of the German powers were not sufficient to quench the blaze, particularly as, even though allies, they remained jealous of each other and their attention was diverted by the Russian move against Poland in their rear. The Austrian Netherlands, the old target of French expansionism, fell with incredible speed into the hands of the revolutionary aggressor.

Now at long last it was Britain's turn to start up in alarm. For two hundred years it had been an axiom of her policy never to allow a dominant Continental power to establish itself in the river deltas, where it could, of course, develop sea power and threaten to upset the ingenious balance of power system. On this point, public opinion was sensitive. Only lately it had repudiated Pitt's change of attitude toward Russia. It flared up swiftly against France, the more so since concern over foreign policy was mingled with moral indignation. The reign of the guillotine aroused in England a storm of anger reminiscent of the wave of wrath touched off by the Massacre of St. Bartholomew and the Revocation of the Edict of Nantes. In every village and town, public opinion denounced the democratic movement, closed ranks behind the Government, and demanded armed resistance, if need be, to the presumptuous French aim to "liberate" Europe by the sword. It was an impressive demonstration of insular independence in the moral sphere. It was more than national solidarity, a concept apt to narrow the view to the political arena alone. We must always bear in mind that in the British Isles, thanks to a history different from that of the Continent, faith and tradition had also preserved a different, fresher, validity. In a country in which the state meant so much less than on the Continent, moral abhorrence had to be added to political reasoning to fire the masses. That is why the execution of Louis XVI played such a significant role in precipitating the outbreak of war. Here we come up against the problems of the crusading spirit and of cant; in his basic attitude to foreign policy even so early an English statesman as Sir Thomas More was a moralist.

Pitt was a past master at forging Continental coalitions, a tradition established by William III. The very first coalition Pitt assembled against France united practically the whole of Europe and even embraced Russia. Anglo-Russian world rivalry, so vocal of late, was muffled by the renewal of Anglo-French antagonism. No one hurled more menacing words at the Revolution than Catherine, but no country took less action against it at the outset than Russia.

Pitt's diplomatic success was not matched by any military victories. The new France continued to develop a dynamic vigor that overshadowed anything achieved by the well-tried armies of Louis XIV. These had soon fought themselves to a standstill in the amphibious territory of the States-General, and the sole result of long years of war had been the capture of a few fortresses. The swiftly mustered armies of the Revolution, on the other hand, overran the Austrian Netherlands, and then accomplished overnight, as it were, exactly what Louis had aimed at in his boldest dreams: they broke the power of Holland and, aided by the native party of the Patriots, erected on its ruins the satellite Batavian Republic. Holland might still rank as the richest country in Europe, but from then on she could be squeezed like a lemon by the rising dominant power.

Were the consequences of this process for Britain and the world really as great as they would have been in the seventeenth century? Certainly, Britain no longer possessed a bridgehead on the Continent, and for nearly half a generation, until she intervened on the Iberian Peninsula, took no part whatever in the fighting on land. During that period she merely nourished the war with vast funds. The Dutch trade, which Britain had inherited, helped to augment these funds, and so did the Dutch colonies, which, together with most of the French colonies, fell one by one into British hands. Conversely, France, lacking a navy with effective striking power, could not make full use of the bases she had conquered. Thus, events which a hundred years earlier might have brought a turning point in the whole system now produced no decisive effects.

While France for years remained unable to engage her main opponent in his own element, the latter meanwhile calmly organized a grand-scale trade war which destroyed the enemy's maritime traffic and either curbed that of the neutrals or kept it under control. For Britain, more than ever before, naval warfare became an enterprise without risks. This partly explains the constant renewal of the cornucopia from which subsidies flowed in torrents. But in the long run, the naval war would not have sufficed to replenish the coffers. Britain's young industry had to join her sea power in supplying the state with the immense resources it needed. British products were indispensable to the overseas territories, above all to the large Spanish and Portuguese territories which had been cut off from their mother countries by Britain's trade war. One may say that the industrial civilization of Britain, spread by private enterprise, helped to outfight the political civilization of France.

But the French stormed on, as if they possessed magic powers—not merely in the Netherlands but also in the German lands along the Rhine and in Italy. Without revolutionizing the technique of communications, the new civilization had nevertheless established a new relationship with space and time.

However, it was not French striking power alone that yielded this result. A contribution was made by a state at war with the Republic—Russia. Catherine would have been overjoyed to acquire the whole of Poland while the German powers, engaged in the West, had their backs turned. Although this proved to be impossible, she could at least resume the old Russian game of playing off the two German rivals against each other. Austria was kept in the dark while the empress arranged the Second Partition of Poland with Prussia; and the procedure was roughly reversed in the case of the Third. By pushing farther forward on one of the traditional outward routes of Russian policy, the central route, she benefited greatly from the conflagration in the West. But to her dismay her action brought palpable relief to the hated revolutionaries, and also led to Prussia's withdrawal from the coalition. At the beginning of the century, Russia's intervention in Poland had weakened one of France's important outposts; it now had the opposite effect, as France no longer had any prestige to lose in Poland. Had Catherine been granted a longer reign, she presumably would have reversed course and inaugurated a more active policy against the French danger.

This was to be the task of her son Paul. She died on the eve of a grandiose application of power that was to reach far beyond the sphere of influence of her own Russia. For in the long run, the eastern flanking power could not, any more than Britain, remain unconcerned at the rise of the French volcano from amid the craters of European policies.

At first, however, general peace was brought about on the Continent by a brilliant campaign on the part of the rising Napoleon. In the Treaty of Campoformio, France gained a position such as had never before been hers. All the aims that her most ambitious rulers since the sixteenth century had set themselves to attain in sequence were now achieved at one fell swoop: in Italy a position of dominance such as Charles VIII, Louis XI, and Francis I had dreamed of; in Germany the near certainty of obtaining the Rhine as a frontier in conformity with the program of natural boundaries; and a partly overt, partly masked control of the Low Countries. In much the same way revolutionary Germany, between 1938 and 1940, saw fall into her lap all the golden fruits to which former generations had aspired. In both cases, only one thing was missing: peace with Britain.

Had France no means of coming to grips with her main opponent? Her disorganized navy was still being rebuilt; but it might be adequate for an expedition to Egypt, particularly as Britain had withdrawn from the Mediterranean since Spain had entered the war on the side of France.

What was the purport of Napoleon's Egyptian expedition? In the Middle Ages the Western world's line of advance, and especially that of France, had lain in a southeasterly direction. The Turks had barred its path and thus diverted the Occident's accumulated energies onto the oceans. But the Turkish barrier had rotted. Could not the stream of Europe's energies once again seek out its old bed?

In any event, from that time on, Continental powers aiming at supremacy have again and again clung to the hope of recouping themselves in that area for their lost command of the oceans. If they could establish themselves at the junction of Africa and Asia, the continental principle would have won a decisive battle over the insular principle, the encirclement of the European peninsula would have been broken, and they would have ducked under the guard of the Russian colossus. In short, the nightmare from West and East that lay over the Occident would have been removed. But removed at what price? At the cost of the freedom of the system. For only a power that had *achieved* supremacy could hope to burst through the fateful ring, and such a power's success must of necessity perpetuate its dominance in Europe.

France's distant colonies had been either lost or cut off because the motherland could not compete at sea with the leading maritime power. But Egypt promised an opportunity for colonizing activity closer to home; for even a weak navy might, if concentrated in the Mediterranean, maintain communications with the mother country. If the gamble succeeded, the state's Continental instruments of power could be applied with far greater force on the comparatively nearby Nile than on the distant Mississippi or St. Lawrence.

Napoleon's Egyptian campaign heralded the change of front in France's colonial aspirations which, in the nineteenth and twentieth centuries, was to bring forth the grandiose, consolidated second French colonial empire; it was to be created in a truly Continental spirit. However, compared to the hopes that Napoleon pinned on his Egyptian expedition, this second colonial empire seems minute. For the conquest of Egypt was intended to jeopardize the second British colonial empire, whose most valuable component was India. Here Britain had found a kind of substitute for the lost American colonies.

What an astonishing phenomenon British India was! A small European island nation was the master of a huge, distant subcontinent, then inhabited by 200,000,000 Asians, some of them highly cultured. The establishment of such dominion by one of the great military states of Continental Europe might not have been beyond imagination; but how could unmilitary, unbureaucratic Britain, of all countries, achieve it? Here, after all, she was not helped, as in America, by a strong flow of emigrants. Portugal and Holland, the two older sea powers, had always been content to occupy no more than stations on the Indian subcontinent. Our astonishment at Britain's achievement grows when we consider that she spread her power through India while she was heavily engaged in armed conflict elsewhere—during the Seven Years' War, the American War of Independence, and the Napoleonic Wars.

The fact is that, in India, Anglo-Saxon private initiative achieved triumphs of no lesser magnitude than those it accomplished in America, although its feats here belonged in another category. In their Indian diplomacy, the British showed consummate skill in playing off against one another the corrupt native potentates, whose fairly well-ordered cohesion had disappeared with the downfall of the Mogul Empire. In the financial sphere, the British succeeded in more than amply recovering all expenditures from profits made on the spot. In the military field, they were able to use predominantly native forces for the effort required; as a rule, the sepoys five times outnumbered the white troops, who, for the most part, were used only for training purposes and as a stiffening. The great leaders, Clive and Hastings, developed quite independently, growing under the challenge of great opportunities. With no instructions to guide them, certainly none from the home government, they acted in the name of the privately owned East India Company; and only a change of policy, designed to counter French expansion in India, secured for their struggles a certain amount of support from official sources at home. This support was trifling compared with the means that the French state, characteristically, placed at the disposal of her pioneers in India. If the British nevertheless succeeded in gradually driving their competitors out of India, they were able to do so because they could rely on the wealth of their Company—in other words, on private resources.

Yet a number of French army officers and Residents had stayed on, still a thorn in the flesh of the British at the end of the century, and had found among the native rulers patrons who might become dangerous to Britain. Napoleon's plan was to co-operate with Indian princes and re-enact, via Egypt, the march of Alexander the Great—that is, to use continental instruments of power to snatch from the British the great prize they had won by maritime means. The old project of building a Suez canal was included in such plans.

(Trump cards later to be used by the Third Reich appear here, though shuffled in a different way; similar situations inevitably and repeatedly breed similar plans.)

In the space of a few hours, the naval battle of Aboukir upset these daring schemes. Now the world realized for the first time the full historic significance of Britain's penetration of the Mediterranean during the War of the Spanish Succession, and of her subsequent stubborn defense of Gibraltar against the most violent attacks. Here, if anywhere, a rent should have been torn in the invisible net that a modest number of wooden warships, dispatched from an island with a relatively small population, had woven around the great and exuberantly vital peninsula of Europe. But the net held. Thanks to Gibraltar, Nelson's fleet sailed into the Mediterranean and, thanks to his and his crews' superior seamanship, destroyed a French fleet of equal size, a feat all the more admirable as Malta was in French hands at the time. Realizing its importance, Napoleon had seized it from the Knights of St. John on his outward journey. From then on, the British strove to gain possession of this key fortress, and soon it was to be caught in a special way in the swirl of high politics.

With the naval battle of Aboukir, the Egyptian expedition was wrecked, no matter how many land victories the French army, now cut off from its base, might win. Once again, the cruel disproportion between the continental military effort and the maritime naval effort was brutally exposed: at the cost of only 900 dead, Britain was able to thwart the grand-scale sortie of a dominant Continental power into the world outside.

The consequences of this French failure could not remain local and limited. They had widespread repercussions in Asia as well as Europe.

First, they encouraged the Turks to declare war on the invaders, thus rupturing an alliance that for two hundred and fifty years had been a stable element in Western diplomacy. Until then, Turkey had been a highly important, though distant, outpost of France. Now she was brought within the scope of Napoleon's expansionist plans, and figured again and again as an objective in his world-wide scheming. This was reason enough for uneasiness in St. Petersburg. Russia could not tolerate, any more than Britain, a breakout southeastward of a European power seeking supremacy, be it France, as at that time, or, later, Germany. To counter such attempts, the two world powers, though rivals, would always join forces.

They did so then once again—in Europe. And this time Russia did not content herself with a demonstration against France. True, it was not only considerations of foreign policy that drove the unpredictable Paul I into battle; the Russian switch was also prompted by Paul's mania for legitimacy. What violent swings of policy might not be brought out by a change of monarch, or even a shift in the monarch's whim, in this Hellenistic realm of despots! Yet Paul's eccentric legitimism did not lack some rational grounds. However backward, indeed fundamentally different, Russia's social and intellectual situation was compared with that of France, France contained inflammable material enough to kindle revolutionary thinking in Russia. The power mechanism created by Peter the Great owed its efficiency to the forcible mating of heterogeneous elements—the orthodoxy of Old Russia and secular techniques. What would happen if these techniques were followed by Western ideas? What if an echo of ill-understood, distant events were to arouse the malleable Eastern peoples, those human instruments in barracks and government offices and the patient peasant masses whose legal status had sunk lower and lower under Catherine? The late Tsarina, who had had to suppress peasant risings, had known only too well why she dreaded the French Revolution: the more artificially the social order had been stabilized on the pattern of Western absolutism, the more confusing the model of Western revolution might prove to be. Any Continental power state tends to develop rigidity; to evolve, it requires a strong initiative from above. If this initiative comes from below, from the depths of society, the state is shaken to its foundations. How very much more all this is true of the Continental giant of the East! Russia needed the West, yet at the same time feared infection through contact with it. She wanted to conquer it, yet shied away from the vanquished victim. Paul subjected all foreigners to the tightest control and put every kind of obstacle in the way of travel abroad by his subjects. Young people were not permitted to study at foreign universities because the pernicious doctrines said to be in vogue there were apt to inflame immature minds. Peter the Great, who had been forceful enough in organizing foreign travel, had always been on his guard against a revolution arising out of the spirit of Old Russia. Now, the specter of a revolution engendered by the Western spirit hovered by the throne of the Tsars. It was never to depart as long as the Russian throne existed.

Accordingly, Russian policy reached out far into the West, beyond the sphere of interest in Eastern and Central Europe on which Peter the Great and Catherine II had systematically concentrated their efforts. Evidently Germany was no longer in a position to provide an adequate counterweight to the new France, as she had a hundred years earlier to the old. Prussia dared not give up neutrality. In the trough between two struggles for supremacy, her strength, coupled with heroic effort, great daring, and extreme dexterity, had enabled her to attain great-power status of a sort. Now, amid the rising din of the new battle for supremacy, the pusillanimous Berlin government believed it could preserve this status by remaining inactive, and could evade the backlash of the tempest by ignoring it. For France, Austria alone was no longer the dangerous adversary she had been before two powers appeared on the German scene; but as Austria was resolved to have the peace of Campoformio revised and her interests both north and south of the Alps made secure, she seized the opportunity to join the new coalition as the *de facto* dominant power in Central Europe.

However, her military performances were completely put in the shade by Russia's. Italy, Switzerland, and Holland, which until then had never seen a Russian soldier, witnessed heroic deeds by these semi-barbarians from the East. The Muscovite soldiery may have had the air of phantoms as they moved through the center of the Occident; but the landing of a Russian force, together with a British contingent, on the island of Walcheren and the wintering of Russian troops in the Channel Islands were indications of the uncanny increase in the range of Russia's activities. Yet with all their heroism, these men were fighting for a madman rather than any clearly conceived state policy; Paul first broke with Austria, then with Britain as well, and finally executed a *salto mortale* to land in an enthusiastic partnership with France and her great ruler.

Napoleon, having returned from Egypt, had in the meantime become the ruler of France by the *coup d'état* of *Brumaire*. With a mighty blow he felled Austria, left in the lurch by Russia, and restored peace on the Continent in a blaze of glory. Peace at sea and victory over Britain still remained to be achieved. Napoleon hoped to achieve both through a coalition with the Tsar.

During the American War of Independence, it had become evident how dangerous to Britain a united front on the Continent could become. What if the two most powerful Continental countries were to join forces now? Could not their alliance solve the riddle of the insular sphinx once and for all? Napoleon feverishly drafted plan after plan. His design was to prepare a direct attack on the island in Flanders and Brittany, while the French and Spanish fleets were to link up in the Mediterranean with the Russian Black Sea fleet. He enticed Paul with a scheme to build a Suez canal, which would facilitate Russian trade with the East Indies. As for the East Indies themselves, Napoleon's aim now was to approach them by overland route and conquer them jointly with his new ally. His powerful imagination completely ignited the sickly fancy of the Tsar. Paul set a Cossack army in motion toward India, urged a French landing in Britain, and soon renewed the Armed Neutrality of Catherine's day. As Denmark joined this compact, Britain found herself prompted to dispatch a fleet to Copenhagen in order to seize the key to the Baltic, and Nelson succeeded in destroying the Danish fleet. But an even greater sensation than the tidings of his victory in the Danish Sound was touched off in London by the news that the Tsar had been assassinated.

Napoleon's fantastic scheme, which had called for a madman's aid to succeed, burst like a gaudy soap bubble. The shattering news from St. Petersburg threw him into one of his fits of fury; for the second time, a weapon against Britain had been struck out of his hand. No longer in a position to hope for early peace through victory, he was now prepared to bargain for a negotiated peace which would give him time to consolidate his huge Continental domain.

But could Britain enter into such an arrangement at a moment when the dominant Continental power was expanding more menacingly than ever? Of all the nations that took the field against France in the years between 1792 and 1815, Britain pursued the most consistent war policy. In fact, this struggle for supremacy, like its predecessor and those that followed, was in essence a struggle between the insular and continental principles.

Nevertheless, in 1802, Britain did for once give way to war-weariness. In France, the new civilization, owing to its political emphasis, served the dynamics of war, while in England, where its effects were seen in private and economic life, it favored the interests of peace. Pitt fell. The British were unwilling to see Napoleon as he was; they saw him as they wished him to be. Britain went out of her way to bring about a lasting peace; without further ado she handed over Belgium, so often a bone of contention, to the French, and did not even ensure the unequivocal restoration of the independence of Holland. She compromised, almost to the point of carelessness, her old and tried principle of never leaving the Low Countries' river deltas in the hands of the dominant Continental power. In fact, one could scarcely speak any longer of a balance of power on the Continent.

As against this, the supremacy of Britain on the oceans was all the more unquestioned—and therein lies something of an explanation of her mild policy. This dominance permitted her to return a large proportion of the recently occupied colonies to their Continental owners, notably to France herself. Less certain was Britain's dominance in the Mediterranean, which, since the Egyptian expedition, had to be regarded as vital for the future of the maritime principle.

Still, the French had been driven out of Egypt, and therefore Britain believed she could risk holding out to the Knights of St. John the prospect of the return of Malta, the key fortress which she had only just won.

If there was any possibility of achieving a long-term settlement through flexibility, not renunciation, on the part of Britain, that chance lay in the conditions to which she assented in the Treaty of Amiens.

The prospects for such a settlement were all the brighter because of the mood of the French people, which was as close as it had ever come to favoring it. After a tempestuous decade, the nation, free of danger from its neighbors and—apart from colonial luxuries—economically self-sufficient enough not to demand expansion on economic grounds, wanted nothing more than to enjoy its incredible gains in peace.

However, on the Continent public opinion does not carry the same weight as in the British Isles. It asserts itself by resorting to revolution only after the state leadership has proved uncertain and hapless. Faced with a strong-willed ruler who knows how to keep a firm grip on the military and bureaucratic apparatus, public opinion will in the end be willing to follow the bold lead of a man who seems to embody the spirit of the nation and its power. The heterogeneous elements of the opposition fail to find a counterpole to rally around; driven to conspiracy and treason, they remain scattered on the fringes of state life. Every member of the *grande nation* harbored a dormant longing for his country to achieve glory, which in the context of the time meant supremacy. Understanding of the perils inherent in efforts to achieve this has always been rare. The French, a great continental people, were not able to appreciate the invisible strength of their small island opponent, and failed to see the narrow boundary between a bold game and a hopeless gamble. Thus they could not shake off the rider who hoisted the nation with him over so many hurdles. They would go on until they collapsed, worn out beneath him, in the midst of catastrophe abroad; and the very qualities of this daemonic man, who had lifted the nation steeply to the heights, would engineer its precipitous downfall. His ephemeral successes would exact a terrible price.

But how could it ever occur to a man of Bonaparte's temperament to stop halfway? The idea of world dominion carries a temptation of unique force. To gain it, even the legitimate Christian kings Philip and Louis had squeezed the last ounce of strength from their peoples; and Napoleon was a son of the Revolution, in which the will to power had cast away all the calming influence of faith and tradition. He was filled with the ruthless Jacobin's sense of superiority toward the old society, an adventurer without ties hailing from the margin of the French-speaking world, continental in all his instincts, though born on an island—a Mediterranean island. How could he, driven by a passionate will to power and at the peak of his Continental triumphs, appreciate the enigmatic durability of the invisible net that encompassed his huge, highly armed empire? The great dominators of the Continent have always been in danger of overestimating their own possibilities. Like all other passions, lust for power tends to throw off checks and balances and bring about decadence in its victim.

Such decadence did, in fact, begin to show in Bonaparte's demeanor after Amiens. It was not at all his intention to have the opportunities of the peace so rapidly exhausted as they actually were. He probably planned to take cover behind the screen of the treaty for years, in order to fortify his position and expand it in one sector after another, on both sides of the ocean, for a new passage of arms. However, in his *hubris* he not only underestimated the enemy but also made mistakes in carrying out his own purpose. Disregarding the letter and spirit of treaties, he spread out in Italy, Switzerland, Germany, and—the touchiest of all places as far as Britain was concerned—Holland; there was no question of his re-establishing her sovereignty. In reality, even the struggle for the Mediterranean went on, treaty or no treaty; Napoleon had his eye on the central sector of North Africa and, again, on Egypt. His gaze was roving once more in the direction of the East Indies. A whole army was shipped to the West Indies to restore discredited French rule there. Even a renewal of the battle for North America seemed to be moving back into the realm of possibility. Napoleon had just acquired Louisiana from Spain. True, he soon sold it to the United States, but only when war was about to break out again in Europe and the good will of the States appeared more important to him than the precarious possession of that distant territory. Moreover, the French navy, which might have secured communications with Louisiana, was not yet ready.

Naval rearmament, pressed with all the means at France's disposal, caused alarm in Britain. As understood there, the treaty, though not designed to stabilize a balance of power on the Continent, was to establish such a balance between the British and French spheres of influence in the world. The British were disappointed, regretted their rash readiness to compromise, and renewed the war. Destiny took its course, and to us Germans, each stage of that route reads like a chapter of our own history.

The first stage was the camp at Boulogne, where the master of the Continent busied himself with plans for a landing as daring as they were amateurish. Some historians have suggested that these preparations were only a feint to camouflage the assembling of an army for use against Continental foes; but this view has been abandoned. Napoleon was in deadly earnest. Gloating sanctimoniously, he told a Russian diplomat that the probable consequences of the new war filled him, as a European, with horror, and that he would be as deeply saddened as Russia if the news should one day come that Britain no longer existed. Hopes at his headquarters ran high; and Talleyrand's diaries for the period use language of the same confidence. At first, the landing was to be effected by fishing craft escorted, to ensure surprise, only by small armed vessels. But according to the final calculation, 2,000 of these escort vessels were required; and the harbors were not large enough to accommodate them. Moreover, trial runs showed how greatly dependent they were on the weather. It was therefore decided to have men-of-war cover the landing and fight to gain control of the Channel, for a few days at least. But the French navy proved too weak for the task. Does not all this sound like the summer of 1940?

Boulogne was the third attempt, after the Egyptian expedition and the plan of co-operation with Tsar Paul, to come to grips with the enemy by maritime means. Once this third project had turned out to be unfeasible, Napoleon made the obvious move and tried to extend his rule still further on the Continent—by peaceful, even if ruthless, methods for the time being—and to bring Britain to her knees by devious means. What resulted were new wars on the Continent. When the guns went off, they fired in the opposite direction, a turn of events typical of all struggles for supremacy from Philip II down to Hitler. Prussian diplomats had predicted that Bonaparte, who had already made certain of

Hanover, would seek further compensation on the Continent if his landing plans came to naught.

Of course, the Continental powers which had retained their independence, Russia at their head, had become alarmed by the numerous encroachments upon their spheres of influence. It was in Russia's vital interest, as well as Britain's, to enter the lists against any European power seeking supremacy. Only Paul's madness had made him deaf to the demands of this principle. Tsar Alexander obeyed them. His Chancellor feared that in the north the French might gain mastery of the Danish Sound and box Russia up in the Baltic, overpower Turkey in the south, and from there infect the Ukraine with Western ideas. But perhaps the deciding factor in the Tsar's own change of attitude toward France was the execution of the Duc d'Enghien. A man of Bonaparte's stamp was incapable of foreseeing the enormous effect that this act of Jacobinism, a relapse on his part, would have on the still active moral susceptibilities of the Western world.

Thus the Third Coalition came into being, the last achievement of Pitt, who was now back in power. The nucleus of the coalition was the alliance of the great flanking powers. Divided Germany was represented in it only by Austria, which, as a minor power, had manifestly joined under pressure. Prussia stuck to her neutrality even at this late stage, only to suffer an early and devastating defeat in isolation.

Sweeping from the Channel coast into the heart of the Continent, Napoleon won a new series of lightning victories, which led him from Austerlitz and Jena to the Treaty of Tilsit. Though they outshone previous successes, these bloody triumphs were no substitute for the action he had failed to take at Boulogne. "As long as there is no peace with England, all other peace treaties are no more than armistice agreements," he said on a later occasion.

The Battle of Trafalgar made sure that the Boulogne plans were not reactivated. As at La Hogue, the French fleet became the victim of a commander in chief who had no understanding of the sea. We cannot but marvel at the small price—449 dead—that Britain had to pay even for this victory, which brought her a command of the sea that was to remain unchallenged for a hundred years. Among those dead, it is true, was Nelson.

How did it come about that this single naval battle gave the victor enduring command of the sea, whereas in the two preceding generations Britain's superiority had been challenged again and again by French new construction? Technical methods had not yet changed. In fact, something of a myth has grown up around this battle. It was indeed the last great naval battle against France; but it was the last only because shortly thereafter Napoleon was destroyed on land, and this defeat, in turn, was an effect of his inability to master Britain at sea, for otherwise he never would have had to march on Moscow. Had he emerged victorious on land, he would have resumed the fight at sea in spite of Trafalgar; and perhaps only the rising in Spain prevented him from renewing his landing preparations. Let us beware of rushing into the fallacy: *post hoc ergo propter hoc.*

At Tilsit, Napoleon tried to use the detour of a friendship with Russia to achieve his main objective—victory over his island foe. (A similar experiment was launched by Hitler. Its purpose in 1939 was to make war with Britain possible in any case, whereas in 1807 the object was to bring the war to an end.) Napoleon had driven Russia back from Central Europe, a region she had been pushing into since the beginning of Paul's reign. But at Tilsit he was only at the Russian frontier: he had not defeated Russia. For all his recent victories, he had not been able to finish the Continental game that had been forced upon him by the abandonment of his landing plans. Despite the incomparable expansion of his sphere of power, he was no better off than Philip II and Louis XIV had been. Suppose, however, he were to succeed in calling the game a draw, and revive the Franco-Russian collaboration which Paul's assassination had ripped apart at its most promising moment?

Paul had been a maniac, whereas Alexander I, a man of many facets, possessed some of the qualities of a ruler. The alliance suited him well as a means of getting out of an awkward war unscathed; but he could not be lured into a common policy that lacked a genuine community of interest. Russia could acquiesce, for a time, in the unparalleled growth of Napoleon's Empire, but only on condition that corresponding concessions were granted to her. As her long-standing westward influence had been checked, and the Polish Grand Duchy of Warsaw set up on her own border, to exercise a magnetic effect eastward, Russia must at least demand that the road to the south not be blocked. Several lines of advance were open to her in that direction. Constantinople would, in any event, have been a compensation.

However, Alexander was to learn that his partner had by no means dropped his ambitions in the Orient; to realize them promised him a breakthrough into open spaces, a move that could be accomplished without an ocean-going fleet. Of course, Napoleon held out vague hints about a partition of Turkey; about plans for co-operation against India, with which he had earlier fired Paul's imagination; and about common action against Sweden. But Alexander must have sensed that his empire was merely being courted as an auxiliary in a *societas leonina*. Moreover, the news of Britain's invasion of the Iberian Peninsula and of the popular rising in Spain made it clear to him that the Tower of Babel was showing cracks in its foundations. Napoleon, then, held out his hand to the empty air. The flowers of the Tilsit friendship bore no fruit. It failed precisely where the Emperor aimed at causing the collapse of Britain's front—in the trade war he had inaugurated through the Continental System. Russia's trade was geared to an exchange of lumber and agricultural products for British manufactured goods. The standstill in this exchange threatened the vast empire with incalculable embarrassment.

To the Orthodox believers of Old Russia, the alliance of their Tsar with the godless Emperor of the West was an odious thing. And if this alliance should achieve its goal and obliterate Britain, the Tsar would only find himself isolated vis-à-vis the Emperor, an ally who even now was unwilling to accord his partner any expansion. The prospect was anything but alluring.

Still, the Tilsit friendship would have been of service to Napoleon if his sole object had been to cover his rear and master Britain by his own strength—master her by maritime means. But this was out of the question since Boulogne, and especially so since Trafalgar. All that France could do was to keep on applying Continental instruments of power—the Continental System, as the term implies, was one of them—and no swift and conclusive success was to be expected from these methods.

Thus the brittleness of the alliance at its foundation, the lack of a community of interest on the cardinal question, had ample time to take effect. Equivocation, mutual distrust, and finally treachery undermined relations between the two men.

The collapse of these relations in 1812 did not occur without the earlier appearance, at numerous other points, of signs of decay in the Napoleonic Empire. Most of these were connected with the ill-starred Continental System, the seat of infection from which a creeping poison spread through Napoleon's great domains. The Continental System, a war without actual weapons, was more exhausting than the bloody campaigns that were waged, in vain, to shorten it. It foreshadowed, to some degree, the rationing and coupon systems of modern wars, except that the shortages it created were not the consequences of a British blockade, but rather those of a voluntary sealing off of the Continent, a counter-blockade. This is not to say that the Continent was then dependent upon sea-borne supplies in order to sustain itself; but, as it turned out, they played a much larger role in its economy than they had in earlier centuries, when armed conflict with the island kingdom had nevertheless caused serious economic complications. In the meantime, manufacturing had flourished in Britain, and the agricultural countries of the Continent had grown accustomed to importing British manufactures, especially textiles and steel goods. Thus Russia was not the only country that found itself in difficulty when these supplies dried up. New industries then arising did not suffice to make good the loss. Wherever it reached, the System sowed hatred against both the tyrant and the *grande nation*, which enjoyed privileges in the economic sphere as well as in others. Smuggling became widespread, the morale of the administration went to pieces, and belief in the soundness of the Napoleonic Empire itself was eaten away.

Outwardly, the tendency toward unification of the Continent continued to make progress. But after the first era, with its stupendous and fascinating expansion of France, there followed a second, which was charged with compulsion, doubt, and indignation. A vicious circle was created. The universal monarchy swallowed up one country after another in order that the blockade, repeatedly punctured, might be more effectively enforced. Garrisons had to be increased to guard against invasions by the British from seaward (and whence might they not come?) and smoldering resistance movements in the interior. Yet neither invasion nor resistance could be prevented on the Iberian Peninsula; they tore open a wound which was not to be healed and which was to drain away the strength of Napoleon's Empire.

While the Continental System boomeranged on the aggressor, it failed to achieve the hoped-for effect on the nation it attacked. The process by which the British manufacturing system increased the vulnerability of the Continental economy also enhanced the invulnerability of the island economy. The Emperor's sanguine calculations that Britain's economic strength would be paralyzed were as little borne out by the facts as were those of the German leaders in a similar situation at a later date. The very products which, in spite of the huge volume of smuggling and other penetrations of the blockade, could not be disposed of on the other side of the Channel conquered overseas markets. They did so the more easily as Britain chased the flags of the neutrals from the oceans and had no competitor to fear except the United States. In 1812 Napoleon himself voiced the gloomy forecast that "in two years the new markets in South America will outweigh the effects of our Continental System." Certainly, many sections of Britain's population had heavy burdens to bear, but they bore them. The insular sense of solidarity gave the unrest so eagerly awaited by Napoleon no chance to develop, and, in spite of embarrassments in individual sectors, the economy as a whole remained crisis-proof. This time, too, the insular character maintained its mysterious strength. Against it, as against some hidden reef, forces with perhaps a tenfold superiority in numbers once more hurled themselves in vain.

What a spectacle! A vast, glittering empire, bristling with armaments, which over more than a dozen years never so much as caught sight of its mortal enemy, and which, writhing like a captive bull in a net, only succeeded, for all its bloody victories, in drawing the net tighter about itself. Facing it, an agile opponent who approached the victim on the distant Iberian Peninsula, a place of his own choosing, at a moment determined by himself. There he inflicted wound upon wound on his victim, until, on the old battlefields of the Netherlands, he gave him the *coup de grâce*—all this with minimum loss to himself. In twenty-two years of war Britain lost no more than 50,000 men on European soil, including the casualties suffered by her German auxiliary troops.

In this era of war, too, most of the battles were fought by Britain's Continental allies. Among them, we have to distinguish between Russia and the group of old Continental states. The former, its approaches damaged but its backbone untouched, needed no fundamental renewal to make it battle-worthy. But how could the old Continental states resume their places in the phalanx after they had been cut down, stripped of their weapons, parceled out, or even replaced by new structures? They needed an infusion of fresh moral energy. They received it from the idea of nationalism.

In the years of the overpowering onrush of the tidal wave, it might have seemed as if the *imperium Romanum* were being revived; as if the tendency toward unity, which during the Middle Ages had been realized in only shadowy outline, would now take on massive substance under the dynamic stimulus of a swiftly advancing civilization. In all countries, the new spirit of the upsurging classes sailed for a while before the wind of France's revolutionary concept of mankind. The peoples of the old Continent seemed as wax in the hands of the Emperor, ready to be molded into a universal form. Let us imagine what the consequences might have been if a unified Europe of Continental stamp had been able to assert itself as the focus of world power and culture. Let us try to gauge the possibilities such a turn of events might have opened up, and what others it might have shut off. Without a great number of freely competing nations, so many of the values created since that time would be as unthinkable as the threat that hangs over them today.

However, the dike held; Britain and Russia remained upright. The universal flood ebbed away, and the historic pattern re-emerged. Compelled to overstrain its resources of power, Napoleon's Empire lost its magic. Once again, Europe's tendency to split up triumphed over the forces of unification, this time for good. Not only did an Occident made up of many states maintain its continuity, but it acquired huge fresh sources of vitality by adopting the new spirit and absorbing the rising social classes. It did so through the medium of the concept of nationalism.

This idea, which had first inspired the revolting masses of France as they repelled foreign enemies, now transformed and inflamed the opponents of France. The giant mass personalities of the nations took the stage full of self-assurance, passionately intent upon giving forceful expression to their nature, never again to be malleable as wax, but from now on hard as crystal. The new national energies, powerful but also disturbing as allies, streamed into the structures of the old states, giving them strength to rise again and take their places in the phalanx opposing the Emperor. Were these states capable of regaining their freedom only with England's help, or could they have done so on their own? If so, by what sacrifices, and when?

At all events, the young eastern flanking power did bring incalculable relief to the old Continent in its struggle for freedom. Not that Russia attacked; in attack, her biggest assets would not have been effective. But the Emperor himself felt compelled to take the offensive if he wished to achieve his main goal, the downfall of Britain. The collaboration with Alexander, begun with so many hopes, had produced as little result as the earlier one with Paul. By her very nature, Russia could never sincerely support any power seeking supremacy in the West. Yet such support was indispensable to the Continental System, which was bound to be ineffective if there were any gaps in its net around the Continent.

Thus the Emperor was left with no alternative but the use of force against a recalcitrant Russia. He also had to consider that if he did not himself attack, his opponent might one day force war upon him at the most inopportune moment. Britain might join up with Russia, start a fire in the east as she had done in the south, in Spain, and roast the Empire at a slow flame. To forestall the enemy before the drain on Napoleon's own strength had gone any further was wiser than to wait—and that meant preventive war! "To rob Britain of every hope of forming a new coalition by undermining the power of the only great state that might still become her ally—that is a great, a sublime thought" (Napoleon to Caulaincourt). In truth, this was the bitter consequence of Boulogne and Trafalgar: Napoleon had to fight his maritime enemy indirectly by means of land wars of ever widening scope. With his fortunes similarly on the wane,

171

Philip II, too, had had to take an extreme decision, but he took it reluctantly. Napoleon, on the other hand, crossed the Niemen on June 21, 1812, inflated with the confidence of *hubris*.

As his calculations had gone awry in the west because of his ignorance of the maritime world, so did they miscarry in the east because of the strangeness of the vast Eurasian expanses. Napoleon was a western Continental. This was continent, too, but it was no longer western. He had been the first man to subjugate the old Continent by force of arms; neither Charles V nor Philip II nor Louis XIV had achieved anything comparable. But in this new continental territory his career was to reach a turning point. The field of action of European politics had been enlarged by the addition of the giant Russian empire; and the significance of this change for the freedom of the European system of states was to be demonstrated at a decisive hour. For even the new civilization offered no adequate means of mastering the immense distances of the East. Thus Russia was now enabled to prove herself as a guarantor of the system alongside Britain, the German powers having shown themselves unequal to the task. Russia could rise to the first rank in world affairs, far above the level of her achievements under Peter the Great and Catherine.

In the war itself, the Russians used all the strong cards that had brought about the downfall of Charles XII: the vastness of the country, the destruction of their own cities, the rigor of the climate. Nor did they, in 1812, play these cards for the last time.

Only when the pendulum was swinging back did the German states and others join in; and finally, under the leadership of the two flanking powers, a solid phalanx was formed. This coalition grasped the power seeking supremacy, and crushed it. Twice the French capital fell into the hands of the victors; a clear demonstration that, in contrast to the reverses suffered by Louis XIV and Philip II, this defeat was a collapse. In the end, a large proportion of the French population welcomed the debacle as the last way out of a situation that admitted of no other.

Unlike the first French wave of power, the second did not ebb away slowly. It had reared up abruptly as a surprise sortie and an attempt to break out into the wide world beyond; now it crashed down, and with it the energies of a profoundly exhausted nation which the Revolution had mobilized to the uttermost limit. All reserves had been thrown into action.

France, in later days, toyed more than once with a claim to supremacy; but she never again put the last of her strength into the struggle. In fact, from that moment she felt herself lagging behind the progress of the victors. Her population figures declined. Her will to power, which had come into tragic conflict with the people's simple will to live, never recovered from the excessive strain. She had passed her peak for good, as had Spain two hundred years earlier. A proud nation that receives from the hand of a victor a constitution, however excellent in itself, and the guarantee of its internal stability, sustains a deep wound from which there is no full recovery, no matter how swiftly favorable circumstances and the victors' wisdom may cause the scar to heal over. However much resilience the nation may retain outside the field of politics, a spring has been broken which cannot be welded together again. The higher a Continental power rises, the more far-reaching the effects of its fall.

While the autumn of France's destiny thus set in, Britain bathed, for the next two generations, in the brilliant glow of high summer. True, her claim to be chief architect of victory was no longer uncontested as it had been a hundred years earlier; Russia was at her side to demand a huge share in the fruits. Nevertheless, Britain at the summit of her power and fortune towered above the proudest of her Continental counterparts.

I shall therefore review the results of the era of war from the vantage point of London. These results confirmed and transcended the outcome of the two preceding struggles for supremacy. Once again the old Continent had shown its inability to give birth to a dominant power and had had to watch its transoceanic relationships wither. These two corresponding phenomena both operated in Britain's favor—indirectly, as a European balance of power, and directly, in the shape of British supremacy beyond the seas. More clearly than ever before, the old Continent had bought the continuance of its free system of states at the price of the migration of its power.

For the time being, this process did not become manifest to its full extent in the changing circumstances of colonial ownership. But the size of the empires retained by the two Iberian nations and the Dutch must not blind us to the fact that the colonies of the latter lay in the British sphere of influence, and that the colonies of Spain and Portugal—aided and abetted by Britain—soon began to move toward secession from their mother countries. The French colonies could obviously be regarded only as fragments of the old empire. Moreover, Britain, by strengthening her position in the Mediterranean, establishing herself at the Cape, and seizing Ceylon, notably expanded her empire in a systematic endeavor to keep the routes to India in her hands. But more important than all these territorial changes was Britain's unchallenged monopoly, not to be found on any map, of sea power, sea-borne trade, and exports. Here was an improved version of Venice on a world-wide scale. Encroachment on Britain's triple monopoly was, in any event, to be feared only from a single power, the United States.

This brings us to a shadow in the bright picture. The hub of the old British Empire had broken away and remained outside it. How and in what direction the potential of North America as a world power was to develop constituted a question of the first importance for the destiny of the world. The United States had come into existence as a result of a conflict with the mother country. Would that conflict persist? At the time, it seemed probable enough.

I have related how Napoleon sold Louisiana to the United States when the peace concluded at Amiens was proving to be short-lived. This renunciation bore fruit; for whatever the disadvantages the Continental System had for the Emperor in Europe, in America it brought him a brilliant success. It touched off British countermeasures at sea which paralyzed the lucrative American trade with the neutrals, and led to a new war between the States and their motherland. This was a memorable moment: while the Emperor was trying to force a decision against Britain in Russia, the Yankees, having previously neglected to conquer Canada, attempted to make good their omission and establish themselves as sole *de facto* claimants to mastery of the huge American continent. Their attempt failed. But if another such attempt were made, how completely it might alter the fate of Europe! How, in the future, could Britain prevent the rise of a dominant power in Europe if she were engaged in the rear and at sea by the United States, a world power in the making? Such a course of events was, in fact, forecast as a probability at that time. But as the Americans turned their backs on the sea and began to direct their attention to the vast interior of the continent, a *détente* between them and Britain made itself felt. The only competition Britain had to fear in the maritime field grew weaker and weaker.

Whereas the unmatured overseas world power only occasionally encroached upon Britain's sphere of interest, the Eurasian world power had already blossomed into a mighty antagonist on the Continent. At the peace settlement a hundred years earlier, London had been concerned only with removing the French danger. Now Britain was certainly no less constrained to pay attention to the Russian peril. Doubtless, the destruction of Napoleon had removed the threat of a new bid for supremacy on the old Continent far more effectively than had the defeat of Philip II or of Louis XIV. But the weakening of France had been dearly bought at the price of Russia's rise in the outer eastern areas of the Continent.

All the more reason for England to attempt to establish equilibrium on the Continent as a counterpart to her supremacy on the seas. Britain's difficulties offered to defeated France an opportunity such as would scarcely come the way of defeated Germany at Versailles after the breakdown of the Tsarist empire. For in 1815 Britain dared not bear down on her vanquished enemy beyond the point of stripping him of the ability to renew his quest for supremacy; in fact, she must keep him strong enough for use as a potential counterweight to Russia. The restored Bourbon monarchy met both these requirements to perfection. Dependent upon continued foreign good will, to which they owed their existence, the Bourbons feared war as such, for it might revive Napoleonic militarism. Their position, while comparable to that of the German Republic after 1919, was more favorable inasmuch as France had better frontiers in 1815 than before the

Revolution, and being economically self-sufficient, could tolerate her exclusion from overseas territories, as she had done under Napoleon. On the other hand, the sizable new kingdom of the House of Orange, comprising the former Republic of Holland and the Austrian Netherlands, was likely to block any new predatory grab at the Low Countries, an area fatefully linked with the European system of states. And the establishment of the Prussian watch on the Rhine served even more effectively to bar the way to any revival of expansionist desires.

The very idea of conceding a relatively favorable position to defeated France had been bound up with Britain's endeavor to forestall, by supple maneuvering, the advance of her victorious Russian ally. France was not compelled to sign any ready-made peace dictated by her enemies. On the contrary, by intervening early in the frictions between the victors and playing Britain's game at the Congress of Vienna, she was able to influence the conditions imposed on her.

The Anglo-Russian antagonism which, shortly before the Revolution, had led to the brink of war, and which had since been kept in the background only by a common fear of the Emperor, reappeared upon Napoleon's collapse. However, the re-establishment of the system of states turned out to favor the main insular power far more than its Continental counterpart. By her very nature, Britain posed a far less formidable threat than Russia to the freedom of the individual Continental states. The smaller coastal states—Sweden (combined with Norway), Denmark, Holland, Portugal, and Piedmont-Sardinia—willingly submitted to the British trident and under it began to enjoy prosperity. And Austria, the inland great power which had so often joined forces with Britain against France in the past hundred years or so, was now beset by the Russian nightmare and stood by Britain at the Congress of Vienna. Only Prussia, bent upon rounding off her territory in Germany as a compensation for the loss of her Polish possessions, joined the group of Russia's protégés. Still, it was Prussia, the weakest of the great powers, who became the victim of the compromise that ended the trial of strength between the world powers.

However, Russia, too, found herself checked, at least indirectly, in her drive to the West. But how great, nevertheless, were her successes! She was pushing forward in all three sectors of her western front of attack: in the south, the Tsar was approaching the Danube delta, one of Austria's self-evident objectives; in the north, he acquired the whole of Finland, thereby giving protection to the exposed location of St. Petersburg and improving his position in the Baltic; and in the west, the Tsar's own new Kingdom of Poland, formed out of most of the territory of the Grand Duchy of Warsaw, was to serve as a two-hundred-mile-wide wedge between the two German powers, and seemed to carry within it the threat of expansion. However, all this progress did not bring Russia into Britain's maritime sphere of interest. The expansion of Russia's position in the Baltic was checked by the continued existence of the Danish barrier and by the growing strength of Sweden, who had found a substitute for Finland in her union with Norway. The important function of the Turkish barrier remained unaffected. Despite all her advances, Russia had not gained access to the Mediterranean, the North Sea, or the Atlantic Ocean. Thus the colossus did not represent as immediate a danger to Britain as had Spain and France. In Asia, the situation was similar. The fact that Russia had reached the northern tip of the Pacific was, as things stood, no cause for concern in Britain; and the southern boundary of the Tsarist empire was entirely confined to the mainland. Although the frontier touched the northern extremities of Britain's maritime sphere of interest and offered ample scope for tensions, the backwardness of Continental communications made an increase in these tensions highly unlikely.

The great world beyond the old Continent was still a power vacuum of immense size. The United States was still occupied in her own huge power sphere; frictions with other powers were rare.

Russia and Britain, though considering each other natural enemies, were still at the stage of suspicious mutual observation, of mutual probing, and of vague jostling. The prospect of an all-out struggle, on the lines of Western wars for supremacy, between the two huge and loosely organized structures was still extremely remote.

That is precisely where the basic difference lies between the world at large and the shrinking Occident, a difference we must keep in mind in assessing the situation created in 1815. This basic difference had, in some areas, been foreshadowed in the seventeenth and eighteenth centuries: we have seen the two European flanking powers grow into the world, followed—outside Europe—by a third, as yet potential, world power, the United States; and we have watched, too, the shrinking of the old Continent's world connections even before 1789. But not until 1815 did these tendencies produce impressive results.

From that date, two theaters of events can be differentiated. The broad world stage, for a long time merely the backdrop of the narrower stage of Europe, became emancipated from it. The two European flanking powers began playing simultaneously on both stages. The United States was still acting only on the broad stage, whereas the states of the old Continent were entirely, or mainly, confined to the narrow stage. While the tensions on the greater stage were still in their beginnings, and space was still available in abundance, the tensions on the smaller stage were temporarily smoothed over in 1815 by natural exhaustion and an artificial new order. However, they were to be renewed on a frightful scale, for the Continental West, having become crowded with people and charged with energies by the progress of civilization, offered even less space for maneuver as opportunities for overseas activities remained comparatively restricted. The old Continent, as Hegel put it, turned into a cage.

In the final chapter of this study, I shall be obliged to keep an eye on both stages, on their parallel evolution and interplay, in order to show how a new wave gradually rose from the deep trough of the period after 1815; how this last, German, fight for supremacy was decided, even more than Napoleon's, by forces outside Europe rather than by inherently European forces; how the two stages merged; and how finally the narrower stage was swallowed up by the broader.

# CHAPTER IV

## The System of States up to the Collapse of the German Bid for Supremacy under Hitler

# THE CONFLICTS SHARPEN

# STEP BY STEP UNTIL THE

# POWERS REGROUP AT THE

# BEGINNING OF

# THE TWENTIETH CENTURY

THE CALM after 1815 was idyllic to a degree not known after earlier struggles for supremacy. It contrasted impressively with the tumult in the era of war just concluded, which in turn had been greater than anything the world had ever before experienced. The calm and the tumult had connected roots. Both are explained by the increasing effects of civilization, which plowed up the entire subsoil of Western existence. This process had channeled new energies into the struggle; once it was over, that very fact created the need to stave off a renewal of the contest through new calming agents. Restoration poured the oil of international solidarity on the waters as the wave fell away, and gave the trough an unprecedented smoothness.

The men behind the Restoration knew that it was a question not merely of saving the freedom of the system of states but also of preserving the social order on which it had rested. They knew that the struggle against Napoleon had been directed not only against the supremacy of French national power but also against the international revolutionary trend that had been its ally. It was therefore not enough to apply proven diplomatic methods to the task of balancing the political power of France in particular; there was also a need to shackle the less palpable social movement in general. Now that the common external enemy had been subdued, the free play of states within the framework of the system must this time not be allowed to start all over again. The phalanx must close ranks against the common internal enemy. The concern for the survival of Western culture, aroused in 1792, could not be lulled to sleep again in 1815. Gone was the rosy confidence of the previous century. The new one posed the question whether the optimistic and fighting will to live, which had once burst through the shell of medieval quietism, would be willing to learn from the perils it had itself brought forth. In other words, would the West, at this late stage, be able to curb the selfishness of individual countries and use the rejuvenated spirit of Christian solidarity to halt the perpetual movement within its system of states? Napoleon had not succeeded in bringing about unification through the violent methods provided by modern civilization. Could the old cultural outlook succeed where he had failed? Could, perhaps, a "United States of Europe" come into being as a voluntary federation which, instead of directing its power against external threats, would counteract internal dangers by spiritual means?

The prerequisite for such a development would have been a drastic change in the way of life of the European nations, both collectively and individually. There was no lack of beginnings in this direction, but they did not signal a new era. They merely had retarding effects, and acted creatively only in alliance with the concrete interests of the old countries and their old social classes. These, threatened by progress, remained as selfish as they were troubled, but managed to lend their halfhearted solidarity the appearance of a spiritual force. The fiery breath of spiritual awakening, which might have fused those selfish feelings into a new collective sentiment, was lacking. The Restoration never got beyond the stage of the anxious defensive. Its leaders tried to make do with small measures. They were afraid of imperiling the balance by the use of larger and more militant designs.

The old Continent, only lately the scene of revolutionary floods, was the natural matrix of the Restoration. The old Continental ruling class, a homogeneous society that considered itself bound together by fate, was inclined to subordinate national interests to the fight against the international movement. But could the wave of restoration also be expected to engulf the two flanking powers? They had, after all, resisted the wave of revolution and asserted their distinctive identities.

Britain's secure insular tradition, though a model for Continental romanticism, was in its ruddy-cheeked robustness itself anything but romantic. Concern about revolution did not dominate men's minds in those islands, as it did beyond the Channel; the spirit of the post-Napoleonic Restoration found no lasting home with the British. Although deep social wounds had been inflicted on the body of Britain, the home of the industrial civilization, the healing powers of her broadly based and flexible way of life were astounding. No collaboration with foreign powers was needed to keep an internal enemy at bay. Britain trusted in her ability to pursue her independent course under her own power—without, at the same time, developing a narrow egotism devoid of spiritual values. Unlike the countries of the Continent, she did not have to make the choice between revolution and restoration. Evolution enabled Britain to represent not merely her own affairs but also a general cause.

How different was the case of Russia! Owing to the primitive rigidity of her social structure, she, too, had remained untouched by the Western upheaval; like Britain on the seas, Russia, thanks to her expansion into the Eurasian continent, had vast spaces at her disposal; and the Tsar, borne by a nebulous sense of mission, in addition to his expectancy of a long career, felt that he above all men had vanquished Napoleon.

But Russia lacked Britain's national harmony. Catherine's worries and her son's manic apprehensions, far from being proved groundless by the great victory, had in fact been confirmed. No sooner had Alexander begun to dream of establishing a new order on the Continent, of uniting under his leadership the monarchs in his mystic Holy Alliance—that Christian League of Nations—and of giving the nations the constitutions they longed for, than the news reached him that his victorious army had brought home with it the revolutionary infection. Alexander, long unbalanced, broke down under the impact of the sinister tidings. The fears that plagued the princes of the old Continent now also overcame the ruler of the new. The very artificiality of the order that had been set up in Russia on the lines of Western absolutism made her particularly susceptible to Western ideas of freedom. The Russia built by Peter the Great lost confidence in herself and took refuge in the solidarity of the Christian Restoration. Under the rulers who followed the neuropathic Alexander, Russia would again and again feel strong enough to expand in Asia and make thrusts at Constantinople. But the Russian drive westward came to a standstill at the very moment when the Continentals, deceived by their traditional thinking as well as the aftereffects of Napoleonic propaganda, more than ever expected its pressure to continue. The drive was not to be resumed for a hundred years. At the Congress of Vienna, Russia's westward advance had been checked only by the outside forces of diplomacy; in 1818—the year in which Alexander received his frightening news—the push was restrained by the innermost nature of Russian society itself. It was to remain at a standstill until Bolshevism removed the restraint through another, modernized, union of Eastern human material and Western techniques.

The Restoration owed a great deal to this pause. Its special beneficiaries were the conservative interests of the German great powers. In the main, Austria and Prussia found their Russian neighbor a patron rather than an oppressor. At any rate, Russia did not undermine these countries, as she had once subverted Poland and Sweden, but, on the contrary, kept them in good order as conservative bastions against the West. The common principles of the eastern powers overshadowed their individual selfishness.

Looked at as a whole, the defensive solidarity of the old states and the old social classes on the Continent was, of course, only the counterpart of the solidarity of the new spirit and the young social classes then on the offensive.

Inside the rigid and artificial structure of the power states, crowded together on the cramped Continent, the vast awakening energies of modern civilization (of which the huge population increase was but one indicator) could not find a broad and appropriate field of activity such as the Anglo-Saxon spaces provided. So these energies, pent up in one form or another, sought outlets in revolutions or wars, in defiance of all the calming nostrums administered by the Restoration. The French Revolution had not cleared the atmosphere. As long as civilization continued to progress, there would never be any lack of new and stormy tensions.

Metternich lumped together all dynamic tendencies under the name of "Jacobinism." Undoubtedly, their roots were connected, to a degree, with the French Revolution. But how many and varied were the growths they had since thrown up!

In France, a regime supported by foreign countries— a regime which, in other words, was the beneficiary of the nation's fall from power—could not possibly become popular. The general feeling of national humiliation was linked to a particular malaise among the middle classes; though thriving in this period of peace, they found their status as semi-*déclassés* hard to bear. They had supported Napoleon's fight against Britain; now they took up manufacturing, which had originated in Britain; and this development soon brought new social tensions.

In Central Europe all longings and discontents were flowing into the reservoir of nationalist ideas. The primary goal of all endeavors was the unity of the state on the Western model; national unification was considered the prerequisite for power and prestige abroad as well as for the free circulation of pent-up energies at home. But that unification could not be achieved without the ripping up of a network of old and new boundary lines, without the re-shaping, or overthrowing, of existing patterns. Disillusioned by the Revolution and the Empire, the young generation had moved closer to faith and tradition during the Wars of Liberation, and in the fight against Napoleon's international empire had labored for a national renewal. Now these young men were disappointed by the results of the fight. The mood of cosmopolitan revolution again began to spread, its object not to disavow nationalist ideas, but to realize them through mutual support among the nations and against their governments. Solidarity among attacking forces, such as then developed, makes conflicts of self-interest easier to adjust.

In this changed atmosphere, the eyes of the Continent again turned toward Paris. The French people seemed no longer to constitute a menace to the liberty of other nations; but France had remained the motherland of all libertarian, nationalist ideas. The victor nations looked for their salvation to an uprising of the vanquished nation. If the French threw off the shackles of the treaties to decide in freedom on their regime, then all the dynamic forces in Europe could count on French encouragement or support. In spite of 1815, the French had not lost their nimbus as the nation that carried the Continent's destinies on its shoulders. Their intellectual dominance had remained unimpaired even after the collapse of their bid for supremacy in terms of power.

In Russia, socially the most primitive country on the Continent, national unification was not a problem that stirred emotions. Instead, the quite peculiar and funda-mental problems that had arisen from Peter the Great's un-organic structure thrust their way to the surface, especially the liberation of the serfs.

Yet hidden under the smooth surface in the halcyon

days of the Restoration was a great and growing array of dynamic forces, which could not come to the top as long as the governments remained united in solidarity. Where these forces were able to burst through, as in Italy or Spain, they were pushed under again by concerted measures. But in the 1820's that solidarity was loosened at the edge. Britain, the most independent of the powers in her attitude toward the Restoration, became the first to emancipate herself from it as she turned her attention to fostering her interests outside Europe. The other flanking power, Russia, followed suit, to pursue her special interests in Asia and the Balkans. Still, the bulk of the Continent proper remained knit together under the banner of the Restoration until the July Revolution of 1830 in France tore a gap in the middle of it. And the February Revolution of 1848 was to unleash the long-restrained selfish tendencies of states and peoples on the old Continent in a new and stormy era of local wars.

As we trace the breakup of the Restoration from the periphery, we are led from the narrow stage of Europe to the broad world stage. In the early 1820's, Britain drew away from the Restoration to look after her interests in the insurgent Iberian colonial empires. For two hundred and fifty years she had tried to penetrate these territories. She had started the War of the Spanish Succession mainly to avoid being forestalled overseas by Louis XIV. I pointed out earlier the role that overseas markets played in maintaining Britain's economic power of resistance during the years of the Continental System. Now, unexpectedly, the danger again arose that France might establish herself in those markets. Entrusted by the Pentarchy at the Congress of Verona with the task of putting down the Spanish liberals, France also took steps to force the colonies sympathizing with them back under the control of their legitimate ruler.

Success would have given France a new foothold in America and allowed her to break through the barrier cutting her off from overseas territories, thus jeopardizing Britain's recently created maritime monopoly. A storm of indignation arose in Britain—characteristically, without regard to party. Then, with its sure instinct, private initiative—the mainspring of Britain's prestige since the freebooters' days— sided with the Spanish insurgents, thus espousing the cause of freedom while at the same time guarding its own interests. The Government followed public opinion. Canning, though a Conservative, emphatically dissociated himself from the Continental Restoration. While the European governments were fearfully suppressing every stirring of movement, a whole continent on the far side of the ocean changed ownership under the protection of Britain's navy. Where was there another naval power to challenge her?

Through the secession of Europe's oldest colonies, the isolation of the old Continent from the overseas territories was carried an enormous step forward, a belated but logical effect of the Napoleonic Wars. And Britain retaliated, as it were, against Spain and France for the role they had played in the revolt of her own American colonies.

This event also demonstrated to the world at large what the Union's independence meant. For the developments in Latin America no longer brought benefit to England alone, but also—and with more important consequences—to her daughter country. The United States proclaimed the Monroe Doctrine. By doing so she ranged herself for the moment at Britain's side; but with her gigantic claim, which might someday clash with Britain's interests, the United States also reached out for a preferential position on both American continents—or, to put it more precisely, she was making a bid for insularity within this broadest of all frameworks.

We know how the character of the English people and the essence of their power grew from their insular background, and how the insular position was consolidated in Scotland and Ireland by great, even terrible, exertions. The Union, too, had striven for an insular position since its inception. The existence of neighbors of equal status on land would have compelled it to build up its military establishment and evolve into a power on Continental lines. In other words, the United States would have been robbed of her birthright, her Anglo-Saxon insular status. Her task therefore was to forestall this danger through expansion on a huge scale.

It was a paradoxical phenomenon: a people proud of their liberty and contemptuous of war as the tragic privilege of the old monarchies and oligarchies nevertheless developed in their foreign policy the same forcefulness that marked their economy and their way of life. In the New World, the expansive powers of civilization, freed from tradition and borne up by faith, surpassed all the experience of the Old World as thoroughly as those German long-range guns of 1918 exceeded all the earlier performances of artillery by hurling their shells into the rarefied layers of the atmosphere. The Peace of Paris in 1762 had doubled the territory of the Thirteen States; the Louisiana Purchase of 1803 redoubled it; and in the meantime the Union had been further augmented by the purchase of Florida. True, the attempt to seize Canada had failed; but then Britain was not an aggressive military power. Could France, the old dominant military power on the Continent, which had been driven from North America in 1762 and 1803, now be allowed to establish herself in South America in the place of a moribund Spain? Was it to be tolerated into the bargain that Russia, the friend of France under the Restoration, should at the same time expand from Alaska to a point south of Vancouver? So the Union proclaimed the imperious principle that no European power might extend its sway into either of the Americas. In spite of the geographical and cultural disparities within this vast area, the United States henceforth considered it, in the last analysis, a single island in which the Union intended to secure for itself the privileges of insular existence, tolerating no rival of equal status. Some people in Europe were heard to say that America would see the emergence of a balance of power system on the European model; in reality the Latin-American states were overshadowed from the moment of their birth by their great northern neighbor. To establish a balance with her would have been possible only through the aid of powers outside America, an unthinkable development as long as the United States was able to implement the Monroe Doctrine. By that doctrine the American continent became a closed preserve. As civilization progresses, the freedom of a system of states can be maintained only in an open area such as Europe was; otherwise, this freedom succumbs to a hegemony.

Still, we must bear in mind that the two Anglo-Saxon powers at that time had parallel interests in regard to French and Russian ambitions in America, and that the benefits of their Pan-American co-operation outweighed their lingering differences over Canada. Certainly, Canada's southern border was vulnerable; but the long straggling coasts of the continent would prove equally sensitive unless they were protected by a good relationship between the Union and Britain, with her command of the sea. For the first time, then, there emerged the outline of a solidarity between the two kindred insular nations against the Continentals such as had once bridged Anglo-Dutch antagonisms. The expansion of each was in itself great enough; now, in addition, the first signs of coalescence between the two became discernible.

In Europe, territories were split up after the periodic convulsions set off by nations seeking supremacy; in the world outside, the course of events led to territorial agglomerations of ever-increasing magnitude. Technical progress in overcoming distance—the telegraph and steamships, soon joined by railroads—though it did not determine this process, no doubt accelerated it. Under the impetus of Anglo-Saxon initiative, technology, European and Anglo-Saxon in origin, found limitless scope for development in the vast empty spaces of North America. The Latin Americans were neither ethnically nor culturally fitted for this kind of civilization. Even after the establishment of free states, the basic dissimilarity between the Anglo-Saxon and Iberian colonial territories did not lose its force.

Thus the Yankees, in the course of their uninterrupted westward migration, were easily able to push aside the Mexicans and reach the Pacific. By the 1840's they had spread from coast to coast, expanding their territory by a full 80 per cent. The process more or less reached its close in February 1848, the very month in which revolution flared up in Europe. There, an explosion of hemmed-in forces; in America, an expansion of untrammeled energies.

Let us now return from the New World to the Old.

The liberal turn in English politics, which loosened the Restoration structure in Europe, had also coincided in a strange manner with Russian policies. Under the upright and manly Nicholas I, Russia began to emancipate herself from the political quietism of the Metternich brand, to which Alexander I had fallen victim. But this emancipation, far from going all the way, mainly took effect in Russia's

Asian and Balkan policies. The Decembrist rising, as well as news of discontent in Poland, had brought home to the new ruler the danger of revolution, a danger that any autonomous power policy directed at the West could only increase. Accordingly, Nicholas, in his Western policy, never showed any lack of rigid adherence to conservative principles. But he could hope to create a diversion for revolutionary discontent—without at the same time bringing it into contact with dangerous Western ideas—by vigorously pursuing Russian interests on other fronts. An aggressive foreign policy is vital to a military despotism.

Thus conservative Russia first took up the cause of the Greek insurgents at the side of liberal Britain, but then bypassed her to plunge into a war with Turkey. Yet in spite of her great sacrifices, she was denied expansion on a grand scale. Russia was unable to force the barrier of the Dardanelles and was not to do so in the two World Wars. Britain was always able to contain her rival in time by combining her maritime strength with the parallel interests of Continental powers, especially Austria and France, in groupings similar to those that had first emerged from the Congress of Vienna. Moreover, Russia never put her full strength into the fight. Fearful of revolution, her eyes were always straying westward. Thus Anglo-Russian rivalry in the world, for almost a century the overriding motif in the general diplomatic scene, never led to a world war. The great Continental power simply kept on probing along the entire Asian-Balkan front, switching pressure from one point to another. Undeniably crowned with success in the depths of the Continent, Russia was checked at, or driven back from, the coasts wherever she impinged on the spheres of interest of the naval power.

In this respect, the 1820's brought a preliminary decision, whose import, we feel, can be fully appreciated only today. Russia began to withdraw from North America, on whose west coast she had gained a foothold, ahead of the Anglo-Saxons, as early as the end of the eighteenth century. But across the uncharted wastes of Siberia and from her poor naval bases in the Pacific, she had not been able to maintain any real position of power in America. Under the pressure of the Monroe policy, she fell back on Alaska, and so left a valuable area free for Yankee, as well as Canadian, expansion. In fact, she was to evacuate Alaska as well some decades later. Russia's expansion, though enormous, was strictly confined to continental territory and mainly to the poorer side of Asia. The expansion remained tied to the state apparatus; it was advanced neither by private initiative, such as the Anglo-Saxons showed in this field, nor by any technical aptitude even remotely resembling theirs. In fact, contrary to Peter the Great, Nicholas I looked upon Western inventions with the same suspicion as he harbored for Western ideas.

Thus the two insular world powers had, from the very outset, a head start in the race for the world's empty spaces.

While all three of these world powers, systematically pursuing their aggrandizement, were reaching out to distant places; while on the fringes of Europe the Balkans were already being drawn into the process; and while France was beginning to take a hand in the Mediterranean region—all this time the Continental West as such was still bathed in the quiet glow of peaceful days.

But in 1830, the old heart of the white world once again started beating faster. In the July Revolution, the French, still the pacemakers of Europe's destiny, tore down the Bourbon flag. In the ancient capital, on which the eyes of all Europe had long been riveted with concern or hope, the

European forces of movement broke through, electrifying the whole Continent. The reins of power were seized by the capitalist bourgeoisie. Intent on peaceful development of the young technological economy, this class was too well aware of the enormous tasks at home to push beyond the borders. But soon civilization was advancing at a faster rate. The forces that had cleared the road in the July Revolution were not appeased by its success, but only spurred to accomplishments on a larger scale.

Were the old powers united and strong enough to drive back these forces and restore the smooth homogeneous surface of the Restoration—as they had after the less violent outbreaks in Italy and Spain? Russia felt confident that she could lead a coalition of the conservative powers in a crusade against the common external and internal enemies, without herself abandoning the attitude of reserve she maintained in her autonomous power policy. But Austria and Prussia felt too weak for action on a major scale; they feared they might provide openings for the revolutionary movement within their frontiers if they fought it outside. The Polish Revolution proved them right. It also struck the Tsar's upraised sword from his hand. Britain found the peacefully commercial July Monarchy wholly akin to her own character and at the same time a useful counterweight to Russia. Moreover, the establishment, at that time, of the Coburg monarchy in Belgium relieved the British of the fear that France might make a revolutionary thrust into their vital sphere of interest in the Netherlands.

The July Monarchy was thus able to hold its own. Although it remained too weak to play for high stakes, it nevertheless caused a palpable increase in international tensions, particularly in the Orient, and, to a degree, unsettled diplomatic relations.

Yet after no more than half a generation, the progress of civilization had washed away the foundations of the July Monarchy itself. Louis Philippe had not succeeded in satisfying the victims of the machine age, the petty bourgeoisie and the working class.

In the same period, far greater social tensions in Britain achieved an evolutionary solution. This was due to opportunities for emigration; to the wealth flowing into the country as the result of uniquely favorable economic conditions; to the ancient flexibility of the social structure, which took the edge off class conflicts; to the unbroken sense of continuity; to a predilection for provisional solutions; to practical self-help; and to the wise spirit of compromise among the ruling aristocratic elite. All these fortunate circumstances existing in Britain were absent on the other side of the Channel. There, only a grand foreign policy, operating from the lofty eminence of state interest, could allay domestic conflicts. The spontaneous forces of society were not adequate to the task. The upper ranks of the bourgeoisie, using the great apparatus of a power state in decline to further their own ends, aroused the hatred of the lower order, which, inflamed by ideologies, were struggling in their turn to seize possession of the state machine. The revolution on the Continent was produced by the concurrence of two phenomena: a great country's decline in power and the melting of a society into a state of flux under the scorching sun of civilization.

The new explosion which occurred in Paris in 1848 shook the whole of Europe, with the exception of the two flanking powers; Britain was immune because of the flexibility of her evolution, Russia because of the rigidity of her reactionary regime. For the nations of the old Continent, the February Revolution was the long-awaited beacon. Social conditions, it is true, were not so ripe for revolt in any other country as they were in France; but what the social movements lacked in strength was supplied, particularly in Central Europe, by the nationalist movements. As the old order melted away, the waters of these great reservoirs of all discontents and longings lapped against the rigid dikes of government and social order. The solidarity of these dynamic forces proved itself in the combined assault, and a breakthrough was achieved along the entire front of the old Continent. This time, the two great German states, which in 1830 had been too weak to seal up the first penetration, were also swept along by the waters.

Would this outwardly unified process result in a new inner unity, a new ordering of the Continent, a "Young Europe" (Mazzini)—a kind of "United States" built on the principles of the revolution after the attempt to build it on those of the Restoration had finally failed? This was not to happen.

Let us review the factors that more than ever accelerated the process of division. The very success of the forces of movement jeopardized their cohesion and exposed their dissensions. This applies to both social and nationalist aspirations. It was the radical social aims of the petty bourgeoisie and the proletariat that had brought about the February Revolution. Before long, wide sections of the propertied classes of France felt menaced: not merely the former ruling classes, which had long since been pushed into the background, and the upper middle class, which had but recently lost its political position, but also the middle ranks of the bourgeoisie and even the broad, healthy strata of the peasantry. These groups were not without weapons: the army opposed the revolution. It smashed the rule of the radicals before July was out and so cleared the way for a new Caesar to ensure the safety of the social fabric. It stifled the danger of a second Reign of Terror, of another eruption of the volcano which might again have sent its lava of propaganda and war pouring across the frontiers. The aging nation no longer hankered after bloody adventure in the grand manner of earlier days.

This setback had immediate effects outside France. Everywhere, the intimidated ranks of the propertied classes clamored for the armed protection of law and order. No sooner had the middle classes—particularly the bourgeoisie which had arisen belatedly in Central Europe—seen their revolutionary *élan* achieve its first, surprising victory than they were paralyzed by fear of the forces let loose from the lower depths.

This fear threw the advance of the nationalist movements into confusion, the more so as mutually conflicting aims had by then become apparent. Indeed, we must not jump to the conclusion that a victory for national democracy might have spared Europe its subsequent struggles. Did not the French Revolution rapidly replace the power machine of the *ancien régime* with a new and far more terrible apparatus? In the last analysis, the forces of modern life, which had found an outlet in the popular movements, fostered expansive tendencies. The expansion they demanded could not be gained by peaceful means on the cramped and crowded Continent. A victory by these forces in 1848 might easily have brought in its train passionate national wars that would have been far more destructive than the brief, methodically conducted wars of the following two decades.

As it was, the disintegration of the popular movements rendered them incapable of seizing that victory, even though it seemed within reach. This failure gave the conservative forces a breathing spell. In Central Europe, too, they had at their disposal armies that were eager to restore the established social order. Moreover, Russia, unbroken, provided support in the East.

To maintain the Restoration had been beyond the strength of its sponsors even in 1830; now a genuine restoration of the old order was inconceivable. Gathering strength under her new Caesar, France ambitiously went her own way. Soon, in the Crimean War, she triumphed over the last stronghold of reaction. Gone forever was the era of an ideological solidarity that could peacefully override the selfish interest of individual states. Its place was taken by increasing division and extreme instability. Now, as in a similar state of flux which had overtaken the system of states in the middle of the previous century, the richest prizes would again fall to those who were swift-footed and bold in exploiting kaleidoscopic changes.

With the field of foreign relations so transformed, the domestic political situation could nowhere be pushed back to its condition before the upheaval of 1848. Henceforth, the creative statesman would exploit whatever confusion arose among the popular movements so that he himself could put into effect those parts of their program that could be reconciled with the interests of the state. This called for a combination of astuteness and daring in zigzagging with the popular winds—which, with the increasingly rapid progress of civilization, could hardly be expected to abate. The methods of an active domestic policy had to be attuned to the aims of an active foreign policy. To keep the wild steeds of the age at a standstill was no longer possible: they must be kept moving if they were not to get out of hand.

Thus, the energies of the state were invigorated by the effects of the frantic events of 1848, although the revolutionary forces had been compelled to retreat—a process like the revival of vegetation in the valley of the Nile as its muddy floods recede. The narrow stage of the fenced-in and divided old Continent again became the scene of exciting action, while out of the world stage developments took place which, though inconspicuous and undramatic, would nevertheless, in their future importance to the destiny of this globe, far outshine the most violent conflicts on the old Continent.

The new era of turbulence did not come to a close until two new major states had spread out over the debris of small countries—a brilliant solution to the problem, posed by the events of 1848, of how to use storms of popular feeling to keep the ship of state on course. From then on, the chessboard of Europe was filled, square by square, with strong pieces which, without adequate room for maneuver, confronted one another in uncanny immobility. No common ideological firmament spanned their conflicting interests, as it had in the tranquil days of the Restoration.

I must confine myself to recalling, from the maze of events in the period from 1848 to 1871, those that throw into relief the growth of a dynamic political trend. I shall trace the ridge rising from the straggling lower ranges of ordinary happenings to the peaks of the two World Wars. Running at first along the French massif, the ridge crosses over into Germany in 1870.

Under Napoleon III, France, which had never ceased to occupy the central position in the intellectual and social sense of the phrase, became once more the center of the Continent in terms of power politics. The Emperor proved himself a master at the enigmatic art which the times demanded of a great statesman, the art of canalizing the swirling waters of chaotic movements and guiding them to turn the mill of state.

The French Revolution had given birth to a great Caesar; the revolution of 1848, a revolution that had broken down inwardly, brought forth a small Caesar. The revolution of 1789 had been eminently French; the revolution of 1848 immediately set off a series of eruptions outside France, and these launched the careers of a number of creative statesmen who undoubtedly possessed some Caesarean traits. They all learned from the new Napoleon, the model Caesar of the day.

He brought the revolution to a halt by ending the decay in the power of the state. He gave security to both the propertied classes and the workers and brought relief to the socially underprivileged. To all, he offered the enjoyment of a prosperity such as had never before existed, while presenting them with brilliant successes abroad in return for shrewdly imposed sacrifices. This was the secret of his reign. He showed how the power of the state and material civilization could be methodically fostered side by side and through each other, a system that had been well understood earlier by the absolute monarchies but disdained by the Restoration. At the same time, he demonstrated once more how a devoted army, a loyal police force, and a pliant bureaucracy could constitute a reliable instrument of power in the hand of a chief of state, and how this strong hand could be concealed in a velvet glove, how propaganda could veil naked force and terror. He taught all the arts of leading and misleading the masses. True, his success was purchased at a price that was difficult to calculate. Restrictions on freedom and falsehood in public life were part of the price; and this compound resulted in the luxuriant spread of a faintly musty civilization at the expense of genuine culture.

The regime's very name, its garb, its gestures, showed that it was toying with aspirations to hegemony. How far would it be able to progress toward realizing them when its protagonist was constantly aware that the mainspring of the national energies, broken in 1815, was beyond repair?

How close Napoleon III did move to the brink of a bid for supremacy can be seen from the fact that friction developed between France and all three world powers in succession—Russia, Britain, and the United States. Had the emperor crossed the threshold of war, the two flanking powers, though rivals, would no doubt have become allies; and the United States might have joined them. In actuality, the life curve of the Second Empire fell away just as it was reaching the level of such a conflict; and this drop was closely connected with the decline in the life curve of the nation itself. Napoleon III's throne was toppled in a limited Continental war. Unlike his uncle, he was swept away without a grand coalition and without the intervention of world powers.

The new emperor climbed the first rung of the ladder in the Crimean War, under cover of the Anglo-Russian conflict. After smoldering for a long time, this antagonism had, since 1848, become so heated that it could not fail to erupt, sooner or later, in war. The prime mover was Russia. The only Continental power that had not been shaken by the Revolution, she had crushed the Hungarian uprising in 1849 at Austria's request, and thus restored one of her two German bastions against revolution. The other bastion was restored the following year when, at Olmütz, the King of Prussia had to abandon his feeble national aspirations. The policies of the three eastern powers were brought into line, as they had been before 1848. Like Catherine the Great before him, the Tsar had been able to assume the role of arbiter over Germany and bring the swaying balance between the two German powers back to rest on terms favorable to Russia. He now felt strong enough to crown, through another war against Turkey, the gains he had so consistently achieved. He expected Russia's second Turkish war to bring the great success denied her in the first.

As it was, this second war disclosed Russia's inherent weakness. In fear of revolution, she had shut herself off from Western civilization, in which Peter the Great had once sought strength. Without an adequate network of railroads and ignorant of the techniques of modern warfare, the ungainly colossus was defeated by the British-led coalition of Western powers which helped defend the Turkish barrier. Napoleon III was the most active of the allies, and the distinction won by his forces brightened the shadow that had lain since 1815 across France and her prestige.

This first war—and to this day the only one—between the two world rivals was anything but a world war. A limited enterprise, it did not call for an all-out effort on either side. Britain's leadership on land was maladroit. But her fleet, threatening invasion from varying directions, availed itself of the peculiar opportunities offered to mobile sea power, and the Royal Navy made no small contribution to the defeat of the Continental giant.

For the next two decades, Russia was occupied with herself and her domestic reforms, though these could not remove the threat of revolution.

For Napoleon, however, the first great success held out the promise of others. He had decided to play the role of protector of the nationalist trends in Central and Eastern

Europe even before these had acquired a new freedom to develop. Borne by the very currents that had driven Napoleon I to his doom, he himself planned to gain for France, by skillful maneuvering and no great effort, a camouflaged version of the supremacy that his powerful uncle, pulling against the stream, had not been able to capture.

In Italy, this method at first worked brilliantly. The great coup was carried out entirely on Napoleon's initiative. Was any Continental power a match for this new imperial France? Was she not already moving toward a bid for supremacy? But according to the old rules of European politics, must not Britain feel threatened now by the Emperor, whom she had but recently used against her Continental counterpart? In fact, the panic that broke out in Britain over the safety of the island was probably the worst in the long series of such scares up to World War II. It was fed by apprehension about the modernized French navy; in particular, its steam-driven vessels. For the first time, modern technology, an Anglo-Saxon growth, hurled a challenge at the Anglo-Saxon insular stronghold. Would technology, then, bring victory to France in a third war for absolute supremacy?

The menacing cloud banks very soon rolled away. Napoleon's policy of low risks, craftily stage-managed, sufficed to achieve surprising initial successes; but it lacked the force to consolidate them. The Emperor disappointed the Italian patriots' hopes for complete national unification. Moreover, he asked to be paid, by territorial concessions, for his support. Britain demanded no reward for hers; and in the course of Italy's unification she easily outshone France in the public mind on the peninsula, without any sacrifice of blood. A nation holding supremacy at sea can afford to be more generous than a nation supreme on land.

Napoleon's policy of furthering nationalist movements lost credit as its contradictory motives were revealed. The new Italy, scarcely born, developed an overmastering urge for unrestricted sovereignty, an urge that is as inherent in the modern European national state as it was in the Greek city-state. The progressive implementation of the nationalist principle only served to deepen the divisions of the Continent.

France had always endeavored to find moorings for her dominance beyond the seas as well as in Europe. Under Napoleon III, she again sought to break out of her Continental confinement. In the Mediterranean, the Emperor found a strong French position already in existence; its foundation had been laid by the July Monarchy, indeed by the Restoration. I shall forgo a detailed account of the development of this position, through the construction of the Suez Canal, along the old line of advance toward Egypt. I shall also forgo a review of French expansion in eastern Asia and the Pacific, which was bound to arouse misgivings in Britain. But I cannot bypass the Mexican adventure, which carried Napoleon across the path of the third world power. For a moment, battles and decisions apt to affect world history seemed imminent, as in 1859, when Britain had feared invasion. But the clouds passed over, as they had then. The vital energies of France no longer impelled her toward action on a grand scale. Mexico remained an adventure. Yet to our contemporary view, it seems charged with problems of world history in more than one respect.

For one thing, it represented France's last attempt to gain a foothold in America, and to revive, and perhaps exceed, the aspirations of three centuries. Could not France set herself up as the protector of Latin America, as she had tried to do in the eighteenth century through her connection

with Bourbon Spain? Could she not help the Latins overseas to attain equality of status with the Anglo-Saxons?
Could she not herself climb again to the rank of a great
maritime power and undo her failure of 1823, when, reaching out across the ocean, she had been smashed by the
combined Anglo-Saxon powers? Now, the bond between
these was torn. More than that, the bonds holding the States
of the Union together were torn.

The States, involved in civil war, were in danger of losing
everything they had gained. A permanent split among them
would end the privilege of their insular existence—regular
armies on the Continental model would have to be maintained; there would be an end to the principle of holding
aloof from European politics; allies would have to be sought
wherever they could be found. Indeed, there would be an
end altogether to the rise to power of this young continent
and its tendency toward unification in a closed area. The
tendency toward division, toward building a system of
states in an open area, must of necessity gain the upper
hand. The relationship of the New World to the Old would
retrogress, and the power that had migrated would return,
as it were, to the other side of the ocean. Then Britain's star
would rise again within the Anglo-Saxon world. In fact,
during the Civil War this beguiling prospect was widely
welcomed in Britain. But cutting across this prospect was
another, which gave Britain cause for concern—the likeli-
hood that in such circumstances France's star would also
rise. By establishing French rule in Mexico, Napoleon
would be able, a hundred years after the event, to make up
for the expulsion of French rule from Canada.

A review of Napoleon's Mexican expedition brings us
close to a historical watershed that is truly global in its
implications. The fact that this was never crossed was due

to the soundly based and clear victory of the Northern states. This prevented the stream of American history from seeking a new bed. As soon as the States became the "United States" again, they were strong enough to drive the Emperor, by means of a mere threat, from the soil of their giant island. To do this, they had no need to combine with Britain, as they had in a similar situation in Monroe's day; this time France was critically engaged in Europe, too. Thus, from a state of threatening decline, the prestige of the third world power soared to even greater heights.

In the hour of need, the Union had learned how the maritime aspirations of a power dominant on the European Continent could jeopardize the vital principle of its own existence. In 1812 the United States had still believed that she could take advantage of Britain's involvement in Europe to attack her in Canada; she had thus indirectly given support to the dominance of Napoleon I. This time the United States merely had to confront Napoleon III, while the relationship with Britain, though cooled off, nevertheless held out through the period of tension. As it was, Britain could then no more wish to see France established in Latin America than she had in 1823. But no one could say whether the two Anglo-Saxon powers would in the future make common cause against a third European power, or whether they would someday fight each other again on Canadian battlefields. In the days to come, the decision between these two possibilities on the world stage was to decide conflicts on the European stage.

Napoleon's failure overseas was both a cause of his approaching collapse in Europe and one of its effects. In Italy, his policy of supporting nationalism had allowed him to preserve the semblance of victory; in the case of Germany, this policy led to a clear-cut diplomatic defeat and to military catastrophe. His policy had summoned up spirits it could no longer control. In the decisive field of foreign affairs, Napoleon could not, in the long run, master the problem, posed in 1848, of weaving the forces of popular movements into the calculations of power politics. The keystone in the structure having crashed to the ground, the regime lost the secret of its success, and France entered the autumn of her career. As she could no longer muster the necessary moral and material strength, her dalliance with aspirations to supremacy proved futile in every respect.

The dynamic forces in politics now moved over into Germany to scale a new ridge.

How did it come about that, after Spain and France, the German nation set out, as the last among the great nations of the old Continent, to storm the unconquered peak of supremacy, only to bring to a close both its own history and that of the European system of states?

We Germans have never lacked natural strength, numerous and geographically spread out as we have always been, compared with other nations. An urge for paramountcy was stirring among us even in the early days of our political existence, and for us those days dawned sooner and with greater promise than among the peoples of the West. But if German power at times towered up like a cloud bank, it also dissolved again in rolling mists. Unformed in formless territory, our power was without core or sequence, always developing, never developed. Its forces boiled over across our frontiers, and at the same time turned against one another within them. The greed of the princes, at the subnational level, eroded the supranational prestige of the Emperor. While, in the earliest days of the European system of states, the three Western national states were assuming their increasingly distinct individualities, the Reich, by contrast, showed a tendency to dissolve into a number of petty states reminiscent of the Italian system in preceding centuries; and the Emperor in his marginal location was inclined to spread his tentacles far across Europe. The breakup of the Occident as organized under the Church, which in the West worked in favor of a concentration of secular power, only accelerated its decay in Germany. The discovery of lands beyond the seas, which in the West opened up possibilities of unforeseeable scope, merely served to atrophy those that existed in Germany. Finally, Russia's rise closed to us the great spaces of the future in the East, and in the Southeast elbowed us off a promising line of advance in the direction of Turkey. Moreover, the rise of Russia at the same time had its effects on the internal structure of Germany; by promoting the rise of Prussia, it gave new impetus to the old tendency toward disorganization. For two centuries, the Habsburgs had striven with varying success to counteract that trend. They had never, it is true, brought the interests of their house fully into line with those of the nation; but the two had undeniably moved, more or less, toward each other. And on the fringes, the Emperor, based on the broad arc of his own possessions, did in fact screen the tangled center from foreign dominion, and shielded it against both the French and the Turks. As his Prussian rival arose on the Empire's northeastern edge, Germany's political existence—the loose, remaining framework of the nation, always more potential than real as a formative force—was placed in jeopardy, together with the dominance of the Habsburgs. For now two marginal powers balanced each other, while in between them the "Reich" languished in its amorphousness.

Who could have foreseen in 1770 that a hundred years later this shadowy and chaotic region, cut off from the world's expanses, would generate forces strong enough to cut their way to the core of decisive world events?

This nevertheless happened, thanks to particularly favorable circumstances and developments whose conjunction lifted the dead weight that had so long acted as a drag on Germany's destiny. But could that dead weight remain eliminated forever?

At any rate, those circumstances made possible a rapid ascent—which, to us as we look back, falls into two parts. The first stage takes us up to Bismarck's Reich, a position of power on the Continent which, however elevated, does not attain heights of global importance. Only the second stretch, covered in the era after the elimination of Bismarck, leads up over the green knolls of the medium ranges to the ultimate peaks and into the deadly solitudes of rocky crags and eternal snows. A book concerned primarily with German history would dwell on the first part of the ascent and the abundance of enduring values that it brought forth. This study, aimed at world history, need deal with it only to the extent of showing how those favorable circumstances and developments were creating the buoyancy that was to launch Germany upon her Icarian flight.

These circumstances and developments can be grouped under three headings: the foreign situation, the economic civilization, and the moral energies.

To begin with the last, national feeling had emerged in the West as the spiritual rallying point for a young, or rejuvenated, society; but it generated its greatest creative effects only as it moved eastward. In the West, it merely invigorated existing countries; in the East, it provided the impetus for the establishment of essentially new ones. In the West, it only gave new weight and scope to entities which had long since been shaped by the proud accomplishments of a great past; in the East, where these feelings had been paraded for many centuries under false colors or had evaporated, they called for a drastic remolding of entities. The fragmented nations of Central and Eastern Europe, shaking off their chaotic history like the memory of a nightmare, felt strong in spirit and eager for action in the dawn of their impending freedom and unity. Their awakening brought amazing forces into the game of politics, forces that favored these nations in their relations with older ones that had long been united.

This applies particularly to Germany and, above all, to her relations with France. On the Continent, a people's national feeling, ripening amid the struggle for existence in a cramped space, contains a combative element. It gathers strength from having an opponent. In the first century of Germany's rise, her nationalism drew spiritual as well as political strength from her rivalry with France. Its first accomplishment was to break through the rules that France had set up in the name of the individual rights of nations. This was a common experience such as the Germans had not known since the early Middle Ages, an ideological point of unity high above denominational and territorial interests. But that breakthrough was far from being a drive for supremacy. German national feeling had simply come out in opposition to French claims to universal dominance. It is true that even these beginnings were not entirely free from stirrings of an appetite for supremacy; but such stirrings lacked any realistic sense of power politics.

If this national feeling rejuvenated what was old, welded where there was division, and infused dynamic life into static conditions, it did so only within the framework of a more general process that embraced everyday economic life as well as political ideals. In fact, the new economic developments, which favored Germany as much as did the awakening of national feeling, were of immense importance. Ever since the age of discovery, the Germans, being cut off from overseas territories, had been at a disadvantage vis-à-vis the maritime nations. But in the era of Napoleon I and the Restoration they had shared this drawback with the whole Continent. Moreover, the rise of modern industry had made the drawback less painful. As time went on, it became more and more evident that on the Continent the development of industry was operating mainly in Germany's favor. Her poor soil was rich in coal and iron, and her rapidly increasing, frugal, organizable, and organizationally gifted people were well suited to factory work. Not being committed to the binding forms of a national culture, Germany was ready to plunge into the economic civilization and the scientific activities that were its concomitant.

Moreover, not only did Germany become charged with new moral and economic energies, but, at the same time, she encountered less pressure from her Continental neighbors to the east and west. Russia was paralyzed by the Tsar's fear of revolution, France wounded by the defeat of 1815. Although the first half of the nineteenth century did not satisfy the German activists, it remains a bright page in the annals of our dark history. It is characterized by a sense of dignity after the victorious conclusion of the Wars of Liberation, by security within a broad framework of conservative policies, and by quiet growth in the midst of a tranquilized Europe, the blessings of whose peace also soothed all German misgivings. The rivalry of the two great German powers was losing its sharpness during this period of slumbering power politics.

For many years, Metternich's Austria effortlessly held a distinguished and key position in the diplomatic councils of the powers. It seemed as though the Restoration, in pre-stabilized harmony between the European system of states and the multi-national Habsburg empire, were intent on transforming its inherent drawbacks into as many assets.

Prussia forgot her old lust for power. Her bleak civilization, fertilized by the German spirit in the Napoleonic era, blossomed into a culture both noble and solid in the years before the revolution of 1848. Almost against the will of her government, Prussia became the hope of the progressive elements among the nationalists and economists, and the *Zollverein* (Customs Union) a sober, unpretentious blueprint for the coming Reich. Since 1815, Prussia had been in a peculiarly suitable position for launching a great national policy. But this position had not been of her choosing. It was Russia's westward drive that had squeezed Prussia out of Polish and into German territory; it was British and Austrian counterpressure that had compelled her to mount the watch on the Rhine and had torn Prussia's territory into two groupings. This painful state of affairs represented a challenge to Prussian statesmanship, inviting a bold man to overcome it in alliance with the nationalist movements. But in the Biedermeier Berlin of that period, there was no one to grasp the challenge.

Not until the revolution of 1848 and the turbulent era it touched off was Prussia awakened to her potential role on the German scene. The greatest of the century's four creative statesmen was to translate this possibility into reality.

True, Austria produced in Schwarzenberg a man of the stature that the times demanded; but from the outset the design of the old ship of state prevented its sails from being unfurled to the popular winds. The Greater Austria toward which the intrepid captain steered might have flattered the self-esteem of the German element in more ways than one;

but in spite of its size, "Greater Austria," would not have offered scope for realization of the national ideals. Moreover, the Tsar easily succeeded in crippling the development of these proud plans by exploiting the rivalry between the two German powers.

On a quite different scale, Prussia was able to imbue her old egoism—the thirst for power of Frederick's day, which had not been nationalist—with German nationalism. Earlier, the Hohenzollerns had been ready enough to sacrifice the interests of Germany in the West to those of their own state. But the frontiers of 1815 had made the interests of both identical, to say nothing of the swing in national sentiment which the Wars of Liberation had brought about and which could not be undone. Thus, the revived Prussian urge for expansion automatically acquired the cachet of a national mission.

There was a resemblance here to the ambitions of Piedmont. Of course, the distribution of emphasis between the nationalist concept and that of the state was basically different in each case. The unification of Italy, an entity pre-formed by nature and fostered by the vying attentions of two great powers, was achieved by the audacious Cavour in harmonious co-operation with the nationalist movement and with almost as little exertion as it takes to pick a ripe apple.

Germany, however, formless by nature, lay at the point where the lines of pressure of Continental high politics intersected. For three hundred years her territorial disorganization had been closely bound up with the organization of the system of states. Integral German unification, if feasible at all, was hardly attainable without revolutionary shifts of power; and only the exploitation of all the favorable circumstances I mentioned earlier—above all, the encourag-

ing situation in foreign affairs—might bring about a qualified unification. However, that situation was encouraging
only if measured by the standards of German history—and
only to a master like Bismarck.

Like Frederick the Great, he knew how to exploit the
system's slackness and instability to the advantage of his
lean but sinewy state. In fact, Bismarck followed Frederick's
line of approach. Both men were products of a trough between two waves of movement toward hegemony. In both
cases, the great powers had to shrink somewhat so that the
small power might greatly expand. Nevertheless, in a fairway so thickly studded with foreign-policy hazards, the
German nationalist movement had only restricted room for
maneuver. Unlike Italian nationalism, the German movement could never play an important role side by side with
the state.

Exactly how dangerous the fairway in which a nationalist policy sailed could be had been shown as early as 1848–9,
when a change in the German attitude toward Denmark
brought about a rapprochement of the two flanking powers,
Britain and Russia. On the appearance of a new competitor,
they put aside their rivalry, and France joined them to complete the ominous encirclement. Only by the most subtle
maneuvering did Bismarck succeed in playing off the three
great powers against one another—and none of them could
possibly wish to see the center strengthened—thereby gaining full scope for his own activity. His conflict with the
nationalist movement, which had seemed to make his task
hopeless, ended by rendering it easier. He used this conflict
as the screen behind which he concealed his strength and
his intentions in order to make surprise sorties and create
accomplished facts. The less dangerous he appeared to the
cabinets of the great powers, the more easily he could work

his way forward in leaps, without being caught in the wake of any of them and so losing the strongest card in his diplomacy, his mobility amid the general instability.

Let us now review Bismarck's relations with the three main non-German powers in the years of his *"grand dessin."*

Until the Crimean War, Russia, herself long hampered by the one-track policy of Nicholas I with its strict adherence to principle, had, of course, also obstructed any expansive German power policy on the part of Prussia. Under Alexander II, she was no longer in a position to do so. Embittered by the attitude of "ungrateful" Austria during the war, and by her efforts at the side of the Western powers to thwart the Balkan plans of the very power that had rescued her in 1849, the Tsar was, if anything, inclined to switch his favor again to his trusty little Prussian friend. Bismarck's conduct in the Polish rising of 1863, a policy he did not allow the opinion of "Europe" to interfere with, fully vindicated that benevolence. In 1864, the Tsar showed indulgence toward Bismarck's success against Denmark, a country friendly to Russia, in order not to impede his meritorious fight against Parliament and revolution. He acted similarly in 1866. Too weak to mediate between the two German powers, as Catherine II and Nicholas I had done, and in spite of painful misgivings, Alexander acquiesced in the outcome of Prussia's lightning campaign which transformed the German scene overnight—but which, at any rate, punished faithless Austria. Moreover, any prolongation or sharpening of the struggle might have brought quite different changes in its train, revolutionary upheavals that would also have been dangerous to Russia and her rule in Warsaw. Finally, the downfall of Napoleon III in 1870 brought vengeance on the main victor of Sevastopol and shook off the humiliating Black Sea clause in the Treaty of Paris of 1856.

Thus, Bismarck was able to complete his work, unhampered by a weakened Russia and indeed protected by Alexander's dislike of his Crimean War opponents and his concern about revolution.

However different from the passive policy of St. Petersburg, the active Paris policy of supporting national movements also afforded advantages to Bismarck. Expecting the Austro-Prussian conflict to end in a draw, France encouraged Prussia's actions in the hope of becoming the arbiter between the two German powers, a remunerative role for which Russia no longer had the necessary strength. As events were to show, Napoleon no longer had it either. His star was waning in America. Snatching nervously at a chance for success, his hand grasped the empty air.

In London, concern over France was still a primary consideration, as it had been, except at intervals, for nearly two hundred years. German affairs had always been a matter of secondary importance. Certainly, Prussia's advance into Schleswig-Holstein in 1864, the strengthening of her maritime potential on two seas, and the humiliation of the Danish outpost in the Sound embittered the great naval power—and declared protector of small nations—as intrusions upon its own sphere of interest. But Britain, her eyes fixed on the Tuileries, tolerated the encroachment. Bismarck, with his great skill, knew how to keep the non-German powers from acting jointly, as they had in 1848–9.

Even when assessing the German question as a whole, London thought primarily in terms of repercussions in France. After Russia's defeat in 1856, prevention of French expansion was the dominant consideration. A climate of peaceful Austro-Prussian relations seemed to offer the best guarantee for this policy. But when, in 1866, it became apparent that Prussia on her own was able to prevent French expansion, Britain was readily able to reconcile herself to the changed situation in Germany and later even co-operate with Prussia on occasion in protecting Belgium. A closer association against France seemed unnecessary. Yet to the British the outcome of the battle of Sedan meant, above all, a release from pressure.

The Machiavellianism inherent in Bismarck's violent practices, with their mixture of Frederick's and Bonaparte's methods, was always regarded as deplorable in Britain. But the British were obliged to learn that Continental Germany was not the same as seabound Italy. In Italy, where British interests and those of the Italian patriots coincided and Britain's maritime instruments of power protected both, the British had been able to create an opening for their mentality and ideals. In Germany, where the patriots themselves did not know what they wanted, where Britain's interests counseled against a drastic change in the status quo and her instruments of power could not be brought to bear, the British had not been able to offer much more than correct liberal doctrines to their numerous admirers in the pre-Bismarck period; and liberal doctrines were of no practical help in achieving progress on the German question. Once Bismarck had established the new Germany as an authoritarian Continental power state par excellence, Britain had to stand by and watch her German admirers dwindle away.

Having recapitulated the special circumstances—utilized by an altogether exceptional man—that were needed to brighten the fate of Germany at such a late stage, we must nonetheless keep in mind the many sinister shadows that had not been removed, as well as those that were now gathering.

The integral unification of the nation had not been brought about; the Gordian knot was uncut. What had been achieved was paid for through losses to the nation's fabric and damage to the nation's psychology. Revitalized, the hard, Old Prussian character could be superimposed on the soft, amorphous German spirit, and Prussia's militaristic-*cum*-political civilization could form the grand alliance, foreshadowed in the *Zollverein*, with a civilization inspired by economics and technology. The middle classes, caught, as they had been since 1848, between the authoritarianism of the state and the demands of the Fourth Estate, completely lost their self-confidence. The spirit of culture, withering throughout the Occident, could put down no deep roots in the stony landscape of the new structure; and in the unsettled atmosphere, the cultural decline was bound to have more grievous effects than in the long-established countries of the West. The national character coarsened. In 1866, the nation's sense of right and wrong having been thrown into confusion, the success of a daemonic, charismatic statesman remolded that character; in the *Kultur-kampf*, it was thrust back from the deep wells of religion, to which the schism had long blocked proper access, and the anti-Socialist law added an element of callousness. The unscrupulous vitality of *Realpolitik* took the place of vanished character traits. Bent on the acquisition of power and wealth, the Germans were at the same time incapable of recognizing the limits of the possible within their policy of realism. Indeed, they were dazzled by sudden good fortune which they failed to understand.

Yet who can say what explosions of then-unformed

energies Bismarck did not stave off, what dangerous forces might have taken the place of the Prussian monarchy? He did not engineer the sudden upsurge of vitality in the rejuvenated nation which plunged headlong into the pursuit of civilization. He guided the inexplicable urge, but also dammed it up. Maneuvering boldly and according to need, he mastered the problem that had been posed in 1848, and trimmed the sails of the ship of state to the hurricane; he alone laid down the course.

After 1871, that course was strictly designed to preserve what had been achieved. He closed the era of turbulence. He was no longer playing the trump card of German unification; the Reich was satisfied. The advent of two great powers in Central Europe had corrected the system of 1815, not made it obsolete. He never so much as toyed, in the manner of Napoleon III, with pretensions to supremacy. The legitimate monarchy stood in no need of glittering adventures. Certainly, during his great enterprise, Bismarck had never recoiled from using revolutionary methods of the Bonapartean brand. But his objective remained the preservation of the arch-Prussian nucleus, for whose protection against the popular movement he had entered the lists in 1848. Ideological sentiments as well as rational considerations kept Bismarck within a tight circle. Without the monarchy, without the royal army, without the established social order, he could not have accomplished anything; and had he been able to do so, this would not have been his wish. There is a close link between Bismarck's policies, after the foundation of the Reich, of preserving the status quo at home and protecting his achievements abroad; in fact, the pupil of Napoleon III seemed at times to have become a disciple of Metternich.

Frederick the Great had acted no differently in devoting

the last two decades of his life to keeping things as they were. There had been reforms since his day. But the Germans had not experienced an upheaval such as the French had in 1789. Even under Bismarck, a sense of stability still reigned in the Reich; and despite drastic changes, German society as a whole had not become fluid in the manner of French society under the impact of the Revolution. Modern life flourished luxuriantly on the trellis formed by an authoritarian and military state of unimpaired validity—a paradox which only the authority and good fortune of its leader could conceal.

# THE QUESTION

# OF GERMAN SUPREMACY;

# WORLD WAR I

W<small>E NOW PASS</small> on to face the question why the Germans so hastily abandoned the plateau of political existence reached in Bismarck's Reich to continue their ascent to the peaks of a bid for supremacy.

To find the answer, let us review the transformation which, in the years after 1871, had come over the three factors I discussed earlier: the situation in foreign affairs, the economic civilization, and the moral energies.

After the foundation of the Reich, the moral energies of the nation were bound to go through a phase of being extended to the limit, which at times passed beyond that to a sense of surfeit and with it a state of disenchantment with the Reich. On the one hand, the scattered elements of reaction rallied in opposition to the young Reich; and on the other, its progressive citizens—for instance, the most recent development, the Fourth Estate—found no satisfaction either. Adjustment to new social patterns has always been difficult for a Continental power state as such; how much more so for the rigid, authoritarian, military state of Prussia-Germany!

If, then, the pressure of national energy slackened for a time, particularly among the older generation, an excess of pressure was soon built up among the younger. This, however, lacked the idealism of the older nationalist movement, its rich spiritual and moral content. Henceforth, the admixture of material interests, which had always been present, pushed its way more powerfully to the surface, thus creating the new sinister shadows over the young Reich to which I have already referred.

Every true culture contains an element that serves to calm the human will; civilization, a stimulant for it. Civilization develops dynamic forces and demands expansion. By its very nature, Bismarck's Reich, which had provided civilization with such fruitful soil, acted unwittingly as a stimulant to the urge for power and wealth. Once the bourgeois class had capitulated to the success of its opponents in the political field, it plunged headlong into economic activities.

Up to now, this economic civilization had filled the sails of the German ship of state with a fair wind. Now its strength swelled menacingly. Originally the urge for expansion had merely aimed at tearing up the network of boundaries inside Germany, and yearned for a large national territory. Now this enlarged territory became filled with rampant forces. The big population increase made a mockery of the Chancellor's assurance that Germany was satisfied. The economic strength which the early stages of industrialization had brought to this agricultural country made it vulnerable as industrialization advanced; self-sufficiency was transformed into dependence on foreign raw materials and markets, and the new tariff law could not remove the roots of the trouble. In the narrow confines of the Continent, prosperity itself became a danger.

After the establishment of the Reich, this sense of constriction also became increasingly tangible in foreign affairs. Now that Germany herself had moved into the forefront on the old Continent, the protection of her policy she had managed to secure in St. Petersburg, London, and Paris began to dwindle.

The loss of Alsace-Lorraine turned France into an ever-present menace for the Reich, just as Prussia through her conquest of Silesia in the eighteenth century had turned Austria into a lurking adversary. German support of French colonial policies, a costly sedative that could not often be applied, brought only temporary relief. Germany's freedom of movement was shrinking.

The relief offered by Anglo-Russian antagonism was problematical. How swiftly that rivalry was put aside when in 1875 the IS WAR IN SIGHT? episode united the three great non-German powers against Germany, just as the Schleswig-Holstein question had in 1848–9! The game of maneuvering independently between the rival world powers involved the risk of complete isolation for Germany. Yet, to opt for one of them would have been tantamount to moving down a step and losing freedom of movement altogether. Doubtless, in the Crimean War, Napoleon III had been able to exploit Anglo-Russian antagonism by siding with Britain; but France was not a neighbor of Russia's. For Germany, the long-term consequences of a victory over the Tsarist Empire, no matter how glorious, would have had perturbing implications. Conversely, to opt for Russia would have exposed Germany to the arrogant demands of St. Petersburg, which would not have been prepared to recognize its Berlin ally as a power of equal status.

To complicate matters, Russia had begun to embark upon a new phase of activity in Europe such as had not been seen since the end of the eighteenth century. True, Alexander II did not succeed in replacing the formidable rigidity of his father's regime with a healthy and modern one. His reforms, by exposing the organic deficiencies of the social fabric all too clearly, increased the threat of revolution. And this situation only served to heighten the new urge for action in the field of foreign affairs. The wave of nationalist sentiment rolling in from the West had reached Russia. Radical Pan-Slavism acted as a ferment. Making common cause with the old expansionist tendencies of Peter's Russia, it sought to restart the long-interrupted advance of the Russian colossus toward Europe, in the direction of the Adriatic and Bohemia. Under the circumstances, Germany's scrupulous cultivation of good relations with Russia on the old conservative lines would be of hardly any use in the long run. Of what avail was Germany's correct attitude during, and after, the Turkish war? On the contrary, the ideological qualms of St. Petersburg, which had thus far prevented its alliance with Paris, were melting away. In much the same manner, Bismarck himself had stripped his diplomacy of all ideological ties. Now, however, he could not but fear that he might lose his eastern support, the fundamental element of his foreign policy, and be caught in the pincer movement that had always haunted him like a nightmare.

The alliance with Austria, a power on the decline, provided no compensating defense, and in any case it was a double-edged weapon in that it provoked the Pan-Slavists. For the alliance had not only deprived Russia of her traditional policy of exploiting the German two-power situation, but also jeopardized her own southeastward drive.

While German relations with Russia were growing cooler and more uncertain, those with Britain did not grow warmer and stable enough to offer a substitute. For all British good will, London did not deem it appropriate to consort with Berlin on an equal footing.

At the root of all these difficulties was the unalterable fact that the two world powers belonged to an order of magnitude different from that of the powers on the old Continent. This was the disease that afflicted the harmony of the system of states, a harmony that Bismarck tried repeatedly and with dogged virtuosity to salvage as the prerequisite for Germany's security.

Accordingly, nothing was further from his thoughts than to provide a foreign policy safety valve for excess pressure at home. The *"grand dessin"* of his early career could not be repeated. So he turned over in his mind the gloomy notion of shortening sail. He thought of suppressing by force the popular movements he could no longer divert into foreign policy channels, thus applying in reverse, as it were, the Caesarian formula of Napoleon III; and, as social legislation alone could not secure peace and order, he considered forestalling any revolutionary unrest by staging a *coup d'état*.

The end of Bismarck's career was darkened more and more by sinister shadows. Had the swift march of events exhausted those statesmanlike ideas that had been brought into play by the ferment of 1848—exhausted them even in the hands of their greatest exponent? Did the aging *Junker* lack the instincts needed for a positive evaluation of something alien to him—the vast forces of modern life? Did he, in short, lack the imagination and audacity to turn to fresh concepts?

Now, as before, it was obviously impossible to remain inactive; forced to a standstill, the horses would bolt. It was equally impossible to use them in an offensive in European high politics. But could this not be done in the setting of world politics—if Germany stepped from the narrow stage onto the broader? The younger generation, the monarch at their head, were confident of their ability to continue the ascent; and they had no doubt that they could find their way among the crags of world politics. The men of that generation allowed themselves to be carried upward by the rising wave, and were intoxicated by the glittering vistas that opened up from its crest.

These men did not hesitate at the crossroads; with their spirits high and glorying in their vitality, they followed their instinct and took the enticing road which was to lead them, by an unexpected detour, toward the horrors of the last struggles for supremacy in Europe. How many of them had even an inkling of the apprehensions that were tormenting the founder of the Reich in his peculiar solitude? Yet his maneuvers were still being carried out on the familiar stage in full view of Germany's neighbors.

However, the capital of accumulated political experience had become worthless in the new conditions of the reconstituted Reich. As inherited wisdom in foreign affairs was scarce even in Prussia, let alone in other parts of the Reich, the new generation in their reckless bravado were all the more tempted to underrate the difficulties of shifting the maneuvers to the world stage. But on that stage, what instincts could be expected to guide the Continental who, with a pounding heart, had only just scaled a dizzy new height of European existence and was still swaying as he tried to get his balance? How was he to exercise judgment in those unknown expanses which were themselves undergoing

a rapid transformation? The Anglo-Saxons knew their way
about these regions; they were part of their own domain.
But their experience was so radically different from that of
the Continentals that a complete two-way understanding
was beyond the capacity of even quite eminent minds. This
lack of understanding had no disastrous consequences for
the insular peoples; for centuries, world history had accorded them the upper hand in the great struggle between
the forces of equilibrium and those striving for supremacy.
The Continentals, on the other hand, had had to pay for
their errors with their blood and their existence. The tale is
told on every page of Spanish and French history in modern
times, but most clearly in the record of post-Bismarckian
German history. It is a sad story of a consistent inability on
the part of the Continentals to appreciate fully the strange
and hidden sources of strength among the insular nations,
a basic phenomenon that peers forth again and again with
wearying regularity from behind all the many-hued masks
of different centuries, peoples, and personalities, and which
is reflected time and again in countless millions of facets,
each with its own individual sheen. It makes a mockery of
every lesson of history. The will to live, stronger than the
intellect, is the master who brooks no irksome warning from
the precocious servant. All the servant can do when catastrophe strikes is to pick up the pieces.

The characteristic element in all the struggles for supremacy since the time of Philip II that I have discussed so
far is a collison between a power dominating the old Continent and the exponent, or exponents, of Western sea power.
A secondary feature, appearing at the time of Napoleon I,
is the collison between the dominant continental power and
Russia.

Now even a Bismarck had had to put forth the last

ounce of his statecraft to exorcise the phantom of a collison
with the Tsarist Empire. But not until a hazardous relationship with Britain was added to Germany's equally precarious relationship with Russia were the feet of the nation
planted on the slippery slope leading to a fight for supremacy. When the new course took the Germans onto the stage
of world politics, they found themselves confronting Britain,
the world power, wherever they turned. Indeed, the conflict
with Britain was henceforth to put its stamp on a whole new
generation of Germans.

The long conflict with France, so fruitful in helping to
mold the modern German nation, was a closed book. And
if the Bismarck era had brought in its train an immense loss
to the nation's historic heritage, the change of front under
William II could not fail to have an even greater effect in
preventing a fresh stabilization of its affairs. The deportment of Germany and the Germans, at once strident and uncertain, was the natural result. In this, the young monarch
set the pace. His qualities were of the kind that enabled him
to lead and mislead. In the face of all criticism, he radiated
about him in his own fashion the sort of confidence that so
easily becomes linked with unreflecting vitality. He again
secured the initiative for the leaders of the state in the manner demanded by the nature of Continental power states if
revolutionary upheavals are to be avoided. In fact, the So-
cialist danger did not increase to the point of explosion. The
cornucopia of prosperity showered the rapidly growing nation with manifold gifts, some of them of a worthier kind
than those offered by the notorious period of stock-exchange
speculation that had followed the founding of the Second
Reich in 1871. But the glittering edifice was built on slim
foundations and mortgaged with a busybody world policy
that lacked clear concepts of its own ends and means. The

tower was being piled up with the Continental's typical insensitivity to the susceptibilities of maritime nations, and, more especially still, with the overweening arrogance of the Johnny-come-lately; at the same time its construction was being hurried forward under the growing pressures and tensions generated by the constricted situation. These pressures, palpable throughout the Continent, were naturally at their most alarming at its center. Thus Germany's efforts to break out into the world were conditioned by a peculiar combination of confidence and concern.

Prussia-Germany had thus far made no bid for hegemony on the Continent; she had striven only for equality of status within the framework of the system. The idea of inheriting the envied supremacy of the British at sea was even now far from her intentions. Nevertheless, she was determined to accelerate the downfall of Britain's dominance. This end was to be served primarily by the construction of a battle fleet capable of seeking a decision in the North Sea, and which, by its very presence, might encourage the opponents of the British and bring all of them within range of the diplomatic activity of the Reich. Through ruthless organization, Frederick William I had built an awe-inspiring army on the slender basis of a poverty-stricken, artificial state; in the hands of his son, that instrument had forced an entry for Prussia into the circle of the great powers of Europe. Now that experiment was to be repeated in a new sphere. The bold and calculating spirit of Old Prussia's military civilization, allied with that of a swiftly expanding economy, turned toward the seas. But that spirit remained thoroughly Continental even while it forged a new kind of instrument for a new theater. Prussia-Germany set herself the task of outgrowing the European system and reaching up to the heights of a global system. Was she attempting the impossible? When all was said, the question at issue was whether such a new world system into which she planned to insinuate herself was actually developing. In truth, all our individual acts of political ineptitude, however imposing their sum total, need not in themselves have prevented our breakthrough into the world—if only our basic conception of incipient developments on the world scene, and our trust in a current that would carry us toward our goals, had been justified.

A good many events—on the surface of the stream, as it were—tended to nourish our confidence. There was, first of all, the new advance of the United States after the rubble of the Civil War had been cleared away, a process that caused Britain embarrassment but benefited German unification. Then there was, for instance, the combined intervention, in 1895, of Russia, France, and the German Reich in the Far East, which demonstrated that the right kind of co-operation between the Continental powers, bypassing Britain, offered opportunities for effective action on the world stage. In 1905, Japan's victory over Russia, which may at first have served the purposes of Britain, Japan's ally, nevertheless again increased the number of possible combinations in the interplay of world forces and also made China's emergence at some future date a not altogether unlikely prospect. It also was quite conceivable that some of the Latin-American countries would become consolidated and strong enough to pursue independent policies. Finally, could the British keep their hybrid empire together in the long run? For all the haste of the new imperialists to expand Britain's colonies and so forestall the competitors that were treading on her heels, her own economic and maritime prestige was passing its Victorian zenith. We Germans had reason to think it feasible that, with world conditions growing more complex and less stable, we could use our youthful and disciplined strength to take advantage of the incipient decline of Britain's power in the same way that Prussia had exploited the decline of Austria and France.

Deep down, however, the stream took a direction that thwarted Germany's hopes. Today we recognize as a fallacy our instinctive analogy between the European and the world systems which fed those hopes. In all previous struggles for supremacy, attempts to unite the European peninsula in a single state had been condemned to failure primarily through the intrusion of new forces from outside the old Occident. The Occident was an open area. But the globe was not, and, for that very reason, ultimately destined to be unified, not split up, unless the progress of civilization, with its conquest of distance, slowed down or came to a standstill. In that event, the divisive tendency might also triumph in the global framework. If, however, the pace were increased, the process of unification must also of necessity increase. And this very process was clearly reflected in both World Wars.

The underwater current that was disastrous for Germany operated at first to Britain's advantage, and compensated to a certain degree for her slow descent from the pinnacle of her fortunes. Russia and the United States, the two other world powers, became Britain's allies; all three of them, after all, were interested in preventing the rise of new world powers either in Europe or in Asia. Thus England was not only able, as she had been in the war against Napoleon I, to bring her Russian rival to her side; she also won over her American daughter nation. She rebuilt on a world-wide scale the grand coalition of earlier centuries against the dominant power on the old Continent.

Looked at in this light, the prehistory of World War I

falls into a clear pattern. British policy at the turn of the century still presented the contradictory picture of a swampy watershed. Britain was still in doubt whether to go on directing her energies at her Russian world rival or to give the close and acute German danger priority over the distant and chronic one. She probed the possibility of forestalling the German menace by making friends with the Reich and thereby gaining support against her Russian opponent. But the British soundings were rebuffed by our pride; we did not wish to be maneuvered into an unrewarding secondary role and were confident that Anglo-Russian antagonism would continue to be a basic element in the world system. As we ourselves knew that we were not seeking supremacy, the idea never occurred to us that Britain might force us into a war for supremacy. We did not stop to think that Britain, following the procedure used a hundred years before, might for a time combine with Russia against us as the common enemy, and even subordinate her opposition toward other countries to the new and paramount consideration.

In the end, Britain made up her mind to view Germany as Enemy Number One, an opponent of the order of sixteenth-century Spain or of France in the seventeenth, eighteenth, and nineteenth centuries—in other words, as a power seeking supremacy. Britain felt no less threatened at the core of her position as a power than she had in those earlier instances, even though Germany, shut in as she was, had no maritime zone that could be compared with that of France, let alone Spain. It was, in fact, the building of the German battle fleet, designed for decisive operations in British coastal waters, that constituted a direct threat to Britain's insular strength. The prosperity of Germany enabled her to embark on a breathtaking armaments race. Moreover, Germany's lunge into the Near East pressed the more disturbingly on the Empire's major artery since the Reich had no need, as France had had under Napoleon I, to make claims on the sea route; across the land bridge provided by the Balkans and Turkey, Germany could use Continental resources of power to make her influence felt in the world outside. With the revival of the old southeastward drive of the Habsburgs, Germany's colonial drive, which cut across Britain's interests—as represented by the Cape-to-Cairo line —was of secondary importance.

Now British diplomacy began to take precautions against Germany with all the wisdom acquired in the country's earlier fights against powers seeking supremacy. Britain wove a net of friendships which was bound to tighten about her opponent if he continued to pursue his present course. But these friendships also put an end to her splendid isolation with its proud freedom from ties.

The Anglo-French entente was the prelude. It was negotiated without difficulty. As France, with the downfall of Napoleon, had ceased to be an opponent to reckon with in a contest for supremacy, large concessions could be made to her, particularly as she had only recently given ground in the Fashoda crisis.

More difficult was the task of laying the groundwork for an entente with Russia, thereby providing the new coalition front with a powerful eastern wing. For Britain to make concessions to her world rival through fear of Germany might prove tantamount to driving out the Devil with Beelzebub. In order to come to an understanding with Russia, Britain's statesmen had to walk a tightrope between abysses. But this feat was made easier for them by the victory of their Japanese ally over Russia and by Germany's policy toward Turkey. Russia's defeat in the Far East diminished Britain's risks in making concessions to the Tsarist Empire, which was in any case undermined by revolutionary activity; and Germany's appearance in the Orient brought the two old rivals together again, just as French Oriental policy had under Napoleon I or Louis Philippe. To stand united and frustrate any effort on the part of a power on the old Continent to break out into the world—this, in the circumstances, was the most pressing concern of both Russia and Britain. What would come afterward could be left to the future to decide. In order to make certain of the Tsar's help in the case of a war against the two German powers, which Britain had in vain tried to pry apart, she further took the risk of incredible concessions to Russia in the Near East and the Balkans. She sacrificed Turkey, a country she had so often protected but which was now siding with Germany, and generously accorded the Russians a large sphere of interest in Persia, regardless of the threat to India that was thereby conjured up.

Once Britain had won the support of the Eastern world power, the task of weaving the second- and third-rate countries into the coalition network was almost a secondary one.

On the whole, none of these diplomatic actions went beyond the circle of the countries involved during the Napoleonic era. The case of the unwritten entente between Britain and the United States was another matter. This entente brought to the surface the underwater current I described earlier. As the two Anglo-Saxon empires united for the first time within the top group of the three global powers, the tendency of the world to form a single conglomerate gained a lasting lead over all tendencies toward division. In the course of this process, leadership passed to America.

After the Civil War, two alternative ways of expansion were open to the United States. She could resume and push to a conclusion the controversy with Britain over Canada and the other British possessions in the Western Hemisphere and so win complete insular status vis-à-vis the one power outside America that could be considered an opponent to reckon with in the hemisphere. Conversely, the United States could join forces with Britain and, following the parallel policies of Monroe and Canning, ward off any threat from the European Continent to their common insular existence. At first it seemed unlikely that the second course would be followed. Britain's equivocal attitude during the Civil War was still remembered with bitterness in the United States. The Alaska Purchase, which drove Russia from the American continent, could be looked at as a preparatory step for similar treatment of Britain; Canada was now clasped on two sides by American territory.

However, in the depths of public opinion a change began to take shape: confronted in Asia and in Europe with peoples and powers of an alien character, both nations gradually found their natural affinity to be of greater importance to them than their old antagonism. The diplomats of Washington and London translated these feelings into the realities of foreign policy. In the seventeenth century, the two sea powers had forgotten their rivalry in order to mount a common defense of their insular character against the dominant Continental power; so, now, the rise of Germany, a Continental power, contributed not a little toward drawing the two insular nations closer together. Then, small and vulnerable Holland, which had reached maturity ahead of England, had to pay with a slow, dignified decline for securing an alliance with the large island which had been later than Holland in turning toward the ocean. Now the relationship of the small British islands with the big American island was to develop along fairly similar lines. The golden age that had followed Trafalgar was drawing to its close, a process reminiscent of the period of Dutch history after the defeat of the Armada. The American island, having consolidated its internal structure through the Civil War, turned its expansive energy toward the oceans, just as the islands of Britain had done after her revolutions. The Americans built a fleet and acquired dependencies. In other words, having used their insular position for defensive purposes, they now discovered its offensive possibilities and began to develop them, soon to outstrip the British in this field. The driving force behind this American activity was technology. Its distance-destroying powers, which were perilously hemmed in on the old Continent, lent wings to the forces of expansion on the new continent. And Britain's white Dominions, which exhibited similar conditions, served as a bridge between the small mother country and the great daughter nation.

The price Britain paid for American backing was her attitude of indifference toward the construction of the Panama Canal. Built by the United States alone, it doubled the effectiveness of her naval rearmament (just as did the new Kiel Canal in the case of the German navy). In the long wall of the American continent, a gateway was opened through which the energies of the Atlantic coast could be poured, in increasing volume, into the vast expanses of the Pacific. Britain stood by—this, too, was part of the price she paid—while the United States was rising to a place of increasing importance in this ocean where power positions had not yet congealed. The two Anglo-Saxon powers appeared to start dividing the oceans between them; and this division was to become manifest after World War I.

Significant in this respect was the attitude of the United States while mediating at the Peace of Portsmouth. Half a century earlier, she had forced an entry for Western civilization into Japan. Now, after the defeat of Russia, she took care that Japan would not derive from her victory any advantages that might turn her into a potential threat; and indeed, during World War I the Japanese still proved unable to break away from the world coalition. So, in the Far East as well, the common interest of the three world powers in keeping any competitor from penetrating their tight circle became visible in a policy of solidarity.

While only the beginnings of a richer variety of states of equal caliber developed on the world stage, this diversity once again asserted itself in Europe on the bloody stage of World War I. Certainly, the old Continent remained the center of events in that war. But Britain, by her foresight in handling relations with the United States and Japan, secured participation by the overseas powers on her side, and made it possible for the action on the broader stage to be co-ordinated, under her direction, with that in the narrower setting.

In this way, and only in this way, Germany was overcome in four years. Who would care to calculate how long this might have taken without the aid of the United States? Did it not become clear that Britain and Russia, the two flanking powers, could no longer match their achievements of the Napoleonic wars? Britain's naval supremacy could not yet be shaken. But how much greater were the losses in blood and treasure she had to bear this time, compared with her sacrifices in that earlier struggle! In fact, those losses sucked at the vitals of her world position. Moreover, Germany, unlike Napoleon's France, had at her disposal a land route to the Near East—a matter of considerable moment. Above all, Ludendorff, succeeding where Napoleon had failed, put Russia out of action. Could he not, given time, have organized Germany's supremacy on the Continent on a more permanent and expansive basis than Napoleon had his? He might have done so, had he not been called upon to face the strength of America, the power which, in 1812, had threatened Britain in the rear.

Although it is true that plans for Continental supremacy in the Napoleonic sense were remote from Germany's original conception, she was nevertheless compelled by circumstances, or beguiled, into moving ever closer to such an aim. By establishing herself in Belguim she entered, almost unawares, the fateful region that had played its part in all struggles for supremacy since the time of Philip II. Without extending her European base, Germany could not secure a base from which to become a world power among world powers, a rise that in spite of all remained the nation's deepest longing. The unexpected struggle against "a world of enemies" merely served to intensify the defiant self-confidence of the nation. It would not settle for an unsecured European existence under the old cramped conditions. The comparison with the Peace of Hubertusburg as the precedent for a victory without territorial expansion was not accepted, for in 1763 Frederick the Great, while agreeing to existing frontiers, had at the same time maintained Prussia's status as a great power. But if William II had brought home nothing but the status quo from the titanic struggle, he would have compromised forever the nation's passionate hopes for world-power status. As long as forty years before, Seeley had predicted that, in view of the rapid developments in world politics and economics, the states of Continental Europe were bound to shrink to the size of pygmies. Germany had a premonition of this fate; and at the decisive crossroads she rebelled with all her vitality

241

against being forced onto the downward path. She did not collapse until American intervention had destroyed every reasonable hope of success.

For the fourth time, a dominant power on the old Continent, within sight of the unconquered peak of supremacy, had been hurled into the depths. And for the fourth time, the task remained to secure the rescued freedom of the system by comprehensive peace treaties.

Alas, the treaties of 1918 did not lay the foundations of so lasting an order as had those established by their predecessors. Was this due only to the general speed of developments in the age of the internal-combustion engine, developments that compressed centuries of change into a few years? There were other special causes at work; and these were closely connected with certain peculiarities of World War I which I touched on earlier.

As I have repeatedly pointed out, the equilibrium of the system had always been kept in balance during its great crises by counterweights operating from new territories outside the old Occident. The price of the maintenance of liberty had always been a decline in power on the divided Continent and its exclusion from these young territories. Thus power had slowly departed from one after another of the old countries in the Occident's heartland. But in World War I this tendency developed an unprecedented momentum and new features. The influence of the overseas territories was no longer felt, as before, only indirectly and via Britain, acting as pivot; American intervention, bypassing Britain, gave a new immediacy to that influence. In 1815 the migration of power had still benefited Britain and Russia, the states on the margins of Europe; now power leaped across the ocean. It was not only the old Continent that, once again, paid for its freedom with a decline in power; this time, an ominous shadow fell across Russia, too, and even across victorious Britain. For despite her grandiose colonial expansion, the maintenance of the balance of power in Europe no longer went hand in hand with a consolidation of British supremacy in the maritime sphere. Her financial and industrial dominance was melting away, and without it colonial possessions were bound to become a burden.

As the military decision had been brought about by the United States, the new peace settlement could be a lasting one only if it drew inspiration from, and were guaranteed by, the United States; only if the actions on both the narrow and the broad stage, which during the war had at first been linked under Britain's leadership, remained integrated in peace under American leadership.

With this end in view, the United States did bring a great plan for a League of Nations to the conference table. After 1815, the monarchist Restoration, which had its deepest roots in Central and Eastern Europe, made an attempt to restrain the egotism of individual states, in order to save culture from the murderous final battles within the European system which the old classes felt were approaching. Now the endeavors to impose such restraint on individual states came from the West, from the Anglo-Saxon democracies, which had always looked down on Continental power struggles from the lofty level of their virtue. In particular, these endeavors came from the American democracy, to which the diplomatic and military collisions on the distant European Continent could not fail to appear quite incomprehensible and even sinful. But where the Restoration had been restricted to the Continent and was both rigid and apprehensive, the Anglo-Saxon concept was designed for global application, based on confidence in progress, and filled with the island spirit of free social evolution, while re-

243

jecting, or even ignoring, the methods of power states. In this idealistic form, Anglo-Saxon world leadership, with the United States in the van, made its appearance for the first time. In the days when the European system of states was in its infancy, how modest and peripheral the insular element had looked compared with the magnificent manifestations of the Continental principle! Now the cutting had grown into a tree that bade fair to overshadow the globe with its foliage. Amazed and shaken, we Germans began to discuss the possibility of a *Pax Anglosaxonica* as a world-wide contemporary counterpart to the *Pax Romana*. Suddenly the tendency toward global unification towered up, ready to gather the separate national states of Europe together under one banner and blanket in a larger cohesion their tendency to split.

But how could this concept be brought closer to realization, if not actually realized, without the purposeful intervention of the United States herself? As it was, America, unprepared in spirit for the global role suddenly proffered her, rejected it, and withdrew into the "splendid isolation" of her giant island. Even in the Pacific, she kept only a negligent eye on her interests. Rome, too, had taken a long time to understand the significance of her world role.

The narrow stage was left to its own devices. It did not even retain its old dimensions, deserted as it was by defeated Russia as well as victorious America. Russia disappeared into the vast, featureless expanses from which Peter the Great had broken out. But she was still strong enough to defend her new, sphinxlike way of life against the inconsistent attempts on the part of the all but exhausted world powers to liquidate it.

Indeed, it was against the tangled background of an unmatured global situation that the peace problems of Europe

were guided toward their solution. Mature and lasting that
solution could scarcely be. It was not shaped by any flexible, farsighted, world-wide vision. Instead, the old Continent's power principle, which had evolved over the centuries, asserted itself once more in all its inexorability; and its
effectiveness was appallingly heightened by the instruments
of pressure that modern civilization placed in its hands.

France embodied this fortified power principle. With the
United States and Russia standing aside, she found herself
thrust unexpectedly into a leading role. Having escaped final
collapse by only a hairbreadth, she was resolved to use
every possible means to keep the superior vitality of her
prostrate enemy from recovering. At this late hour, it was a
case of to be or not to be. France could not rely on immediate aid from the world powers in case of emergency. If the
thread of French history were not to be broken in a final
catastrophe, the danger of another war with Germany must
be methodically eliminated.

This purpose was served by the policy of promoting
nationalism. It had preoccupied French politicians since
1815. Under Napoleon III, it had encountered disaster. The
alliance of the two great Central European countries had
proved dangerous to France. Therefore, France's objective
was to counterbalance this danger by alliances with the me-
dium-sized and smaller countries that had emerged from the
wreckage of the three old Eastern powers. It was not sufficient to put a mechanical gag on Germany and nibble away
her frontiers; living counterforces, natural allies who could
be relied on to stick with France in fair weather and foul,
must be enlisted to keep watch on Germany's rear. All
things considered, the policy of France under the *ancien
régime* had had no other aim.

However, the belated triumph of France's policy of supporting nationalism could not obscure the fact that times had changed. In days gone by, French encouragement of nationalist movements had had about it an air of joy and high hope for the future. Now the position of France, outwardly so proud, was overcast by the nation's concern for its own security.

And Britain? In 1815, taking the long view, she had mitigated the lot of the vanquished. At that time, France had remained an indispensable figure on the European chessboard, particularly as a counterweight to the Russian colossus. But there were no grounds of equal force that called for Germany to be treated with indulgence. For the time being, Russia was out of the picture. Could Germany really be relied upon as a counterpoise to Russia? Her tight links with that country at the time of the genesis of Prussian power argued against this. Moreover, Britain had long since ceased to regard France as a nation that might again make a serious bid for supremacy. There was no need for a German counterweight to France. Thus, the young German Republic, on the whole, received British backing only to the extent that seemed needed to protect her bourgeois social order from the blandishments of Communism.

# WORLD WAR II

This peace settlement, then, being built of contradictory compromises, created no lasting pattern of existence.

A hundred years earlier, it perhaps was still possible to wipe countries off the map and set up new ones. Political passions were still slumbering. Economic conditions were stable and robust. How different things had become in the twentieth century! There was so much intermingling and overlapping among the peoples of Eastern Europe that the new national states possessed no convincing frontiers. National feelings, satisfied in one place, were outraged in another; but everywhere they were inflamed and spurred on to open or legally camouflaged violence. Then there was the matter of the economic consequences of the new boundary lines. The progress of civilization had made ever-increasing masses of human beings dependent upon the smooth functioning of an ever more complicated economic machine. Now its functioning was impeded. Large economic entities were broken up, and their fragments burdened with the exigencies of a costly administration, stepped-up armament, and economic self-sufficiency.

If these difficulties were felt by the new countries, the beneficiaries of the new order, how much more was conquered Germany called upon to bear! Let us leave aside the bitterness caused by the political effects of defeat. Its economic effects threatened life itself. Germany's twentieth-century inflation was more terrible than the French inflation of the eighteenth century. The cession of highly valuable territory, the loss of loan capital, colonies, and world-wide connections, combined with the nightmare of reparations, brought misery on a scale which the primitive economic patterns of earlier centuries had been proof against. The concern for markets, raw materials, food, and living standards—the concern that had led the nation into world politics—was transformed after the collapse into dire need. American loans could for a time cover up these conditions; they could not eliminate them. So sources of infection accumulated in the newly organized territories of Central and Eastern Europe. Could the governments and the various national bodies deal with them before they merged into centers of disease?

Recovery was disastrously hampered by the situation into which the Continent as a whole has slipped vis-à-vis the territories outside Europe, particularly those overseas. The decline in importance with which the European system of states had paid for its freedom, more so than ever in the recent struggle, became evident in economic terms, both through indebtedness on the part of Europe to America—a reversal of prewar conditions—and through the growth of industrial competition overseas. These were accompanied at times by Russian dumping of exports. The old Atlantic states, still in possession of colonial empires, rich reserves of foreign capital, and large merchant fleets, did not as yet feel the force of the opposing currents so disastrously as did Central Europe, an overpopulated and highly industrialized region lacking such "lifebelts." In theory, co-operation between the European states could have brought a beginning of relief; civilization, if it is to prosper, needs ever-widening spaces in which to operate. But co-operation remained a daydream. The tendency of the Continent to split up, once again triumphant, proved to be nothing less than the indelible hallmark of the system.

Toward the end of the 1920's there was a darkening of the picture of prosperity even in the white world outside Europe, to say nothing of Russia in her seclusion. The economic civilization had become so interrelated throughout the world that a world-wide crisis of unprecedented proportions became possible. This crisis expressed—negatively, as it were—the tendency toward global unification. With the League of Nations atrophied, there was no global organization that could have taken steps to counter the crisis. One might say that political processes, which in Europe were developing in contradiction to economic requirements, had been equally unable to keep pace with these in the outside world. Unemployment and stagnation in commerce spread from country to country. Even the most powerful countries had to look to their own economic ills, and were unable to help the weaker.

The setbacks that took place in all these areas had their most severe effects in Central Europe, a region already disorganized and in danger. How could its lacerated and inflamed tissue heal when the entire organism was sick? Thus, in Italy and, above all, in Germany, centers of disease were formed, spreading a new fever across the world.

From the yawning depths into which the last wave in the long race for supremacy had crashed, carrying down with it an appalling toll of victims, there came, unexpectedly, a new wave, with no more than half a generation gone by.

Central Europe was not the only place where forces were gathering to oppose the status quo of 1919. This was happening also in Russia and Japan, far mightier and more independent power structures than Italy, let alone Germany. Yet those were not the areas in which the new world conflict took fire.

By joining the world powers in the great coalition against Germany, Japan had done well. Now she felt confident in her ability to become a world power herself. Being, like Germany, charged to the bursting point with dynamic energy, Japan believed that she could achieve in the vast expanse of Asia, not yet saturated with power, what the Reich had failed to achieve within the narrow confines of Europe. Like the Germany of 1914, Japan possessed a well-trained army and navy of technical perfection and excellent morale. Over and above this, she had her precious island location. Why had she never produced even traces of a free insular character comparable with that of Venice, Holland, Britain, and the United States? Perhaps because this long-secluded island empire had never wished, nor been able, to assume a great intermediary role between two worlds.

While Asian Japan, inscrutable in her mingling of the ancient East and Western civilization, lay ready to spring, Russia, whose offensive power had always been limited, was still paralyzed by her collapse; but more than ever there was an incalculable Asian streak about her. Out of the agonizing chaos of defeat, she was silently developing original creative powers that appeared utterly alien to the Western observer; these forces, as it turned out, were engaged in a process of *reculer pour mieux sauter*. In this Hellenistic hybrid, composed of two layers, the Asian features now became more pronounced than those that looked to, or were fertilized by, the West. Yet the Western component remained constantly tangible, and was even greatly strengthened in certain special fields.

It is worth remembering that the Bolshevik Revolution had its western predecessor in the Terror of the French Revolution. That earlier totalitarian system, too, had transformed state and society; it, too, had melted down all fixed, inherited patterns of life and, in so doing, released unsuspected energies to turn the wheels of the revitalized state apparatus. Indeed, the Terror had accomplished the same paradoxical transition from tumultuous destruction of the rusting old machine to erection of a brand-new one. It, too, had concentrated its revolutionary energies in a ruling party which, alongside the army and the bureaucracy, the two old instruments of power, had invaded the center of authority to become the dominant element. There, too, the spirit of Christian culture had been eliminated, wherever possible, as an impediment, and all the instruments of terror and propaganda used to exalt a civilization based on politics and economics. There, too, foreign intervention had been repulsed. But even while we detect a typical element common to the development of both these continental power states, despite the time interval between their revolutions, the complete difference in historical background becomes obvious. In Russia, we are not dealing with an ancient, organic culture; life there is based on a more recent, hybrid Hellenistic civilization, characterized by a fusion of heterogeneous elements through despotism. The revolutionary process in Russia strained to return to this familiar despotism almost as a matter of course; and whereas in France the improvised totalitarian system had been able to maintain itself only for a short time, totalitarianism established itself in Russia for good—an old state of affairs rejuvenated under new colors. In more than one respect, the work of Peter the Great was renewed, at a fresh level of development, by the very method he had employed—a grafting of the most modern Western techniques onto the malleable Eastern human material. The fear of revolution, which had impeded continuance of Peter's work under later Tsars, disappeared with Tsarism itself, and thus the way was cleared for a fresh infusion of dynamic vigor into the colossus.

The intellectual resources of the Revolution strengthened this process. Peter the Great's system had lacked intellectual support of comparable power; he had been a man of Western orientation who had ravished the self-esteem of Old Russia. The new Russia proudly detached herself from the West, however much she might learn from it in the technical field. To enhance national self-esteem she used her own methods. The new Russia preached fanaticism to fill the vacuum left by the banished forces of religion, and thereby delivered up the individual, as an instrument more pliant than ever, into the hands of the state.

The Western origin of the state doctrine in no way conflicted with the new self-esteem. The practical conclusions drawn from this doctrine all served to enhance the power of Russia; they fortified both her nucleus, still military as before, and the projection of her spirit beyond her frontiers. If Russia had previously been on the whole a pupil of ancient Europe, she now also had the capacity to teach and supply the large groups of her adherents abroad with doctrines and directives. And if the democratic League of Nations held out to the tormented peoples the prospect of an end to murderous power struggles, so also did the Bolshevik world revolution. Not merely in the West but in the East, too, the emphasis began to shift from the fragmented and battered old Continent with its ancient culture to the broad new expanses where civilization was thriving.

In the early 1930's, Russia's achievements were, to be sure, still a matter of controversy. The Bolsheviks had set themselves the tasks of infusing vitality into apathetic masses and of conquering huge virgin spaces, a program too enormous even for their fanatical energies. Vast areas of Asia were still in process of being linked to the blood stream of modern civilization; and when Japan ventured on her leap into Manchuria, Soviet Russia was still laboring, with planning and vigor, to develop her apparently boundless internal potentialities. But the regime could count on the fact that the manifestations of socio-political disintegration in the European and Asian approaches to its own territory had not yet reached their height. Facing no threat from outside, the colossus could afford to bide its time.

There was no danger whatever of Russia's opening an assault upon the status quo. Nor did Japan's action set this assault in motion. That privilege was reserved for the great German upheaval.

The old volcanoes in Europe still towered so high that an eruption releasing their immense pent-up energies was bound to threaten the world far and wide with streams of fiery lava; no power shift in the loose framework of the Far East need necessarily produce anything like the same immediate effects. Once again, the action on the narrow stage determined the course of events on the broad stage. Once more, Germany was the operative element in this action. Bottled up in a tight corner of the narrow stage, she was haunted by dim dreams of unused reserves of power that might enable her, under the right kind of leadership, to break through the fateful ring.

Even under William II, confidence and concern had

combined to make the German people regard it as possible, or even necessary, to grow out of their tight confinement. Now the hardships of actual destitution emphasized that concern. Misery kept fanning the embers of confidence, which defeat had not extinguished, until a bright flame flickered forth.

Had the Weimar Republic been able to assure adequate means of support for the masses, the memory of departed power might have been confined to the elite of the old classes, and would perhaps have lost its lure. But who can maintain this with certainty? A nation does not so readily forget a draught from the cup of power. Even the proletariat, incorporated as it had been in the armed forces with their spirit of comradeship and self-sacrifice, had sipped from that cup. However that may be, misery, with perplexity and even panic in its train, utterly undermined the domestic prestige of the Republic, which could not boast of a national effort as could the Soviet Union or France. The Weimar Republic, in fact, suffered so greatly from the consequences of defeat because that defeat was the source of its own existence.

The compressed nationalism of the old classes began to expand again. All parties had from the start embraced the idea of using Germany's defeat at the hands of democracy to make a reality of *Grossdeutsch* expansionist aspirations and bring about the *Anschluss* of the German-speaking parts of the former Habsburg empire. The decisive factor in the development, however, was the attitude of Germany's youth. Despairing, partly *declassé* by inflation, it deserted the republican parties and, in fact, rejected the party system as such. The young were not willing to wait for the ripening of modest achievements. Viewing them in the light of the frustration of national hopes, and with the specter of indefinite unemployment before them, they did not believe that

254

those achievements would satisfy them. They no longer looked for salvation in a closing of ranks toward the center—a movement bent on preserving existing values—but in a flight to the extremist parties, to totalitarianism, in which revolutionary *élan* under tough leadership would be combined with rigid organization. In this they only followed the typical instinct of the latter-day Continental power state. That instinct had operated creatively for the first time in the crisis of the French Revolution; it had but recently saved Russia's freedom; and it had stood sponsor at the establishment of a new order in Italy, Spain, and Turkey. It is the instinct which seeks, in times of stress, to reinforce the old, familiar principle of the power state through revolution.

The Republic's last authoritarian regime—senile and impotent as it was, and already a dubious guardian of the spirit of Weimar, but still a dike against the totalitarian flood—was unable to retain a hold on the hopes aroused by the name of Hindenburg, its leading figure.

The question now was which of the two extremist parties would have the better prospect of seizing power.

No doubt, Communism was, on the whole, regarded as the pacemaker for future Russian expansion, and as the harbinger of a process that was questioning the very *raison d'être* of the national states and their social structures by challenging the ability of both to offer, within their narrow framework, a viable future to the masses. In other words, Communism was, on the whole, considered a menace, from the nation's midst, to its existence. This peril aroused the defensive forces of the nation's body. Its vitality was still unbroken. It was stored up for the last-hour call. This vitality clung to the memories of, and drew additional vigor from, whatever testified to its own energies: population figures, the health of the nation and its will to work, the undestroyed potential of its economic civilization, and, above all, the great tradition that united the veterans of the armed forces and kept alive in these men an awareness of possibilities not yet exhausted. The outcome of the war made no sense to the nationalist activists; they refused to realize that it had only confirmed the results of earlier struggles for supremacy, and that the war had been decided through a fusion of the old European main tendency with the new global tendency. These men lived and moved in the atmosphere of Prusso-German history. They never paused to consider how limited had been the area in which our history had attained glory, and how much circumstances peculiar to that period had favored that rise. In an individual, the intellect has difficulty in damming up the will to live; how much more so among the masses! Their unbridled will to live scoffs at the lessons of history, a record capable of many interpretations.

Moreover, the narrowing of the field of vision that accompanied the withdrawal of Russia and the United States from the world scene made it easier for the impulsive optimists to misread the situation. They reasoned that after the seeming downfall of Russia, only France and her small satellites were left to be faced on the Continent—opponents of whose inferior vitality they found cause to persuade themselves. All the old Continental resentments, envenomed now by the "humiliations of Versailles," came to the fore again, and kept the attention of the nation riveted close to home.

And Britain? Would she not reconcile herself to a rehabilitated Germany—a counterweight, after all, to France and Russia? Was Britain, in fact, still strong enough to keep her traditional blocking position?

Once the Germans closed their eyes to the capacity and

readiness of the world powers to resist a new German bid for supremacy, their imagination could indulge in a great many enticing lines of thought which, by daring twists and turns, would side-step facts that their minds failed to grasp. Once again, the mirage of a loosened global system of states took shape. The examples of Japan, Turkey, and, above all, Italy proved that the bold could still break through the dead weight of the status quo and unexpectedly move upward. The Prussian spirit, like a badly wounded lion, heaved itself up from its stupor.

What was there to attract that spirit in the despised Republic's policy of cautious probing? Alarmed by the country's misery, Germany's former enemies made some concessions to the Republic and enabled it to show some achievements. But the masses, in their blind passion, did not wish to acknowledge them. And what was the scope of those achievements? This is a question we must not brush aside if we are to review the subject coolly in retrospect. Did the virtual repudiation of the financial obligations imposed on Germany suffice to remove the deep causes of the nation's malaise? Actually, this malaise, while of course sharpened by the Versailles Treaty, did not stem from it alone. Rather, it originated in the nation's consciousness of defeat as such, and in the general decline of Europe, which produced its earliest disastrous repercussions in the wretchedly depressed area called Germany.

Certainly, "chance" plays an even more obvious role in periods of crisis than in normal times. But Hitler's "chance" occurrence must also be seen as the acute symptom of a chronic sickness. Only in desperate conditions can a desperado make his mark. Probably Hitler could have been eliminated. But would not other, and no less acute, symptoms have come to the surface sooner or later, such as internal disorders combined with intervention by neighboring powers? Every bridge has its maximum load. If this is exceeded, ominous fissures appear; individually, they may have "chance" causes—a flaw in the building material in one place or negligent construction in another.

The advent of Hitler meant something quite different from what a large part of the nation, led astray by demagogy, imagined; far from being the magic potion that would cure the chronic sickness, it was the anesthetic before surgery. Under a fog of ambiguous assurances, action was switched from the track of domestic politics to that of foreign affairs. Ever since the French Revolution, all governments close to Caesarism had acted in this way. But never before had the very life of a nation been at stake.

Before 1914 the objectives of German policy had been hazy but limited; contrary to expectation, they had led to a fight for supremacy. This time they were completely clear in the dictator's mind, and utterly limitless. Although Hitler may have hoped to approach his goal in single bounds and avoid another World War, he was nevertheless determined from the outset not to recoil from any fight likely to advance the realization of his objectives.

Thus, the time had come for Germany to mobilize her last reserves of strength by using all the possibilities open to the administrative techniques of the Continental power state. Reinvigorated, the military and bureaucratic traditions of Old Prussia were fused with the most modern revolutionary methods. The enormity of the ends had to be matched by the enormity of the means. Of course, these were made ready behind a veil. As the beast of prey crept toward its victim, it concealed its talons, to use them only when the time came to pounce.

As modern German history drew to its close, familiar

features reappeared, though magnified to lurid proportions. Bismarck's Reich, like Prussia's status as a great
power, had been created in the face of Europe's guns
through a combination of autocratic leadership at the top
and disciplined devotion to duty below, both marks of the
genius of the Continental power state as such. But now,
in this perilous borderline case, these signs were evident in
maximum sharpness from the start. They were to determine the course of the final fight.

When a man is battling with death, those elemental
forces in his nature that fight for sheer survival thrust their
way to the fore with terrifying power. They seek to crowd
out the more noble feelings that balanced them in hap-
pier days. Yet how unfair it would be to judge a man's
true nature by his moments of agony, and interpret his entire previous life as if it had been no more than their prelude.
It would be similarly unjust to stress only the dark lines of
German history which lead to its last phase and, in so doing, to overlook the harmonious features of previous epochs
—to note only its inherent weaknesses and their perils without also being mindful of the wholesome counterforces that
compensated for them. Nor, above all, must we interpret
the last act of Germany's history solely through the events
on the German stage. Only by visualizing the all-embracing
shifts of pressure on the shrinking globe—those shifts that
helped to warp and distort Germany's history with such
terrible effects—can anyone comprehend that last act.

In the Third Reich, for the first time, one of the great
nations, a nation still vigorous and vital, was in fact engaged
in a death struggle. Poland had once been carved up before
she awoke to full national consciousness. Only the history
of the ancient world offers genuine parallels. Standards
taken from more recent history are inadequate for measur-

ing events that were without precedent, though they may set precedents for others to come.

Precedents there may not have been, but there were warning signals. France had been the prototype of the Continental power state in crisis which at home totally melts the traditional forms of life in the crucible of revolution and aims at boundless totalitarian domination abroad. It was the French Revolution and the Napoleonic Empire that first created the motifs, episodic and fragmentary, on which the Hitler regime, using the full instrumental equipment of an advanced civilization, produced variations in crashing rhythms.

In many ways too, the Russian Revolution represented an intensified version of the French Revolution. It systematized the French improvisations, keyed them to a different civilization, and transposed them to another milieu. There, too, the state of flux inside the country enabled a power state in decline to exhibit surprising strength abroad; but the Soviet Union, secure behind its vast peripheral belt, had no need to break out forthwith from its successful defensive position into a risky bid for supremacy, let alone stage a fight for national existence as Hitler did.

Fascism in Italy, using basically similar methods, endeavored to wrench a sinking great power up to the heights again. But conditions in that country were easier to master, and the regime had no need to resort to extremes, either at home or—as long as Italy was free—abroad.

The Spanish *Falange* system, more than any other, is just an offshoot of the totalitarian wave. Like its Turkish counterpart, it has been limited in scope. Both of them, characteristically, have grown on the soil of power states long since fallen low.

The Third Reich now became the reservoir into which

the ideas of revolutionary Caesarism flowed from far and near; they formed fresh combinations and were heated to the boiling point. As the years went by, the Russian component dominated the others—a symptom of the shift of emphasis to territories outside the Occident and, at the same time, proof of a continuance of the manifold intermingling of Prussian affairs with Russian affairs dating back to the days of Frederick William I and Peter the Great. But what was happening now had an altogether new significance: on the most ancient Western soil, indeed shooting up from it, a system of government was consciously initiating a total break with all the values of human personality honored in the West. And this dark, terrorist civilization appeared more sinister and sinful against the bright background of European culture than in the gloom of a semi-Asian setting. Assuredly, even in the old Occident, the Continental power state had for centuries widened its influence at the expense of the metaphysical values of the individual—at first slowly, then with growing purposefulness. But in the course of Germany's last battle, this drive was pushed to a degree of exclusiveness never before imagined. Encouraged by developments in Russia, this effort went beyond them in many respects. Bolshevism, like the French Revolution in earlier days, was still able to appeal to certain ideals of mankind; the Third Reich could not. Its "ideology," concerned solely with the demands of Germany and the gang that ruled her, failed to generate the strength of a world mission. Here, power showed itself in all its crude nakedness, stripped of any spiritual veil; on the brink of its own destruction, power was pushed to its extreme form.

Hitler's methods of mobilizing Germany's strength to the limit must be viewed in conjunction with his virtually unlimited plans for domination abroad. In his book he

prophesied that the nation able to protect its racial substance will gain mastery of the globe; by sheer logic, a policy
guided by such Napoleonic impulses was bound to lead to
a struggle for supremacy; that is, to a simultaneous collision
with Britain and Russia. Hitler tried, by his limited coups,
to undermine the strength and the morale of the world
powers before they realized the extent of their danger; but,
despite all his arts of diplomacy and propaganda, he failed
in these attempts. He wanted to fight the Russians while
the British held back, and battle with Britain while Russia
remained passive; but the two world powers joined hands
across an ideological abyss. Their World War I alliance,
which had been based on common interests, was renewed
—an extension of their alliance of a century earlier. It was,
in fact, a basic principle of the policy of both countries to
unite against any power that showed signs of outstripping
them. Their tight circle would tolerate no extension through
the entry of rising powers, either in Europe or in Asia.

In the end, the solidarity of the Big Three prevailed
against Japan as well as Germany. Germany's alliance with
Tokyo, while delaying Hitler's downfall, could not avert it.
On the old Continent, Prusso-German history had tri-
umphantly vindicated the idea that a bold leader could over-
run the status quo and raise his country to the heights; in
the framework of world politics, this idea was shown once
again to be a will-o'-the-wisp. Neither heroism nor crimes
could master the opposing current, and all efforts to reach
the far shore proved fruitless. How many of them suggested
efforts in earlier wars for supremacy! There was the renewal
of the old battle for the Low Countries; there were the
schemes, so often hatched, for landings in Britain; and then,
after their failure, the familiar drive for compensating Continental expansion. There was the attempt to subdue Russia

after fruitful co-operation against the island forces had proved as unattainable with Stalin as it had been with Alexander I. And there was the effort to break out of the ring, in the south and southeast, toward the Near East and Africa, in order to escape—notwithstanding the lack of sea power—from the constricting boundaries of Europe. In other words, the world once more witnessed a Continental power's desperate attempts to offset and outmaneuver the naval power, unshakable in its command of the seas, by extending its own continental position. It is not difficult to derive from the earlier great wars a complete genealogy for each of the aims of the Third Reich.

Even the outcome of the last great struggle for supremacy shows its predecessors' features, albeit tragically sharpened. Once again, the assault of the dominating Continental power was repelled at the peak of its ascendancy. But this time the aggressor paid a higher price for his *hubris* than ever before. In spite of their failures, Philip II and Louis XIV had been able to maintain, on the Continent, a strong position vis-à-vis the naval powers. The outcome of the Napoleonic Wars forced the vanquished to a much lower level, and even more so the outcome of World War I. In 1945, the losers lost their political existence and saw their physical existence imperiled.

More than that. If we ask ourselves whether the old Continent might ever again give birth to a new struggle for supremacy, we cannot make an affirmative answer. Today it seems to us that the great game of the modern era, which kept Europe, and ultimately the world, breathless with suspense, has been played to a finish.

This becomes abundantly clear if, while observing the fate of the dominant power, we examine what happened to the perennial antagonist of any such power, the European system of states. Doubtless, it experienced a last triumph as it helped once more to prevent one of its members from suppressing the freedom of the others. But this triumph cost the system its life, just as the Reich, the assailant, paid for its defeat with its existence. It was as if two men fighting a duel had run each other through at the same moment.

I have stressed again and again how the old system of states paid for its freedom by increasing indebtedness to the young outer territories in the west and the east. The balance of power in the Occident was preserved only because new counterweights from territories beyond its frontiers could again and again be thrown into the scale against forces seeking supremacy. But even in World War I, the proportion of actual Western forces to those from outside the Occident shifted emphatically in favor of the latter. In World War II, the forces that had left Europe in successive emigrations—and which, thanks to the lightning spread of civilization in the vast expanses of the new territories, had grown to enormous economic and political power—unexpectedly turned back toward the region from which they had come, just as an echo unexpectedly returns to the mountain climber whose call has touched it off.

The old pluralistic system of small states was completely overshadowed by the giant young powers which it had summoned to its aid, being less able than ever before to defend itself. France, for centuries the Continent's land of destiny, which had so long withstood the Kaiser's attacks, collapsed before Hitler's onslaught as if felled by a stroke. In the age of the aircraft engine, the safety of Britain's insular stronghold hung by a hair. To be sure, the island nation once more played out its old role with great poise. But what would its fate have been if the great daughter nation had not taken up station at its side? Not until victory was won did the magnitude of Britain's exhaustion become apparent. To a far greater extent than World War I, World War II had eaten into the marrow of her financial and industrial position in the world.

The United States moved in to take over the evacuated positions, as Britain herself had done in the case of those vacated by Holland. The great role of intermediary between two worlds, to which Britain owed her greatness, melted away. The world overseas emancipated itself from her mediation. Colonial possessions of immense value slipped from her enfeebled hands. As the old Continent passed into decline, its fate cast a deep shadow over the island, now seemingly closer to it.

The European states, on their own, had been unable to contribute decisively toward their liberation from the German yoke. They derived no fresh impetus from the liberation. Previously a battlefield for foreign armies, they now became a battleground for foreign diplomacy. This time the European states were unable to re-erect their free system. They broke up into two groups, each assigned as a sphere of interest to one of the giant world powers. This division into a Western and an Eastern sphere had been in the making since the eighteenth century, but had now acquired a fresh meaning: loss of independence. The European volcanoes collapsed on themselves.

None of the European states, except Britain, any longer possesses full sovereignty in the old style. This may open up a possibility of limiting the process of division, but it would be limited at the behest of the two world giants, not voluntarily. The character *indelebilis* of the Continent faded only when its life force was spent.

Thus the old framework that had encompassed the European scene—the center of the entire world until 1945

—is breaking up. The narrower stage is losing its overriding importance as a setting for a strong cast of its own, and is being absorbed into the broader proscenium. On both stages the two world giants are taking over the protagonists' roles.

Will a new pattern with a promise of permanence take the place of the one now crumbling, a pattern whose vitality survived four and a half centuries and six great crises? Will the last struggle for hegemony result in a peace settlement which, like those negotiated up to and including the Congress of Vienna, will end the tension, or, like the treaties of 1919, at least allow us to hope for such a *détente?* To pose the question is tantamount to answering it in the negative. A divided system of states reverts again and again to a condition of flux. But the old European tendency toward division is now being thrust aside by the new global trend toward unification. And the onrush of this trend may not come to rest until it has asserted itself throughout our planet.

The global order still seems to be going through its birth pangs. The world has reached only the state of bisection which was foreseen by Seeley. For the moment, the refurbished League of Nations, whatever its role in the more distant future may be, can do nothing to change this state of affairs. For, after the final disappearance of the old European problem of supremacy, the more recent global problem of the Anglo-Russian conflict, which today is a conflict between Russia and the English-speaking countries, automatically moves into the foreground. Already discernible in the early eighteenth century, this problem held the eyes of the world from 1815 throughout the nineteenth century. It did not, however, touch off the expected world conflagration; in a wide and unorganized world, the two rivals still found room enough for expansion. A vigorous European continent lay between them and claimed their constant attention. Necessity brought them together as Germany began menacing them both, just as Russia and the United States found themselves coupled in Asia by common resistance to a rising Japan. Today, these retarding factors have lost their force. With the last tempest barely over, a new one is gathering. The shrinking of distance resulting from civilization moves hand in hand with a shrinking of time; every invention accelerates the speed of events. Once again, the continental and insular principles are face to face, stripped down to their essence and at the same time magnified to global proportions. On the one side, Russia, the successor of the great European continental powers of earlier centuries, growing, out of their tradition, to global status; on the other, the United States, spreading her influence through the world on the foundation of the European insular tradition.

A special dispensation of Providence enabled this insular principle, increasingly upheld by a single ethnic strain, to develop from the most modest beginnings to its present stature. Having so often smashed the dominance of others in Europe, it is now itself staking out a claim to supremacy in the world. Yet, in the atmosphere of a tempered struggle for political existence and despite its alliance with a technological civilization, the insular principle is not losing its basic element—a free and flexible humane spirit.

By contrast, what a malevolent twist of fate caused the continental principle, in all its puissant national manifestations, to suffer defeat after defeat, until a relentless struggle for existence hammered it into a rigid, depersonalized state machine!

But let us beware of using the record of earlier conflicts between the two principles to draw conclusions about the outcome of any future trial of strength. The peculiar mechanism of European history is unmatched anywhere else in the world. Today, the two contenders are faced with dangers and hopes of a new kind. Let us, above all, be wary of making projections into the future based on lines that are emerging at this moment. Let us not forget that, in the mad rush of events, the clouds now darkening the sky may be dissipated by unexpected developments. Indeed, it would be presumptuous to predict the roads and byways by which the trend toward the unification of this daily shrinking globe might reach its goal. Only one thing is certain: it will not abandon that goal, unless a miracle happens and men everywhere suffer a simultaneous change of heart; unless they leave the road of civilization and power struggles, on which, lured or lashed by a rampant will to live, they are now plunging forward headlong, in dread or triumph.

# EPILOGUE

## (1960)

My STUDY has dealt with a structure that has ceased to exist; it is, in a manner of speaking, the result of an autopsy. Observations on the new global system that has taken shape since 1945—and the manner in which it will evolve is still uncertain—cannot represent more than the diagnostic examination of a living body. Any such examination involves imponderables. It can be based only on today's findings, and designed only for today's use. This Epilogue should, therefore, be read as an addendum *sui generis*, not as an organic extension of the foregoing study.

How will the old conflict between the insular and continental principles develop in the context of the world's new division into two blocs? The great divide of 1945 has invalidated all earlier experience. All the same, on the assumption that civilization grows at a constant rate, a tendency toward global unity seemed discernible. But how has the new situation, with its open possibilities, actually progressed?

To lay the groundwork for an answer, we must look at the world as it was when the fires of the last struggle for supremacy in the old European style were dying. In order to avoid confusion amid the welter of events, I propose to climb to the highest lookout points, the Russian and the Anglo-American peaks of power.

Let us take the Anglo-American viewpoint first.

At the end of the last struggle, as in all the great crises of the system during the past four centuries, sea power emerged as the most potent force. In fact, it towered higher than ever before above the forces of the old European continent. But even then, one of its supports was the new, the American, continent.

Naval power stood forth as a phenomenon probably unparalleled in the entire course of world history. Where could an analogy be found to match its uninterrupted rise in recent centuries? Of course, there have been other ages in which sea power achieved prominence, and other places where it evolved from a favored geographical situation of insular character. But never before had such a rise been assisted by events comparable in importance to the discoveries that were made on the threshold of the modern age. Only by gradual exploitation of these discoveries, from a secure insular position, did modern sea power in all its aspects achieve its unprecedented development. Only by this means was it repeatedly able to gain the upper hand in grand contests of policy. Only thus did it finally grow into the giant tree whose branches bore the fruits of fortune in such variety and abundance. In 1945 all the attributes of sea power were displayed in incomparable splendor. As we proceed to list them in loose sequence, we must nevertheless keep in mind their deeply rooted kinship.

Let us examine insularity, in peril in Britain for short periods, but never in the United States. In World War II, the heart of the leading Anglo-Saxon power beat even more serenely than had Britain's in Napoleon's time. The United States was threatened neither from the sea nor from the air. The eldest offspring of insularity—sea power, with all its blessings for merchant shipping and sea-borne trade—had become a monopoly of the English-speaking peoples in an even more drastic sense of the phrase than after Trafalgar. The exploitation of discoveries, operating reciprocally with the insular position, had enhanced the opportunities of sea power; this exploitation, too, had developed into a near monopoly of the English-speaking peoples, embracing the oceans as well as the Mediterranean, the sea-girt continents of America, Africa, and Australia, together with the Atlantic coasts of Europe and Asia and the richest of their hinterlands deep in the Eurasian interior. In short, sea power controlled most of the globe. It controlled almost all of the former colonial world. No wonder, then, that its industrial, technical, and financial potential, springing from the same sources, had grown to an extent that beggared comparison. This potential was applied with particular vigor in the field of technological warfare. It added almost absolute air supremacy to supremacy at sea, outclassed the enemy in the field of production, and inspired unprecedented improvisations in amphibious warfare which combined a maximum of striking power against the continental enemy with a minimum of continental operations on the part of the naval powers themselves. All this had its effects in the diplomatic field. It made possible the organization, in insular style, of the greatest coalition the world had ever seen. And, again, it was the free spirit of humanity that had brought about these achievements. The shield of insularity had helped for centuries to maintain and protect this spirit, which, against the dark background of totalitarian inhumanity, again assured the English-speaking peoples, though sore beset, of the nimbus of humanity. Only the use of the atom bomb marred their record.

No matter how many mistakes the naval powers may have made before and during the war, nor how many defeats they suffered, in the end they again became the conductors of the orchestra of war—thanks to the advantages the gods had conferred upon them ever since the sixteenth century.

But the problems left unsolved after World War I reappeared, in sharpened outline, at the end of World War II. If the victors were not to lose the peace, these problems had to be mastered. Doubtless, Europe was no longer the center, and its system no longer the main structure, of world politics. A gaping vacuum had taken the place of both. The task of filling this vacuum, and of bringing order to the world, had not devolved upon the leading naval power as the fruit of planned initiative. At the height of success, which had been gained somnambulistically, as it were, and at small cost, the United States became conscious of her mission to heal the world's sufferings with the aid of the spiritual and material strength she had lately demonstrated. In other words, the United States became aware of the need for her to complete Wilson's work, or rather to rebuild what he had had to leave behind in ruins. The "One World" of the United Nations was to be the blessing bestowed upon mankind by the American century. The world-wide reign of peaceful democracy would prevent a recurrence of power politics and all its horrors. This seemed to be the logical

conclusion to modern history, and at the same time its conciliatory crowning feature. As the sun disperses mist, so
common sense would wipe away doubts and resistance. The
example of fortunate America, her generosity born of abundance, would replace domination, oppression, exploitation,
Bolshevism, and colonialism with the spirit of free co-
operation. New exertions in the field of power politics,
which became necessary after disarmament had been carried out with typically insular haste, were regarded as ab-
normal, passing expedients; they were contrary to the country's own character. In defiance of all disappointments, the
hope would not die that democratic good sense—the product of a long and happy history to which defeat was practically unknown—might have a strong appeal for the world.

As this hope became more and more clouded, memories
of the events after 1918 grew more and more vivid. Once
again, the alien spirit of continental power politics was bar-
ring the path to a democratic world order. But this time, it
sprang, not from the territory of old Europe, but, the more
threateningly, from the depths of Eurasia.

Let us now observe the scene from the Russian position.

In World War II, Russia was as little on a par with the
leading naval power as she had been in World War I, or, for
that matter, even in the Napoleonic era. Her technical resources proved inadequate, and once again her very heart
was threatened. What would have become of her without
the aid of the allies she so detested? She paid for this aid
with a sacrifice in blood twenty times greater than theirs.
She sullenly accepted the role of "Continental sword,"
though an intractable one. Out of consideration for her
democratic allies, she even masked her Bolshevik counte-
nance.

Compared with the position held by her allies at the

end of the war, Russia's own gains could in no sense be called overwhelming. Her advance into the European continent was saddled with inter-allied agreements which, honestly implemented by her, would have prevented the Bolshevization of today's satellites; she had gained access neither to the North Sea nor to the open waters of the Mediterranean; and the Manchurian harbors which the United States had precipitately yielded to Russia lay in the shadow of nearby American air bases. As at the time of Alexander I, Russia, under Stalin, seemed to have been left in her strait jacket—proof that the Anglo-Saxon nations held the whip hand.

However, even before the end of the war, a number of ruthless actions on Russia's part had heralded the turnabout which was to become manifest in the cold war. Victor No. 2 gained ground on Victor No. 1. Today, he has hopes of leaving him behind.

How could this happen? A comparison of the apparently paradoxical developments after 1945 with those of the postwar periods that had followed previous struggles for supremacy may help us understand the most obvious reasons. Earlier, the insular peoples had lent permanence to their successes by restoring the balance of power in peace settlements of great scope; they had not only prevented a recovery on the part of the dominant power among the defeated, but also blocked the pretensions of the most powerful nation among their own allies. This time, the mechanism of the European balance of power had been totally destroyed, and a settlement depended upon the good will of the great ally, Russia. But what counterweight was there to put Russia in a mood for compromise, now that Germany was stripped of power, Western Europe exhausted, Japan smashed, and the Chinese engaged in internecine strife? In

274

effect, this state of affairs gained for Russia's conventional army a monopoly throughout Eurasia; and to that extent, the triumph of sea power had benefited the great land power. Although Russia thus did not stand in need of peace treaties, she was nevertheless anxious, in her exhaustion, to put an end to war. So she risked a third course, one that no nation had ever attempted before—unceasing "cold war." She set out to wear down her opponents by every means at her disposal, while denying them, through her own armaments, the opportunity of resorting to hot war. In fact, Russia herself did not want to fight, however often she might threaten war in the course of her tactics of attrition.

These tactics were assisted by the fact that technology, which had for so long smiled on naval power, now transferred its favors to land power. Hitler's dream began to come true. What a twist of fortune! The free society of the insular peoples had only recently proved its mastery of technology; by means of technology, it had succeeded in opening up the giant American continent; indeed, this society as such was based on a form of technology, the technology of the sea. However, Bolshevism was, in an entirely different fashion, no less geared to technology. To achieve mastery of it through its own, totalitarian means was the very heart and core of its thought.

Communist world domination at the expense of the naval powers was to be brought about, in economic terms, by means of a highly organized global factory, as it were; the technological development of the Russian continent was to be the first step on that road. This latter experiment, the object of so much doubt before the war, succeeded as soon as Russia could breathe more freely—and at a pace that silenced all doubts. This success was achieved at the expense of countless human lives, the living standards of the entire population, and the right of all to individuality. The objective of all these exertions was to increase the war potential of the state, not its citizens' welfare. While Russia was tightening her grip on her sword, the English-speaking peoples allowed theirs to slip to the ground. Russia's enormous conventional armament was supplemented by an array of superweapons which is showing signs of outstripping those of her opponents. No longer was mere quantity aimed at, but also quality; original inventions must take the place of mere imitation, and scientific research pave the way for practical application. In other words, Russia succeeded in penetrating the apparently impregnable domains of the free societies. For one thing, she challenged Western air superiority, which had determined the outcome of the war. Indeed, the Russians jumped into the lead at the start of the battle for outer space, and thus, retroactively, lent symbolic (and not only symbolic) support to their claim to global pre-eminence. A new era of discovery was launched, and this time it was launched from the continental mainland. A totalitarian technological civilization challenged the technology of the ancient, free, cultural world which had sired it.

At the same time, these successes lent wings to the expansion of Communism, which arrogantly showed its true face again. Unassailable both militarily and economically, Communism manipulated the cold war to further its expansion, with world domination as its long-range objective.

In Europe, it is true, that expansion succeeded only where the Red Army was ready to hand—even though Europe had itself given birth to Communism. As a missionary doctrine, Russian Communism achieved its first striking success among the colored peoples in the huge colonial and semi-colonial areas which had appeared on the world stage in 1945 as a factor of global importance. More than anything else, it contested with the West the fruits of its victory. There had, of course, been earlier movements for emancipation among the colored races, particularly after World War I had lowered their masters' power and prestige and had given birth to Communism. But these earlier endeavors had been unable to unite in a single stream. They had been kept apart by the frictions in Europe, which determined world politics; in both wars, colored people had fought on opposing sides. Since 1945, the pluralistic system of states has been reduced to a world of two blocs, and the underprivileged colored peoples now face only two centers of power. Can they, on the whole, feel any doubt about their preference? All their demands in the area of foreign policy are claims on the ruling white races, and since 1917 Russia has not been one of these. Nor has the United States, particularly since the Philippines were given autonomy; but for all her deeply rooted anti-colonialism, the United States cannot fully detach herself from the colonial powers, her European allies. The role of championing the demands of the colored peoples has fallen to proletarian Russia. Moreover, she is widely viewed as a model by these backward peoples, who are impatient to forge the economic and military weapons which will enable them to rise from their inferior status. They readily accept fraternal help from proletarian Russian preceptors. To former colonials, Western concepts of the liberty of the individual are nothing but sound and fury, the unattainable Western living standard only an irritant. Of course, the price they pay for accepting Soviet aid is the risk that their own ancient cultures, in all their diversity, will be smothered by a monotonous European civilization in Communist garb; moreover, social up-heaval inevitably accompanies industrialization, which is the prerequisite for national emancipation.

These interlocking factors, paradoxical and yet so logi-cal, were demonstrated on the greatest possible scale and with the utmost consistency in China. The Chinese revolu-tion was soon followed by the pronunciamento of Bandung, which proclaimed to the world the solidarity of all colored races. The self-assurance of these peoples vis-à-vis the white man has undergone a radical change; anti-Western resent-ment has spread among them like subsoil water, which, though found at different depths in different locations, nevertheless exists everywhere. Feelings of inferiority have been reduced to a common denominator, in Asia, in Africa, and even in Latin America.

Although this general emancipation as a political and psychological phenomenon is undoubtedly interwoven with the rise of Communism, and in one way or another pro-motes the spreading of it, the new self-assurance may in certain cases nevertheless turn against Russian efforts at domination. Nations just awakening to independence have no desire to exchange a Western master for a Russian ruler. The old animosities of countries that have been threat-ened by Russia live on. Men and classes in power dread Red revolution; religious communities fear Communist atheism. Moreover, altered Western attitudes are healing many wounds. The West, after all, is interested in ensuring that the inevitable emancipation of these peoples produces strong and independent states, not satellites of Moscow or Peiping. To that extent, the interests of yesterday's Western masters and of today's emancipated nations coincide, and they may even lead to co-operation. Might not this process soften the cold war and bring about the *détente* so ardently desired by the West? In other words, might not the appearance of a third force change the two-bloc world into a world system? And might not the existence of such a system strengthen the United Nations, an organization torn today by the very conflicts it was set up to overcome, and turn it into a conciliatory superior forum?

It would, of course, be presumptuous to answer this fateful question, let alone generalize about it. Individual peculiarities have not been sufficiently weakened by the world-wide tendencies toward homogeneity. Too many imponderables are at work within the two giant powers, as well as among the colored peoples, and fluctuations in the prestige of the two countries will influence the trend of events.

It may be appropriate to recall how similar hopes for the emergence of a "third force," and the replacement of the European system by a genuine world system, were nullified shortly before 1914. In those days, German imperialists dreamed of enlisting powers outside Europe, including colored peoples, to bring relief to the Reich in its rivalry with Britain. But even at that time, this hope for a world system on the lines of the European system proved to be vain. The European system owed its durability, above all, to the unique role of modern sea power and its repeatedly proven ability to preserve the plurality of states in Europe by making use of a special conjunction of geographical and historical circumstances. But how can a multiple grouping of world states conceivably be supported from outside in the framework of a finite globe? Moreover, those emancipated nations—which, thanks to the immense populations they bring into play, provide the focus of hope for a "third force"—are themselves involved in a turmoil of early evolution; and anti-colonialism is the one thing that breathes life into their loose and disjointed structures. How can countries of such origin take up a middle position between the two giants? How can they fail to lean toward Soviet Russia? How can these states, themselves constantly disturbed by hasty industrial and social changes, consolidate their foreign policies and become effective as independent forces?

If, however, the world remains divided into two blocs, Communism's position of advantage in the territories of the colored peoples will persist. The Kremlin holds the ostensible trump cards—the overexcited, anti-colonial nationalism and the social unrest it stirs up. With these two assets, the Soviet Union can outmaneuver the West even in the face of America's generous foreign aid. The trend of events in Asia and Africa is only too clear; and the same may soon apply to developments in strife-ridden Latin America, that old Achilles' heel of the United States, where even today the Monroe Doctrine and the safety of the Panama Canal no longer seem assured. If China is taken into account, the majority of the world's population is involved in this process, a majority with a much faster rate of growth than that of the West.

What a shift these changes have produced since 1945 in the power relationship between the two world rivals! Our earth has become so crowded and small that neither can expand without making the other shrink. Each of them shapes the other. World War II's No. 1 Victor has at times lost the initiative to Victor No. 2 and, despite all his defensive efforts, continually faces the danger of losing the cold war imposed upon him by his adversary. His sanguine conception of democracy's world mission has tended to agree but little with everyday reality.

Let us consider the role of sea power in modern history

before 1945 as a background for a clearer assessment of the changes that have taken place. In this way we may be able to penetrate the surface of contemporary happenings and reach their common roots, thus facilitating a summing up.

What has become of the insularity of the English-speaking peoples? Even the insularity of the United States is gravely menaced, and, leaving aside the threat posed by such new means of delivery as rocket-carrying submarines, the sea has begun to lose its importance as a protective belt; the techniques of aircraft and rockets, which soar above ships and oceans to hurl doom upon any island, are superseding the techniques of sea power. In fact, we have seen the great continental power contesting the leading naval power's mastery of these modern techniques. This does not mean that the English-speaking peoples are about to be robbed of their defenses. But the enormous advantages of their geographical position seem to have been greatly reduced; the gods, who for centuries gave them those advantages, seem to be whittling them down. Similarly, the commercial importance of sea communications appears to be declining with the swift improvement of overland communications. Moreover, these changes cannot fail to affect the entire way of life of the maritime peoples, a pattern molded by the conditions of insular existence.

This applies particularly to the exploitation of discoveries, for which command of the sea from a secure island position was the decisive prerequisite. Both are now being challenged. The more brittle the strategic situation of the white rulers, the more rapidly the general emancipation of colored peoples will spread. One oceanic region after another is slipping from the hands of the naval powers and their allies. The strength with which they once clasped their continental adversaries in a throttling grip is dwindling. It is no longer they who do the clasping; they, in their turn, now must fear the clasp. No longer is the insular security of the United States exposed to danger only at long range; soon such threats may come from nearby Latin America.

Naturally, this swing of the pendulum—this reversal of the strategic situation—is making itself felt in matters of industrial, technical, and financial potential. The Anglo-Saxon nations are losing ground in these fields to the opposing camp. No longer do they threaten to outclass their enemies in production; it is they themselves who are threatened. Most perilous of all, the shift in the field of technology has an alarmingly direct and immediate impact on strategic realities. But all the phenomena I have listed are, in actuality, interrelated and must be looked at as a whole. Fading leaves signal a general change in a plant's condition.

Obviously, this change shows itself daily in the diplomatic field. Prior to 1945, the island nations, with mastery of the oceans as the backbone of their policies, had always been able to forge, with all the assurance of inherited wisdom, those great coalitions that encircled their continental opponents. Today, their control of the seas has been weakened, and opponents of limited stature, such as had been fenced in on the old Continent by rivals of comparable size, have been replaced by a power of a quite different order, without rival in the whole of Eurasia. That power is, moreover, rapidly growing in domestic and external strength. The United States has spared neither effort nor sacrifice to implement a policy of containment. But this policy has not been functioning satisfactorily in the colonial and semi-colonial areas. Dams are scarcely erected before the Red flood surges against them or infiltrates them. No *cordon sanitaire* can prevent the Red cancer from erupting, in metastases, at remote points in the previously healthy tissue.

The picture is, of course, radically different in free Europe. There the Anglo-Saxon nations can seek recompense for the losses they have suffered in the oceanic regions and the territories of the colored peoples. The great divide of 1945, which robbed the English-speaking peoples of long-standing opportunities, also presented them with new ones. It was this new situation that forced them to make a virtue of necessity; for, viewed against the isolationist tendencies of sea power, it was necessity, in the shape of the cold war, that prevented the Anglo-American powers from withdrawing, once more, from Western Europe. As the young American nation zestfully shouldered the unexpected task of safeguarding its way of life and its existence by holding its shield over the old nations from which it had sprung, it indeed made a virtue of that necessity. It is true that the naval powers had always joined forces with Continental states whenever a dominant power threatened them all. But those alliances had never outlived the overthrow of the dominant power. The permanent state of cold war enforced a permanent alliance; indeed, it was almost the foundation of a new federation of states, a European integration embedded in an Atlantic integration. The downfall of the European system of states, a negative process, produced a positive result—the Atlantic *orbis terrarum,* an enlarged Occident, an entity united in its destinies. Up to and into the era of the two World Wars, the nations of the West felt powerful enough to think of nothing but individual expansion and to contend for it among themselves. Now, for the first time in their modern history, they feel sufficiently menaced to turn their thoughts to a concentration of strength, to solidarity, to the construction of a common defensive position.

This development has shifted the elements of the *raison d'état* of all countries within this new *orbis terrarum*—most strikingly in that of the leading state. In both World Wars, the United States held strictly to the policies of an insular naval power. Today she has adopted a different policy, which, like the whole body of contemporary events, still eludes definition in terms of current usage. Future observers are likely to admire the speed with which American public opinion underwent this fundamental change of outlook. Its most trying tests may lie ahead; the will-o'-the-wisp of yesterday's isolationism may still return often enough to glow seductively in the darkness. How difficult it is for a victorious nation to realize that its own victory has shattered the world-wide foundations of its aloof and affluent earlier existence! How hard it is for such a nation to appreciate the fact that the spasmodic improvisations of the past must be replaced with permanent exertions, systematically increased, and that the perils threatening insular existence implicitly menace the American way of life!

However, the European allies of the United States, though saved by her intervention, find it even more difficult to realize the gravity of the transformation that has taken place. They are old and they are patrician, and they have come down in the world. They are weighed down by special problems—such as German reunification—that are as difficult to push aside as to solve. How much can America do to help settle them? The collapse of the European system of states, which has undermined the sovereignty of the Continental nations, has made them dependent upon transatlantic backing. Exhausted, their time-honored political ethos has been thrown into confusion, and a new one is being only hesitantly pieced together. All the less easy is it for them to adopt an attitude of lofty impartiality toward the social tensions which the permanent socio-economic revolution is producing everywhere and which hinder a clear-cut decision between East and West. Resentments going back to the days of the system of states—in particular, memories of the frightful conduct of the Germans in their pursuit of world dominance—exert a similar influence on European feelings. There is no need to detail the opportunities that such factors of weakness present to the ingenious tactics of the Communists, nor to emphasize the defensive strength that the Western world has shown in a series of different groupings.

And Britain? She experienced the great divide of 1945 in a mitigated form, but nevertheless with bewildering effects. In spite of her victory, they have cut deeply into the fabric of her life and that of the Commonwealth. Nor has Britain's political ethos, the most firmly rooted in Europe, escaped these effects. There, too, social tensions have grown beyond anything that could have been imagined in the periods of secure insular life. And even there, in that old citadel of the libertarian outlook, the decision between East and West is not an easy one; to the nation that found itself all but exhausted at the end of the war, the memory of yesterday's threat to freedom by totalitarian Germany clouds the view of the threat to freedom posed by totalitarian Russia today.

Amid the turmoil of constantly changing events, my observations are certainly inadequate for even a fleeting *tour d'horizon*. But looked at against the background of the interplay of powers before 1945, they may nevertheless suffice to make us conscious of the different nature of those relationships today and their characteristic effect upon every single phenomenon of present-day life. Do not leaves stirring in a breeze provide evidence of the basic structure of a tree?

Even as I was writing this study of the history of power relationships, the insular-continental "dualism" of the postwar world was clearly discernible. Is this global "dualism" developing, as did European pluralism before it, along the lines of a spiral shaped primarily by the conflict between the insular and continental principles? Is the insular principle once more gaining the upper hand?

It almost seemed so in the immediate postwar period. But even then I felt obliged to warn my readers against the temptation to apply earlier experience to the new situation. "The peculiar mechanism of European history," I said then, "is unmatched anywhere else in the world."

As it is, all my observations converge in the conjecture that a broad and deep current in world politics has begun to favor the continental principle, and that the much-discussed decline of the West might move out of the realm of speculation into that of reality. For a decline of the island peoples, the last guarantors of Occidental culture, could not fail to result in a decline of the whole area of the enlarged Occident.

Of course, it would be rash to prophesy. The historian, a "backward-looking prophet," must know, more than other men, that the future is incalculable.

Even ocean currents can divide or alter course. But for the West to ponder the nebulous possibilities of chance relief would be a perilous pastime. The free world must think only of its own efforts: *aide-toi, le ciel t'aidera!*

Although the English-speaking nations can no longer rely upon the trump cards they held for so long, they have by no means lost the game. But it cannot be won without patience and the kind of prolonged, systematic effort that the West was spared in the past. No longer can final victory be counted upon to follow initial setbacks; the first battle may be the last.

But must the decision be brought about by war, simply because past decisions were made on the battlefield? Is not the nightmare that weighs upon us—a third world war—the product of experience in an earlier epoch unthinkingly applied to the present?

To answer this question in the affirmative, and to ignore the need to prepare for the worst, would be a dangerous error. On the contrary, now as never before we must keep our eyes trained on the *ultima ratio regum* as the determining factor in all our exertions, and thrust aside the easy-going ways of yesterday. How else can we hope to withstand blackmailing threats which in the age of superweapons may bring about decisions without the firing of a single shot?

In our affluent society, hectic demands for greater affluence, unless held in check by an awareness of the deadly peril menacing the society as a whole, become a danger in themselves. On a listing luxury liner, would it not be senseless to fight for the best accommodations instead of rushing to the pumps? Dangerous, too, is our stultifying mass luxury; dangerous the insatiable materialism that impels us to pursue it and at the same time erodes faith—the foundation of man's dignity and his freedom. Not the least of the dangers comes from the outdated attitude of pacifism, a well-nigh mathematical formula for suicide in the face of our adversary's terrorism.

Such tendencies might not only spread through the

battle-weary old Continent but also reach the undefeated and, on the whole, far more youthful island world. Leadership has fallen upon the shoulders of the United States. She cannot relinquish it without sealing the doom of the entire free world, together with her own. An action that had serious consequences in 1919 would today be fatal. A strong America, on the other hand, an America that holds high the banner of freedom, inspires the energies of her allies and can move them to overcome their own conflicts.

If these allies saw only technical parity restored, a nightmare would be lifted from them and the prestige of the West would at the same time rise again in the eyes of the colored peoples. Technical parity would drive away the lowering clouds of war and create the prerequisite for honest disarmament and coexistence (in the true sense) within a peaceful world order.

The technological developments of our time cannot but lead to such a world order. It is bearing down upon us, whether we like the prospect or not. Today's two blocs will merge into a single entity. God grant that in it there may be a secure place for human ideals as understood in the West. God grant that the world of Western culture may not suffer the fate of the ancient world when the cry of *"panem et circenses"* could still be heard even as the barbarians, thirsting for plunder, burst into the *limes*. Schopenhauer once said that freedom, like health, is appreciated only after it has been lost. His words must not be borne out.

# CHRONOLOGICAL TABLE

### CHAPTER I

*ORIGIN OF THE SYSTEM OF STATES;*
*CHARLES V*

1492    Conquest of Granada and expulsion of the Moors from Spain. Columbus's first voyage.

1494    Charles VIII of France invades Italy. Beginning of the struggle for the Italian peninsula between France, Spain, and the Emperor.
Treaty of Tordesillas. Division of the colonial world between Spain and Portugal.

1508    League of Cambrai.

1517    Luther's 95 Theses against Indulgences.

1519    Charles V elected Emperor.

1526    Bohemia and Hungary pass under Habsburg rule.

1527    Sack of Rome.

1547    Charles V defeats the Protestants at Mühlberg.

1552    Maurice of Saxony revolts against the Emperor.
France acquires the bishoprics of Metz, Toul, and Verdun.

1556    German-Spanish division of the Habsburg possessions.

1558    Death of Charles V.

## PHILIP II

1554    Marriage of Mary the Catholic of England to Philip of Spain.

1556    Accession of Philip II.

1558    Accession of Elizabeth of England.

1559    Peace of Cateau-Cambrésis; Spain retains Italy and Burgundy.

1562    Outbreak of the French Wars of Religion.

1566–
1572    Pope Pius V. The Counter Reformation at its height.

1572    Outbreak of the Revolt of the Netherlands. William the Silent, Prince of Orange, Stadholder.

1580    Portugal united with Spain.

1584    Murder of William the Silent.

1587    Mary, Queen of Scots, beheaded.

1588    Defeat of the Spanish Armada.

## CHAPTER II

### THE SYSTEM OF STATES UP TO THE ASSUMPTION OF PERSONAL POWER BY LOUIS XIV IN 1661

1618    Outbreak of the Thirty Years' War.

1629    Holy Roman Emperor at the height of his power.

1630    Countermoves by France and Sweden begin.

1640    Portugal breaks away from Spain.

1642    Outbreak of the English Civil War.

1648    Peace of Westphalia.

1649    Execution of Charles I of Britain. Cromwell.

1652–   First Naval War between Britain and Holland.

1654    The Dutch recognize the First Navigation Act.

1660    Restoration in Britain under Charles II.

## LOUIS XIV

| | |
|---|---|
| 1661 | Louis XIV assumes personal power. |
| 1667–1668 | War of Devolution, launched by Louis XIV against Spain in the Netherlands. |
| 1670 | Secret agreement between Louis XIV and Charles II against Holland. |
| 1672–1678 | Second War, waged by France against Holland, Spain, and the Empire. |
| 1672–1674 | Second Naval War between Britain and Holland. |
| 1680–1682 | French colonial empire in North America from Quebec to the mouth of the Mississippi. |
| 1681 | Strasbourg becomes French. |
| 1683 | Vienna besieged by the Turks. |
| 1688 | The Glorious Revolution. |
| 1688–1697 | Third War (War of the League of Augsburg). |
| 1692 | Defeat of the French fleet at La Hogue. |
| 1710–1714 | War of the Spanish Succession. |
| 1710 | Fall of the pro-war Ministry in Britain. |
| 1713 | Peace of Utrecht between France and the naval powers. |
| 1714 | Peace of Rastatt between France and Charles VI and the Holy Roman Empire. |

## CHAPTER III

### THE THREE "WORLD POWERS" UP TO THE FRENCH REVOLUTION

| | |
|---|---|
| 1689–1725 | Peter the Great. |
| 1700–1721 | The Northern War. |

| | |
|---|---|
| 1700 | Peter defeated by the Swedes at Narva. |
| 1709 | Peter defeats the Swedes at Poltava. |
| 1713–1740 | Frederick William I of Prussia. |
| 1720–1721 | Prussia acquires Western Pomerania from Sweden. |
| 1722–1725 | Peter's War against Persia; Baku becomes Russian. |
| 1733–1735 | War of the Polish Succession. Annexation of Lorraine to France assured. |
| 1736–1739 | Austria's hapless war against the Turks. |
| 1739–1741 | Britain at war with Spain in the West Indies. |
| 1740–1786 | Frederick the Great. |
| 1740–1742 | First Silesian War. |
| 1740–1748 | War of the Austrian Succession. |
| 1744–1745 | Second Silesian War. |
| 1755 | Britain attacks France at sea. |
| 1756 | Convention of Neutrality at Westminster between Britain and Prussia. Treaty of Versailles between Austria and France. |
| 1756–1763 | Seven Years' War, concluded by Treaty of Hubertusburg. |
| 1762 | Death of Elizabeth of Russia. Murder of her successor, Peter III. |
| 1762–1796 | Catherine the Great of Russia. |
| 1768–1774 | Russo-Turkish War. Mouth of the Dnieper and the Crimea annexed to Russia. |
| 1772 | First Partition of Poland. |
| 1775–1783 | American War of Independence. |

1778 Alliance between France and the United States.

1779 Short war between Austria and Prussia ends with Peace of Teschen.
Spain declares war on Britain.

1780 Russian-sponsored League of Armed Neutrality at sea.
War breaks out between Britain and Holland.

1788 Russia's relations with Britain and Prussia deteriorate.

## THE FRENCH REVOLUTION AND NAPOLEON I

1789 Outbreak of the French Revolution.

1792 France declares war on Austria.
The September Massacres.
Battle of Valmy.
Revolutionary propaganda abroad.

1793 Louis XVI executed.
Britain, at the head of the First Coalition, declares war on France.
Second Partition of Poland.

1794 Fall of Robespierre.

1795 Batavian Republic in Holland.
Third Partition of Poland.
Treaty of Basel between France and Prussia.

1796 Paul I succeeds Catherine the Great.

1797 Treaty of Campoformio between France and Austria.

1798 The Egyptian Expedition. Battle of Aboukir.

1798 Anglo-Russian Alliance.

1799 Outbreak of war between France and the Second Coalition.
Napoleon seizes power in the *coup d'état* of *Brumaire*.
Russia leaves the Coalition.

1801 Treaty of Lunéville.
Murder of Paul I.
Nelson's victory at Copenhagen.

1802 Peace of Amiens between Britain and France.

1803 War breaks out again.

1804 Camp at Boulogne.

1805    The Third Coalition.
        Napoleon victorious at Austerlitz.
        Destruction of his fleet at Trafalgar.

1806    Battle of Jena.
        Inauguration of the Continental System.

1807    Treaty of Tilsit.

1808    Insurrection in Spain.

1812    Napoleon's Russian Campaign.

1815    Congress of Vienna.


## CHAPTER IV

### THE CONFLICTS SHARPEN STEP BY STEP UNTIL THE POWERS REGROUP AT THE BEGINNING OF THE TWENTIETH CENTURY

1815    The Holy Alliance.
        The "Pentarchy" of the Great Powers.

1821    Absolute rule restored in Piedmont and Naples by Austria.

1823    Absolute rule restored in Spain by France.

ca.     Secession of the Latin-American colonies from their
1820    mother countries (Chile in 1816, Argentina in 1817, Brazil in 1822, Mexico in 1823, Peru in 1824).

1823    Monroe Doctrine.

1825    Nicholas I succeeds Alexander I as Tsar of Russia.
        The Decembrist Rising.

1828–   Russo-Turkish War.
1829

1830    July Revolution in France. Louis Philippe, the "Citizen King."
        Coburg monarchy in Belgium.

1830–   Polish Revolution.
1831

1848    February Revolution in France.
        Revolutions in Italy and Germany.

294

General Cavaignac puts down the rising of the Parisian workers in June.
Louis Napoleon elected President in December.

1849    Hungarian Revolution suppressed with Russian help.

1850    Britain, Russia, and France resolve to maintain the integrity of the Danish State.
The Punctation of Olmütz.

1852    Louis Napoleon Emperor.

1859    War for the Unification of Italy.

1861–
1865    American Civil War.

1862–
1867    Napoleon III's Mexican Expedition.

1864    Denmark's war against Prussia and Austria.

1866    Austro-Prussian War.

1870–
1871    Franco-Prussian War.

## THE QUESTION OF GERMAN SUPREMACY;
## WORLD WAR I

1868    Beginnings of the reform era in Japan.

1875    The "Is war in sight?" episode.

1877–
1878    Russo-Turkish War.

1878    Congress of Berlin.

1879    Alliance between Germany and Austria.

1881    France in Tunis.
Triple Alliance (Austria, Germany, Italy).
Social legislation in Germany.

1882    The British occupy Egypt.

1883–    German colonies.
France in Tonkin and Madagascar.

1888    William II.

1890    Fall of Bismarck.

1894    Franco-Russian Alliance.

1898    Fashoda; France yields to Britain.

1899–
1902     Boer War.

1900     Second German Navy Bill.

1901     Britain sounds out Germany on the possibility of an
         alliance.

1902     Berlin-Baghdad Railway.

1904     Anglo-French Entente.

1904–
1905     Russo-Japanese War. Peace of Portsmouth with United
         States as mediator.

1907     Anglo-Russian Entente.

1914     Era of the World Wars opens.

# INDEX

Aboukir, battle of, 153
Alaska Purchase, 238
Alexander I: action against Napoleon, 163; Treaty of Tilsit, 165–6; breakdown, 186
Alexander II, 227
America: discovery, 52; development of political will in the colonies, 116; control of New World by Britain, 116–17; migration of power to colonies, drive for freedom, 118; character of the colonies, 119–20; role of Europe in struggle for freedom, 120–1; freedom, 122; trade with England, push to the west, 122–3; trade with Continent, war with Britain, 175; Monroe Doctrine, 191–3; internal expansion, 192, 194; Anglo-American solidarity, 193–4, 237–9; Civil War, 208; thwarting of French try for Mexico, 209; consolidation and expansion, 239; intervention in World War I, 242; League of Nations, 243–4; posture after World War II, 271–3; epilogue, 284–8
Aragon, 31
Armada, Spanish: make-up, 55–6; defeat, 56–7
Austria. See Germany

Bismarck, Otto Eduard Leopold von: diplomatic technique, conflict with nationalism, 217–18; relations with Russia, 218–19, 227; relations with France and Britain, 219–20, 228; effect on Germany, 221–3; end of career, 228
Bolshevik Revolution, 251–3
Britain. See England

Canning, George, 191
Catherine the Great: removal of Peter II, foreign policy, 125; hatred for French Revolution, 144–5

Cavour, Camillo Benso di, 216
Charles I of England, 70
Charles V: election, 34; unifying tendency, 34–5; antagonism of the Papacy, 36–7; victory of the German princes, 38; Turkey as counterweight, 40–1. See also Habsburg, House of; Spain
Charles XII of Sweden, 104–5
Church: source of unification in Middle Ages, 19–20; effects of consolidation of the West, 20–1; assumption of political character, its effects, 21; transmission of Greco-Roman civilization, 22; militant Catholicism a unifying tendency in Counter Reformation, 36; alliance with Spain, effects of Counter Reformation, 45–6; break with Spain, renewal of ties with France, 61; relations with Napoleon I, 141–2
Civilization: defined, 9 n.; common denominator, 96; evolution in the West, 132–3; increasing effects, 183–5; outlet in revolutions and wars, 188, 198; expansion in the New World, 192; and freedom of a system of states, 193; the impact of technology, 194; as a unifying tendency, 234; epilogue, 269–88
Cluny Reform, 45
Coburg monarchy, 197
Colbert, Jean Baptiste, 73, 76
Columbus, Christopher, 52
Company of Merchant Adventurers, 53–4
Congress of Vienna, 177–8, 187
Continental System, 166–8
Counter Reformation: origin in the fall of Italian free states, 36; regaining of territory in Germany, consolidation of Spanish possessions on the Rhine, 44; threat to the British Isles, 45; and the Papacy, 45–6; unifying tendency, 45–6; role in the Netherlands, 49; role in England, 54; death of Mary Stuart, 55
Crimean War, 201, 204–5

i

Cromwell, Oliver: solving of domestic problems, 58–9, 66; author of British maritime imperialism, 70

Culture: defined, 9 n.; bearers of culture, in antiquity and in the West, 22

Decembrist Rising, 195

Demarcation, line of, 52

Divisive tendencies: role of Turkey, 41, 93–4; role of Russia, 41, 93–4, 111, 170, 237; role of England, 54, 60, 79, 111, 170, 206; role of Holland, 60; shifts in the balance of power, 72–3; rise of revolution and nationalism, 169–71, 184, 186–90, 195–9, 207, 227, 245–6; opposed by progress of civilization, 234. *See also* Power, balance of; Unifying tendencies

Drake, Sir Francis, 56, 57

East India Company, 152

Edict of Nantes, effect of revocation, 80, 146

Elizabeth I: encouragement of shipping trade, piloting of England to anti-Spanish leadership, 54; denial of support to war party, personal union with Scotland, 57–8

Enghien, Duc d', execution by Napoleon, 163

England: modified insularity, position in 1494, 29–30; Henry VIII, 39; origin of counterweight policy, inability to enact it, 39, 44–5; role of England in the system of states, 50; first voyages, under Italian tutelage, 53; private initiative in shipping, buccaneering, 53–4; role of Counter Reformation, 54; Elizabeth I, 54, 57–8; raids on Spanish ships, protection of Holland, death of Mary Stuart, 54–5; make-up of fleet opposing Armada, 56; Sir Francis Drake, 56, 57; Oliver Cromwell, domestic problems, 58–9, 66, 69, 70; competition with Holland, 66, 70–1; a world power, 71; Restoration, 71; alliance with Spain against Holland, 76–7; insistence of Parliament on peace, 78; ascension of William of Orange, the European coalition, 80; maritime character, final form, 80–1;

England (*continued*)
alliance with Holland, 81; defeat of French fleet at La Hogue, 81; role in War of Spanish Succession, 82–3; Duke of Marlborough, 83; break-up of European coalition, separate peace with Spain, penetration of the Mediterranean, 84–5; overseas expansion, 85–6; colony development, private initiative in emigration, 86–7; state of the colonies in the New World, 88–9; notice of Russian threat, 106–7; protection of Sweden, 107; at Peace of Utrecht, 107–8; Austria as ally, 108, 111, 113; English colonies battle French, 109–10; war with Spain and France, in New World and Old, 110; posture after first two Silesian Wars, 113, 114; colonies develop political will, drive for freedom, 116, 118; sole heir of Continental power in New World, 117–18; fall of Pitt, lack of island spirit in George III, 120; privateering destroyed, Continental alliance, 121–2; loss of American colonies, 121–2; hold on Canada, trade with free colonies, 122–3; attitude toward Russian progress, 126; revival of Anglo-Russian antagonism, 128; William Pitt (the younger), 128–9, 146, 158, 163; advance of civilization, role of the state, 134, 135; discovery of coal, Industrial Revolution, 134–5; rise in population, 135; alarm at expansion of French Revolution, 145–6; trade war against France, joining of industrial and maritime power, 148; India, 151–2; Nelson, 153, 157, 164; control of Mediterranean, role of Gibraltar, 153; defeat of French fleet at Aboukir, 153; alliance with Russia against France, 154; Russia breaks with Britain, joins Napoleon I, 156–7; defeat of Danish fleet, 157; Treaty of Amiens, 158–9; failure of invasion by France, 162; effect of victory at Trafalgar, 164; prosperity despite Continental System, 168–9; losses in Revolutionary and Napoleonic Wars, 169; posture after defeat of Napoleon, 174–5; unchallenged monopoly of sea power and trade, 174–5;

England (*continued*)
war with America, 175; support of France to balance Russia, 176–7; indifference to revolutionary trend and post-Napoleonic Restoration, 185–6; support of Iberian colonial insurgents, 190–1; Anglo-American solidarity, 193–4, 237–9; ties with July Monarchy, 197; social tensions, evolutionary solution, 198; Crimean War, 204–5; relations with Bismarck, 219–20; passing the zenith of power, 233–4, 238–9; view of Germany as prime danger, 234–6; Triple Entente, 236–7; decline, 264–5; epilogue, 285. *See also* Power, balance of; System of states

February Revolution of 1848, 198–201
First Coalition, 146–7
France: position in 1494, prototype of national power state, 28–9; alliance with the German princes, 38; alliance with the Grand Turk, 40, 41; religious civil war, 44, 61; conversion of Henry of Navarre, re-establishment of strong monarchy, 61, 68; external situation, internal resources, 72–3; Louis XIV, 72–8, 81–2, 84; Colbert, 73, 76; national spirit, first standing army, expansion overseas, 74; attack on Spanish Netherlands, checked by maritime-power diplomacy, 75–6; attack on interior of Continent, continuation of overseas expansion, 78; naval defeat at La Hogue, 81–2; War of the Spanish Succession, 82–3; decline, 82, 83; state of New World colonies, 87–9; role in War of Polish Succession, accession of Lorraine, 108; French colonies battle English, 109–10; war with England on the Continent, 110–11; attack on the Netherlands, 111; posture after first two Silesian Wars, 113; Canada, Louisiana, military planning, 116; lack of sea communications, fall of Quebec, loss of North American colonies, 116–17; loss of East Indies, West Indies salvaged, 117; rigidity of structure, rise of middle class, 135–6; the Revolu-

France (*continued*)
tion, 137; rhetoric, chaos, rise of a new power state, 137–8; role of Jacobins, 138–40; war and domestic dissension, 139–40; Reign of Terror, 140–1; Napoleon I, 141–3, 147–53, 156–8, 160–8, 171–2; revolutionary propaganda abroad, 142–3; background to Napoleon's struggle for supremacy, 143–4; revolution in land warfare, 144; war against Austria, 145; successes in Netherlands, 147; maritime weakness, 147, 150; successes in Germany and Italy, 148, 149; Treaty of Campoformio, 149; drive to Egypt, new attempt at colonization, 150–1; naval defeat at Aboukir, wreck of Egyptian expedition, 153; Treaty of Amiens, 158–9; public opinion and will of Napoleon, 159–60; renewal of expansion, naval rearmament, renewal of hostilities, 160–1; victories at Austerlitz and Jena, 163; naval defeat at Trafalgar, 164; collapse after defeat in Russia, decline, 172–3; restoration of Bourbon monarchy, favorable position, 176–7; national sense of humiliation, turn to industry, 188; motherland of nationalism, intellectual dominance, 189; July Revolution of 1830, 196–8; Louis Philippe, 198; February Revolution of 1848, 198–201; Crimean War, 201, 204–5; Napoleon III, 202–10; expansion in Mediterranean, Asia, Pacific, 207; failure of try for Mexico, 207–9; defeat in Germany, 209–10; Triple Entente, 236; encouragement of nationalism to keep Germany in check, 245–6
Frederick the Great: diplomatic character, 111–12; successes, his method, 112–13; failure to grasp importance of colonial struggle, 115

George III, 120
Germany: attitude toward the system of states, 10–13; position in 1494, state of flux and dynastic growth, 32–4; victory of the princes over Charles V, 38; rise of a system of states, 38, 67;

Germany (*continued*)
Maurice of Saxony, 41; Rudolf II, 44; rise of Prussian kingdom, 84; Austrian acquisition of Spanish Netherlands, Spanish lands in Italy, 84–5; Prussian acquisition of Swedish Pomerania, 106; Austria expelled from Italy by Spain, 108; Austria as ally of England, 108, 111, 113; War of Austrian Succession, 111; rise of Prussia, 111–13, 125, 155–6; Frederick the Great, 112–13, 115; posture after the first two Silesian Wars, 113, 115; posture after the Seven Years' War, 126; relations with Russia, 126–7, 128, 148–9, 178, 187; Prussian betrayal of Poland, 129; loss of Austrian Netherlands to France, 145; Austria a member of Anglo-Russian alliance, 156; Prussian neutrality in Napoleonic Wars, 163; Austria a member of Third Coalition, 163, 172; Prussian watch on the Rhine, 177, 215; Austria's support of Britain at Congress of Vienna, 178; fear of revolution, 197; background to bid for supremacy, 210–12; rise of nationalism, 212–13; economic developments, 213–14; easing of pressure from the east and west, 214; background of Prussia in rise of Germany, 215, 216; Bismarck, 217–20, 227–8; successes in Denmark, Austria, 218; cultural decline, coarsening of national character, 221; moral pressures, 224–5, 232; the urge for expansion, 225–6; effect of economic civilization, 225–6; Prussian alliance with Austria, 227; William II, 231; Prussian determination to break English dominance, 232; construction of Prussian battle fleet, 232, 235; move into Near East, 236; World War I, 240–2; state after World War I, 248; Weimar Republic, 254; attitude of the youth, 254–5; rise of totalitarianism, 255; new bid for supremacy, 255–7; Hitler, 257–8, 261–2; characteristics of Third Reich, 258–9, 260. *See also* Holy Roman Empire; Habsburg, House of
Glorious Revolution, 80
Great Britain. *See* England

Habsburg, House of: policy of dynastic inheritance, 33–5; rise to power with election of Charles V, 34–5; division into German and Spanish branches, 43; Rudolf II, territorial expansion, 44; under Philip II, 46; common cause of the two branches, 66–7, 78; War of the Spanish Succession, 84; War of the Austrian Succession, 111; as force for German unity, 211. *See also* Germany; Holy Roman Empire; Spain
Henry VIII, 39
Henry of Navarre, 61
Hitler, Adolf: objectives, 258; methods of mobilizing German strength, 261–2
Hohenzollerns, 216
Holland. *See* Netherlands
Holy Alliance, 186
Holy Roman Empire: source of unification in Middle Ages, reason for decline, 19–20; Reformation, start of final disintegration, 38; Charles V, 38–41; Philip II, 43–7; condition after defeat of Armada, 61–2; impotence a result of warding off Habsburg supremacy, 67. *See also* Charles V; Germany; Habsburg, House of; Philip II; Spain

India: achievement of British private initiative, 151–2; Napoleon's plan of conquest, 152–3
Industrial Revolution in England, 134–5
Insular principle: Venice, 25, 27; England, 29, 50, 71, 168–9, 185–6, 192; Netherlands, 49; attainment of world stature, 57, 71; value of the people, 60; Russia, 101; American colonies, 122, 191–2; struggle with continental principle, 150, 158, 267; the phenomenon of its strength, 230; Japan, 250; role of technology, 264–5; epilogue, 269–73, 281–4. *See also* Power, balance of
Italy: role in Middle Ages, 20, 23–4; Renaissance system of states, 24–7; in 1494, the prize of battle, 28; fall of the free states, 35–7; spirit transformed in Counter Reformation, 36; rise of nationalism, 206–7; unification by Cavour, 216. *See also* Venice

Japan: defeat of Russia, 233; rise, 250

July Revolution of 1830, 196–8

League of Armed Neutrality, 128
League of Cambrai, 37
League of Nations, 243–4
Lepanto, battle of: role of Venice, 37; advantage to Philip II, 45
Louis XIV: ascension to throne, 72; background to struggle for supremacy, 72–4; plan of attack, 75; securing of support of England against Holland, 76–7; victories on the Continent, 78; miscalculation of England, naval defeat at La Hogue, 81–2; bargain for peace with England after War of Spanish Succession, 84; defeat sealed at Peace of Paris, 117
Louis XVI, execution, 146
Louis Philippe, 198

Marlborough, Duke of, 83
Mary the Catholic, marriage to Philip II, 44–5
Massacre of St. Bartholomew, 146
Maurice of Saxony, 41
Metternich, Prince Klemens von, on dynamic social tendencies, 188
Middle Ages: unifying tendencies of Church and Holy Roman Empire, 19–21; role of the Italian peninsula, 20, 23–4

Napoleon I: stabilization of revolutionary society, 141; Caesarism, 141, 143; peace with Catholic Church, eventual conflict, 141–2; suppression of intellectualism, 142; successes in Holland, Germany, Italy, 147, 148, 149; reason for Egyptian expedition, 150–1; plan for conquest of India, 152–3; return from Egypt, defeat of Austria, 156; plot with Russia against Britain, 157; negotiation for peace after death of Paul I, 157–8; world domination and will to power, 160; decadence, hubris, 160–1; plans for invasion of England, 161–2; failure of invasion, turn to Continent, 162; execution of Duc d'Enghien, 163; victories on land, defeat at sea, 163–4; Treaty of Tilsit, 164–6;

Napoleon I (continued)
Continental System, 166–8; attack and defeat in Russia, 171–2

Napoleon III: master of power politics, 202–3; internal policy, 203–4; plan to support nationalist trends, 205–6; action in Italy, 206; the Mexican adventure, 207–9; diplomatic and military defeat in Germany, 209–10
Nationalism, rise of, 169–71, 188–9, 198–9, 227, 245–6
Navigation Act, 71
Nelson, Viscount: defeat of French fleet at Aboukir, 153; defeat of Danish fleet, 157; victory at Trafalgar, death, 164
Netherlands: rise of merchant shipping, middleman role, 47–8; comparison with Venice, 48, 49; Revolt of the Netherlands, 48–9; role of the Counter Reformation, 49; lack of true insularity, vulnerability, 49–50, 58–9; superior maritime potential, overseas trading empire, 58, 60; domestic friction, 59; House of Orange, 59; political life, 59–60; saved from Spain by Sweden and France, 66; competition from England, 66, 70–1; Navigation Act, 71; storm center, importance to England, 76; separation from England, 76; survival of attack by England and Spain, 77–8; William of Orange on British throne, realliance of the maritime powers, 80–1; power broken by France, 147; posture after the Napoleonic Wars, 177
Nicholas I: policy in East and in West, 194–5; attitude toward West, 196

Orange, House of, 59, 77, 177

Panama Canal, 239
Papacy. See Church
Partitions of Poland, 126–7, 129–30
Paul I, 154, 156, 157
Peace of Augsburg, Religious, 67
Peace of Cateau-Cambrésis, 45
Peace of Paris (1762), 116–17, 192
Peace of Portsmouth, 239–40
Peace of the Pyrenees, 65–6, 67
Peace of Utrecht, 84, 89

Peace of Westphalia, 67
Peter the Great: comparison with Philip of Macedonia, 95–6; reign of terror, imposition of European techniques, 96; founder of a new Russia, 97; rebuilding of navy and army, 97–8; manipulation of church organization, bureaucratization, 99
Peter II, 125
Philip II: background for his struggle for supremacy, 43–5; marriage to Mary the Catholic, 44–5; battle of Lepanto, 45; national hero, his strength, 46–7; victories in France, 60–1; subjugation of Holland thwarted by Sweden and France, 67
Pitt, William, on the conquest of Canada, 115
Pitt, William (the younger): refusal to declare war on Russia, 128–9; First Coalition, 146; fall, 158; Third Coalition, 163
Poland: attack by Catherine the Great, 125; Partitions, 126–7, 129–30; revolution, 197
Polish Revolution, 197
Portugal: first colonial power, extent of overseas bases, 51; line of demarcation, loss of possessions to Spain, 52; lack of security, 52
Power, balance of: Papacy and the Holy Roman Empire against external enemies, 19–20; consolidation of the West, decline of the Holy Roman Empire, 20; rise of the Papacy, 20–1; decline of the Papacy, rise of the Italian states, 24; cultural strength and political weakness, the external enemies, 28, 31–2; France, England, and Spain in 1494, 28–31; equilibrium in Italy, 34; rise of the House of Habsburg, 34–5; role of Turkey, 40–1; division of the House of Habsburg, 43–4; Counter Reformation and rise of Spain, 44–7; rise of England as counterweight, 50, 53–5; rise of Holland, 57; decline of Spain, 60–1; rise of France, 65–6, 67, 72–4; England and Holland's break with the Continent, 66; England a world power, 71; decline of Holland, 71, 81; decline of France, 82, 83, 111; at Peace of Utrecht, 84; summary, 90; contribution of Eastern continen-

Power, balance of (continued)
tal territories, 93–4; the movement of power, 94; rise of Russia, 94–9, 124; Anglo-Russian rivalry, 106–7, 128, 195, 226, 235, 266; rise of Prussia, 111–13; leveling of the Continental states, 111, 113, 114; summary, 113–15; migration of power to New World, 118, 123, 174, 242–3; equilibrium on the Continent, 120–1; impossibility of maintaining maritime balance as extension of European, 123; rise of Napoleon, 141–2; loss of balance on the Continent at Treaty of Amiens, 158; decline of Napoleon I, 168–70; Restoration, 184–90; secession of Iberian colonies, 191; beginning of Anglo-American solidarity, 193–4; Napoleon III, 203–10; rise of Germany, 210–12, 229; the characteristic element in struggles for supremacy, 230; England passes the zenith, 233–4, 238–9; America gains leadership, 237; extra-Occidental counterweights, 242, 264; Continental power principle, 245; rise of Japan, 250; new German bid for supremacy, 256–7; World War II a reprise of past attempts, 262–3; decline of England, 264–5; the two world giants, 265–8; epilogue, 274–80. See also System of states
Prussia. See Germany

Ranke, Leopold von: optimism and glorification of the state, 7; political and cultural unity of the West, 7, 8–9; limited view of Russia and Britain, 8; European culture, 9; limited historical point of view, 9–10; attitude toward, 10–13
Reformation, role in disintegration of Holy Roman Empire, 38
Renaissance: background, 21–2; growth of the system of states, 23–4; rise of politics, 24; Venice, 25–7, 37; struggle for Italy, 28–37; posture of France, England, Spain, and Germany, 28–34; rise of House of Habsburg, 34–5
Revolt of the Netherlands, 48–9
Revolutionary Wars, 139, 144, 147, 148
Rudolf II, 44

Russia: kinship with West, 94; Peter the Great, 95–9; geography and character, absolutism, 95; civilization in, 96; mutiny of the army against reform, 98; bureaucratization of Orthodox Church, caesaropapism, 98–9; education and bureaucracy, 99; internal tensions, 99–100; urge for expansion, 100; before Peter the Great, 100–2; comparable insularity, 101; Siberia, 101–2; entry into West, 102; expansion along western frontier, 103; abortive move to the south, 103–4, 106; alliance with Poland, war with Sweden, 104–5; defeat at Narva, 104; victory at Poltava, 105; Baltic expansion, 105–6; relations with China, expansion in Asia, 106; after Peter the Great, 107; posture after first two Silesian Wars, 113, 114–15; leadership of Continental alliance against England, 121; new expansion, 124; enterprises against Poland and Turkey, 125; Catherine the Great, 125; relations with Germany, 126–7, 128, 148–9, 178, 187; advances in the south, 127; revival of Anglo-Russian antagonism, 128; League of Armed Neutrality, 128; absorption of Poland, 130, 148–9; alliance with Britain against France, 154, 156; Paul I, 154, 156, 157; the specter of revolution, 154–5, 186–7, 195; break with Austria, Britain, 156; alliance with Napoleon, death of Paul I, 156–7; member of Third Coalition against Napoleon, 163; Alexander I, 163, 165–6, 186; attack by Napoleon, his defeat, 171–2; posture after fall of Napoleon, 178–9, 186; lack of national harmony, revolutionary infection, 186–7; Restoration and halt of advances to the west, 187; Nicholas I, 194–5, 196; containment by Britain, 195; gradual withdrawal from North America, 195; Crimean War, 204–5; Alexander II, 227; Pan-Slavism, 227; defeat by Japan, 233; Triple Entente, 236–7; posture after World War I, 250–3; Bolshevik Revolution, 251–3; emergence as world power, 266–8; posture after World War II, 273–4; plan for

Russia (continued) the cold war, 274–6; technological development, 275; expansion of Communism, 276–8; epilogue, 278, 280, 285–8. See also Power, balance of; System of states

Sardinia, 84
Second Coalition, 155–6
Seeley, John Robert, trends in world politics, 13–15
Seven Years' War, 115–17
Spain: position in 1494, concentration and expansion, 30–1; union of Castile and Aragon, 30–1; rise of the House of Habsburg, 34–5; Charles V, 34–8, 40–1; Philip II, 43–7, 60–1, 67; Counter Reformation, consolidation of Spanish possessions, penetration of France, 44; alliance with Papacy, 45–6; universal policy, 46; result of expulsion of Jews and Moors, 47; economic backwardness, wealth from the colonies, 47; conquest of southern provinces of the Netherlands, 48–9; extent of colonial holdings, 50, 51–3; line of demarcation, gain of Portugal and possessions, 52; shipping losses to English freebooters, 54–5; result of death of Mary Stuart, 55; make-up of Armada, 55–6; its defeat, 56–7; the results, 60; victories in France, 61; break with Papacy, squandering of substance, decline, 61–2; on the defensive, 66; War of the Spanish Succession, 82–3; ascension of a Bourbon king, 84; expulsion of Austria from southern Italy, 108; war with Britain in the colonies, 110; invasion by Britain, popular rising, 166; loss of colonial empire, 190–1; Falange system, 260
States. See System of states
Sweden: intervention in Spain's reach for the Netherlands, 67; war with Russia, 104–5; defeat at Poltava, end of great-power status, 105
System of states: state as central factor of history, 5; highest principle of state action is foreign policy, 5, 14; results of friction among Hellenic states, 21–2; origin of Western system, 23; Renaissance Italy, 24–7; beginnings

System of states (*continued*)
of the European system, 28–34, 39, 43–5, 47–50; death struggle of the Italian free states, 35–7; beginnings of a German system, 38, 67; role of Turkey, 41, 93–4, 154; role of England, 50, 53–5, 79, 111, 123, 124, 153, 170, 237; role of overseas expansion, 50–4, 74, 78, 85–6; role of Holland, 57, 58, 76; summary, 90; role of Russia, 93–4, 100–1, 111, 170, 172, 237; friction from the colonies, 109–10, 116; Continental alliance, 121; dynamic rise of the will to power, 132–3; split of Europe into two armed camps, 142–3, 265–8; role of junction between Africa and Asia, 150; rise of nationalism, 169–71, 188–9, 198–9; re-establishment after fall of Napoleon, 177–8; Restoration, 184–90; revolutionary trend, 184–90, 195–9; state of flux, 201–2; disease of difference in order of magnitude, 228; variety in World War I, 240; League of Nations, 243–4; state of new countries after World War I, 247; decline of European system, 248–9; Third Reich, 259–63; final collapse, 265–7; epilogue, 283–5. *See also* Power, balance of

Third Coalition, 163
Treaty of Amiens, 158–9
Treaty of Campoformio, 149
Treaty of Tilsit, 164–6
Treaty of Westminster, 115
Triple Entente, 236–7
Turkey: counterweight to unifying tendency of Charles V, 40–1; decline in the time of Philip II, 45; stimulation of exploration, 51; league with Louis XIV against Continent, 78; Crimea annexed by Russia, 125; on the side of Germany, 237

Unifying tendencies: in the early Middle Ages, 19–21; Charles V, 34–5; role of extra-Occidental forces, 40–1, 93–4, 111, 170, 234; peninsula of the West a natural support, 41–2; Spain under Philip II and the Counter Reformation, 43–6; Spain's expand-

Unifying tendencies (*continued*)
ing empire, 52–3; rise of France, 72–5; rise of Russia, 124–30; rise of Napoleon, 141–2, 169–70; Napoleon III, 204–6; rise of Germany, 229; alliance of Anglo-Saxon empires, 237–9; Anglo-Saxon world leadership, 244; world economic crisis a negative expression, 249; rise of totalitarianism in Russia, 252; rise of totalitarianism in Germany, 254–5, 261; spread of Communism, 255. *See also* Divisive tendencies; Power, balance of
United Nations, 272, 279
United States. *See* America

Venice: forerunner of England, 25; intermediary between cultures, 25; maritime empire, limitation by the Turks, 25–6; advantages of insular character, 25, 26; compared with Athens and Carthage, 26; land power, 26–7; domestic character, 27; only survivor of Italian states, 37

War of the Austrian Succession, 110–11, 115
War of the Bavarian Succession, 126
War of the Polish Succession, 108
War of the Spanish Succession, 83–5
Weimar Republic, 254
West: tendencies toward unification and disintegration, 19; source of vitality, 21–3; bearers of culture, 22; role of the East, 41, 93–4, 242, 264; the movement of power, 94; growing importance of the New World, 122–3; evolution of civilization, increasing effects, 132–3, 183–5, 188, 192; role of nationalism, 212–13; epilogue, 269–88. *See also* countries by name
William II, 231
William of Orange: deliverer of Holland from England and Spain, 77; European statesman, 79–80; ascension to throne of England, 80; his diplomacy entangles Louis XIV, 82
William the Silent, 54
Wolsey, Cardinal, 39
World War I, 240–2
World War II, 257–65

LUDWIG DEHIO was born in 1888 in Königsberg, Prussia. Educated at Berlin and Strassburg, he received his doctorate from the latter university. In 1922 he started working as an archivist in the Secret State Archives, at Berlin-Dahlem, and in 1933 accepted the position of director at the Archives of the House of Hohenzollern.

From 1946 to 1954 he was the director of the German State Archives, at Marburg an der Lahn. In 1948, when it was decided to resume publication of the *Historische Zeitschrift*, the famous organ of German historical scholarship, Professor Dehio was selected as its editor in chief. He held this position until his retirement in 1956.

A member of the Munich Academy of Science, he is the author of several books, among them *Germany and World Politics in the Twentieth Century*, which was published in this country in 1959.

*August 1962*

## A NOTE ON THE TYPE

THIS BOOK is set in ELECTRA, a Linotype face designed by W. A. Dwiggins (1880–1956). This face cannot be classified as either modern or old-style. It is not based on any historical model, nor does it echo any particular period or style. It avoids the extreme contrasts between thick and thin elements that mark most modern faces, and attempts to give a feeling of fluidity, power, and speed.

*Composed, printed, and bound by*
*Kingsport Press, Inc., Kingsport, Tennessee.*
*Typography and binding design by*
VINCENT TORRE